GO MATH!

GEORGIA

HOUGHTON MIFFLIN HARCOURT

HOUGHTON
MIFFLIN
HARCOURT

Printed in the U.S.A.

ISBN   978-0-547-86302-3

9 10 11 12 13 14 15 2421 20 19 18 17
4500652403   C D E F G

Dear Students and Families,

Welcome to **Go Math! Georgia,** Grade 3! In this exciting mathematics program, there are hands-on activities to do and real-world problems to solve.
Best of all, you will write your ideas and answers right in your book.
In **Go Math! Georgia,** writing and drawing on the pages helps you think deeply about what you are learning, and you will really understand math!

By the way, all of the pages in your **Go Math! Georgia,** book are made using recycled paper. We wanted you to know that you can Go Green with **Go Math! Georgia.**

Sincerely,

The Authors

Made in the United States
Text printed on 100% recycled paper

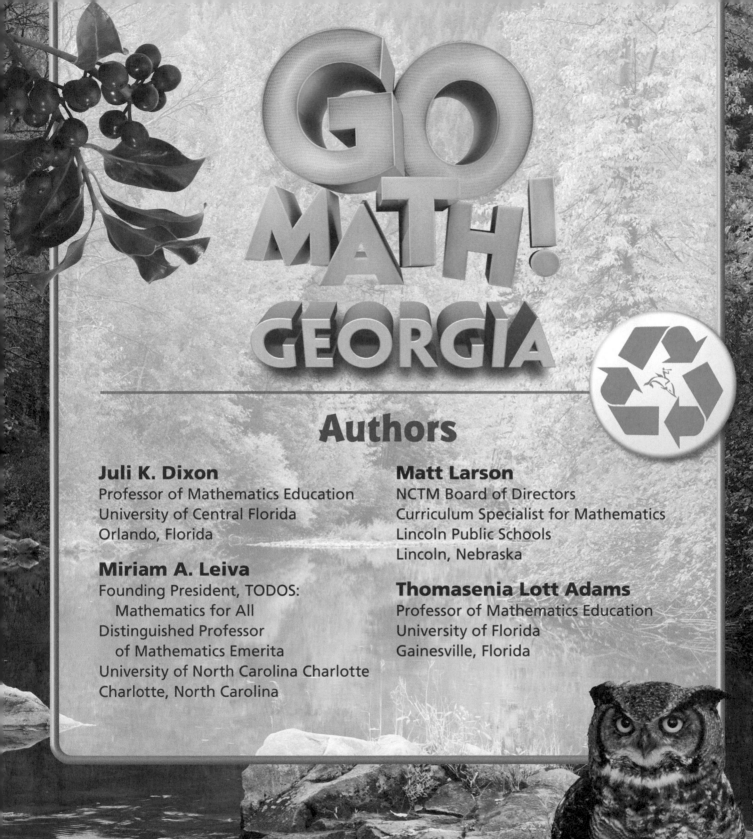

GO MATH! GEORGIA

Authors

Juli K. Dixon
Professor of Mathematics Education
University of Central Florida
Orlando, Florida

Miriam A. Leiva
Founding President, TODOS:
    Mathematics for All
Distinguished Professor
    of Mathematics Emerita
University of North Carolina Charlotte
Charlotte, North Carolina

Matt Larson
NCTM Board of Directors
Curriculum Specialist for Mathematics
Lincoln Public Schools
Lincoln, Nebraska

Thomasenia Lott Adams
Professor of Mathematics Education
University of Florida
Gainesville, Florida

Numbers and Operations in Base Ten

MODULE 1 Addition

MODULE 2 Subtraction

MODULE 3 Graphing

DIGITAL PATH
Go online! Your math lessons are interactive. Use *i*Tools, Animated Math Models, the Multimedia *e*Glossary, and more.

Look for these:

REAL WORLD

H.O.T.
Higher Order Thinking

Connect to Reading
p.36

Use every day for Standards Practice.

DIGITAL PATH
Go online! Your math lessons are interactive. Use *i*Tools, Animated Math Models, the Multimedia *e*Glossary, and more.

Look for these:

REAL WORLD

H.O.T.
Higher Order Thinking

Connect to Reading
p. 76

STANDARDS PRACTICE BOOK

HOUGHTON MIFFLIN HARCOURT

GO MATH!
GEORGIA

Use every day
For Standards Practice.

COMMON CORE

Unit 2

Operations and Algebraic Thinking: the Relationship Between Multiplication and Division

MODULE 5

Multiplication Concepts

Use every day
For Standards Practice.

vii

DIGITAL PATH
Go online! Your math lessons are interactive. Use *i*Tools, Animated Math Models, the Multimedia *e*Glossary, and more.

Look for these:

REAL WORLD

H.O.T.
Higher Order Thinking

Connect to Science
p. 204

Connect to Reading
p. 194

Use every day for Standards Practice.

COMMON CORE

Unit 3

Operations and Algebraic Thinking: the Properties of Multiplication and Division

DIGITAL PATH
Go online! Your math lessons are interactive. Use *i*Tools, Animated Math Models, the Multimedia *e*Glossary, and more.

Look for these:

REAL WORLD

H.O.T.
Higher Order Thinking

Connect to Reading
p. 222

Use every day for Standards Practice.

Operations and Algebraic Thinking: Patterns in Addition and Multiplication

COMMON CORE | # Unit 5

Geometry

MODULE 16 Geometry—Polygons

MODULE 17 Geometry—Triangles and Quadrilaterals

Look for these:

REAL WORLD

H.O.T.
Higher Order Thinking

Connect to Reading
p. 342

Use every day
For Standards Practice.

DIGITAL PATH
Go online! Your math lessons are interactive. Use *i*Tools, Animated Math Models, the Multimedia *e*Glossary, and more.

Look for these:

REAL WORLD

H.O.T.

Higher Order Thinking

Use every day for Standards Practice.

COMMON CORE

Unit 6

Representing and Comparing Fractions

MODULE 18 Fraction Concepts I

MODULE 19 Fraction Concepts II

COMMON CORE — Unit 7

Measurement

MODULE 21 — Time

Look for these:

REAL WORLD

H.O.T.
Higher Order Thinking

Connect to Reading
p. 430

Connect to Science
p. 458

Use every day
for Standards Practice.

COMMON CORE Unit 8

Show What We Know

Unit 1 · Numbers and Operations in Base Ten

Show What You Know

Check your understanding of important skills.

Name **Diana**

▶ **Think Addition to Subtract** Write the missing numbers.

1. $9 - 4 = 5$

Think: $4 + 5 = 9$

$4 + \underline{5} = 9$

So, $9 - 4 = \underline{5}$.

2. $13 - 7 = 6$

Think: $7 + 6 = 13$

$7 + \underline{6} = 13$

So, $13 - 7 = \underline{6}$.

3. $17 - 9 = 9$

Think: $9 + 9 = 17$

$9 + \underline{9} = 17$

So, $17 - 9 = \underline{9}$.

▶ **Addition Facts** Find the sum.

4. $\begin{array}{r} 4 \\ + 3 \\ \hline 7 \end{array}$
5. $\begin{array}{r} 2 \\ + 7 \\ \hline 9 \end{array}$
6. $\begin{array}{r} 8 \\ + 6 \\ \hline 14 \end{array}$
7. $\begin{array}{r} 9 \\ + 4 \\ \hline 13 \end{array}$
8. $\begin{array}{r} 7 \\ + 9 \\ \hline 14 \end{array}$

▶ **Subtraction Facts** Find the difference.

9. $\begin{array}{r} 8 \\ - 5 \\ \hline 3 \end{array}$
10. $\begin{array}{r} 11 \\ - 2 \\ \hline 9 \end{array}$
11. $\begin{array}{r} 10 \\ - 6 \\ \hline 4 \end{array}$
12. $\begin{array}{r} 18 \\ - 9 \\ \hline 9 \end{array}$
13. $\begin{array}{r} 15 \\ - 7 \\ \hline 8 \end{array}$

MATH DETECTIVE WITH CARMEN SANDIEGO™

Manuel's puppy chewed part of this homework paper. Two of the digits in his math problem are missing. Be a Math Detective to help him figure out the missing digits. What digits are missing?

$\begin{array}{r} 3\ \_ \\ + 2\ \_ \\ \hline 72 \end{array}$

Vocabulary Builder

▶ **Visualize It** ••••••••••••••••••••••••••••••••••••

Sort the review words with a ✓ into the Venn diagram.

Review Words

✓ add

✓ difference

  even

✓ hundreds

  odd

✓ ones

✓ regroup

✓ subtract

✓ sum

✓ tens

Preview Words

Associative Property
  of Addition

bar graph

compatible numbers

estimate

frequency table

horizontal bar graph

key

line plot

picture graph

round

scale

vertical bar graph

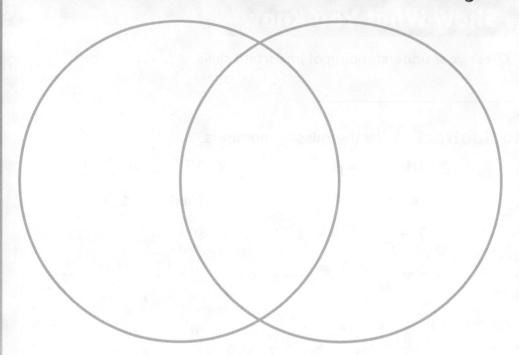

Addition Words   **Subtraction Words**

▶ **Understand Vocabulary** ••••••••••••••••••••••••••

Complete the sentences by using preview words.

1. A number close to an exact number is called

   an _____.

2. A _____ uses marks to record
   each piece of data above a number line.

3. _____ are numbers that are
   easy to compute mentally.

4. A _____ uses small pictures
   or symbols to show and compare information.

GO Online • eStudent Edition • Multimedia eGlossary

Name _____

Estimate Sums

Essential Question How can you use compatible numbers and rounding to estimate sums?

COMMON CORE
Georgia Performance Standard MCC3.NBT.1
Use place value understanding and properties of operations to perform multi-digit arithmetic.

🔑 UNLOCK the Problem REAL WORLD

The table shows how many dogs went to Pine Lake Dog Park during the summer months. About how many dogs went to the park during June and August?

You can estimate to find *about* how many or *about* how much. An **estimate** is a number close to an exact amount.

Pine Lake Dog Park	
Month	**Number of Dogs**
June	432
July	317
August	489

🔒 One Way Use compatible numbers.

Compatible numbers are numbers that are easy to compute mentally and are close to the real numbers.

$$
\begin{array}{rcr}
432 & \rightarrow & 425 \\
+\,489 & \rightarrow & +\,475 \\
\hline
\end{array}
$$

Math Talk MATHEMATICAL PRACTICES
Will the sum of the compatible numbers 425 and 475 be greater than or less than the exact sum? **Explain.**

So, about _____ dogs went to Pine Lake Dog Park during June and August.

1. What other compatible numbers could you have used?

_____

2. About how many dogs went to the park during July and August? What compatible numbers could you use to estimate?

_____

🔑 Another Way Use place value to round.

432 + 489 = ■

First, find the place to which you want to round.
Round both numbers to the same place.
The greatest place value of 432 and 489 is
hundreds. So, round to the nearest hundred.

STEP 1 Round 432 to the nearest hundred.

- Look at the digit to the right of the hundreds place.
- Since 3 < 5, the digit 4 stays the same.
- Write zeros for the tens and ones digits.

$$432 \qquad 432 \to \\ \uparrow \qquad +489 \qquad +$$

STEP 2 Round 489 to the nearest hundred.

- Look at the digit to the right of the hundreds place.
- Since 8 > 5, the digit 4 increases by one.
- Write zeros for the tens and ones digits.

$$489 \qquad 432 \to 400 \\ \uparrow \qquad +489 \to +$$

STEP 3 Find the sum of the rounded numbers.

$$432 \to 400 \\ +489 \to +500$$

So, 432 + 489 is about _____.

Math Talk MATHEMATICAL PRACTICES

How would you round 432 and 489 to the nearest ten? What would be the estimated sum? Explain.

Try This! Estimate the sum.

A Use compatible numbers.

$$47 \to \\ +23 \to +25$$

B Use rounding.

$$304 \to 300 \\ +494 \to +$$

Name _____

Share and Show

1. Use compatible numbers to complete the problem. Then estimate the sum.

$$428 \rightarrow \boxed{}$$
$$+286 \rightarrow +\boxed{}$$
$$\boxed{}$$

Math Talk What other compatible numbers could you use for 428 and 286?

Use rounding or compatible numbers to estimate the sum.

2.
$$65$$
$$+23 \quad +$$

☑3.
$$421$$
$$+218 \quad +$$

☑4.
$$369$$
$$+480 \quad +$$

On Your Own

Use rounding or compatible numbers to estimate the sum.

5.
$$19$$
$$+54 \quad +$$

6.
$$39$$
$$+42 \quad +$$

7.
$$327$$
$$+581 \quad +$$

8.
$$27$$
$$+78 \quad +$$

9.
$$267$$
$$+517 \quad +$$

10.
$$465$$
$$+478 \quad +$$

11.
$$186$$
$$+460 \quad +$$

12.
$$817$$
$$+118 \quad +$$

13.
$$632$$
$$+244 \quad +$$

14. $278 + 369$

$$\boxed{} + \boxed{} = \boxed{}$$

15. $523 + 195$

$$\boxed{} + \boxed{} = \boxed{}$$

Problem Solving

REAL WORLD

Use the table for 16–18.

Dan's Pet Supplies Sold

Month	Pet Bowls	Bags of Pet Food
June	91	419
July	57	370
August	76	228

16. About how many pet bowls were sold in June and July altogether?

_____

17. **What's the Question?** The answer is about 800.

_____

_____

18. **H.O.T.** **Write Math** Dan said the total number of bags of pet food sold in June, July, and August was about 1,000. How did Dan estimate? **Explain.**

_____

_____

_____

_____

_____

SHOW YOUR WORK

19. ⭐ **PARCC Test Prep** Tracy ordered 325 pet toys and 165 bags of dog food for her new pet store. Which is the best estimate of the total number of items Tracy ordered?

Ⓐ 400

Ⓑ 500

Ⓒ 600

Ⓓ 700

Use the Break Apart Strategy to Add

Essential Question How can you use the break apart strategy to add 3-digit numbers?

COMMON CORE
Georgia Performance Standard MCC3.NBT.2
Use place value understanding and properties of operations to perform multi-digit arithmetic.

UNLOCK the Problem REAL WORLD

There are more zoos in Germany than in any other country. At one time, there were 355 zoos in the United States and 414 zoos in Germany. How many zoos were there in the United States and Germany altogether?

You can use the break apart strategy to find sums.

Math Talk MATHEMATICAL PRACTICES
Do you think the sum will be greater than or less than 800? **Explain.**

Example 1 Add. 355 + 414

STEP 1 Estimate. 400 + 400 = _____

STEP 2 Break apart the addends.
Start with the hundreds.
Then add each place value.

$$355 \quad = \quad 300 + \boxed{} + 5$$
$$+\,414 \quad = \quad \underline{\boxed{} + 10 + 4}$$
$$700 + 60 + 9$$

STEP 3 Add the sums.

700 + 60 + 9 = _____

So, there were _____ zoos in the United States and Germany altogether.

Example 2 Add. 467 + 208

STEP 1 Estimate. 500 + 200 = _____

STEP 2 Break apart the addends.
Start with the hundreds.
Then add each place value.

$$467 \quad = \quad 400 + \boxed{} + \boxed{}$$
$$+\,208 \quad = \quad \underline{\boxed{} + 0 + 8}$$
$$600 + 60 + 15$$

STEP 3 Add the sums.

600 + 60 + 15 = _____

So, 467 + 208 = _____.

Try This! Use the break apart strategy to find 343 + 259.

Estimate. 300 + 300 = _____

$$
\begin{array}{rcl}
343 & = & 300 + \boxed{} + \boxed{} \\
+259 & = & \underline{\boxed{} + \boxed{} + \boxed{}} \\
& & \boxed{} + \boxed{} + \boxed{} = \boxed{}
\end{array}
$$

1. **Explain** why there is a zero in the tens place in the sum.

   _____

   _____

   _____

2. How do you know your answer is reasonable?

   _____

   _____

Share and Show

1. Complete.
   Estimate: 400 + 400 = _____

$$
\begin{array}{rcl}
425 & = & 400 + \boxed{} + 5 \\
+362 & = & \underline{\boxed{} + 60 + \boxed{}} \\
& & 700 + \boxed{} + 7 = \boxed{}
\end{array}
$$

   So, 425 + 362 = _____.

2. Write the numbers the break apart strategy shows.

$$
\begin{array}{rcl}
\boxed{} & = & 100 + 30 + \ 4 \\
+\ \boxed{} & = & 200 + 40 + \ 9 \\
\hline
\boxed{} & = & 300 + 70 + 13
\end{array}
$$

© Houghton Mifflin Harcourt Publishing Company

MATHEMATICAL PRACTICES

Math Talk Explain how the break apart strategy uses expanded forms of numbers.

Name _____

Estimate. Then use the break apart strategy to find the sum.

☑ **3.** Estimate: _____

$$142 =$$
$$\underline{+436} =$$

☑ **4.** Estimate: _____

$$459 =$$
$$\underline{+213} =$$

5. Estimate: _____

$$291 =$$
$$\underline{+420} =$$

6. Estimate: _____

$$654 =$$
$$\underline{+243} =$$

On Your Own ....

Estimate. Then use the break apart strategy to find the sum.

7. Estimate: _____

$$435 =$$
$$\underline{+312} =$$

8. Estimate: _____

$$163 =$$
$$\underline{+205} =$$

9. Estimate: _____

$$634 =$$
$$\underline{+251} =$$

10. Estimate: _____

$$526 =$$
$$\underline{+357} =$$

Practice: Copy and Solve Estimate. Then solve.

11. $163 + 205$ **12.** $543 + 215$ **13.** $213 + 328$ **14.** $372 + 431$

15. $152 + 304$ **16.** $268 + 351$ **17.** $413 + 257$ **18.** $495 + 312$

Problem Solving REAL WORLD

Use the table for 19–20.

19. Which two schools together have fewer than 600 students? **Explain**.

_____

_____

_____

Number of Students

School	Number
Harrison	304
Montgomery	290
Bryant	421

SHOW YOUR WORK

20. The number of students in Collins School is more than double the number of students in Montgomery School. What is the least number of students that could attend Collins School?

_____

21. 🔆**H.O.T.** **What's the Error?** Lexi used the break apart strategy to find 145 + 203. Describe her error. What is the correct sum?

$$
\begin{array}{r}
100 + 40 + 5 \\
+\ 200 + 30 + 0 \\
\hline
300 + 70 + 5 = 375
\end{array}
$$

_____

_____

22. **Write Math** ➤ Is the sum of 425 and 390 less than or greater than 800? How do you know?

_____

_____

_____

23. ⭐**PARCC Test Prep** What is the sum of 421 and 332?

   Ⓐ 653   Ⓑ 751   Ⓒ 753   Ⓓ 763

Name _____

Use Place Value to Add

Essential Question How can you use place value to add 3-digit numbers?

COMMON CORE
Georgia Performance Standard MCC3.NBT.2
Use place value understanding and properties of operations to perform multi-digit arithmetic.

 UNLOCK the Problem REAL WORLD

Dante is planning a trip to Illinois. His airplane leaves from Dallas, Texas and stops in Tulsa, Oklahoma. Then it flies from Tulsa to Chicago, Illinois. How many miles does Dante fly?

Chicago

585 miles

Tulsa

236 miles

Dallas

 Use place value to add two addends.

Add. 236 + 585

Estimate. 200 + 600 = _____

STEP 1	**STEP 2**	**STEP 3**
Add the ones. Regroup the ones as tens and ones.	Add the tens. Regroup the tens as hundreds and tens.	Add the hundreds.
$\begin{array}{r} \overset{1}{2}\,3\,6 \\ +\,5\,8\,5 \\ \hline \end{array}$	$\begin{array}{r} \overset{1}{2}\,\overset{1}{3}\,6 \\ +\,5\,8\,5 \\ \hline 1 \end{array}$	$\begin{array}{r} \overset{1}{2}\,\overset{1}{3}\,6 \\ +\,5\,8\,5 \\ \hline 2\,1 \end{array}$

236 + 585 = _____

So, Dante flies _____ miles.

Since _____ is close to the estimate of _____, the answer is reasonable.

 ERROR Alert

Remember to add the regrouped ten and hundred.

- You can also use the Commutative Property of Addition to check your work. Change the order of the addends and find the sum.

$\begin{array}{r} 5\,8\,5 \\ +\,2\,3\,6 \\ \hline \end{array}$

Try This! Find 563 + 48 in two ways.

Estimate. 550 + 50 = _____

A **Use the break apart strategy.**

$$563 = \qquad 500 + \boxed{} + \boxed{}$$
$$+\ 48 = \qquad\qquad 40 + \boxed{}$$

$$\boxed{} + \boxed{} + \boxed{} = \boxed{}$$

B **Use place value.**

$$\begin{array}{r} 563 \\ +\ 48 \\ \hline \boxed{} \end{array}$$

🔑 **Use place value to add three addends.**

A **Add.** 140 + 457 + 301

Estimate. 150 + 450 + 300 = _____

STEP 1 Add the ones.

$$\begin{array}{r} 140 \\ 457 \\ +\ 301 \\ \hline \boxed{} \end{array}$$

STEP 2 Add the tens.

$$\begin{array}{r} 140 \\ 457 \\ +\ 301 \\ \hline \boxed{}\,8 \end{array}$$

STEP 3 Add the hundreds.

$$\begin{array}{r} 140 \\ 457 \\ +\ 301 \\ \hline \boxed{}\,98 \end{array}$$

So, 140 + 457 + 301 = _____.

B **Add.** 173 + 102 + 328

Estimate. 200 + 100 + 300 = _____

STEP 1 Add the ones. Regroup the ones as tens and ones.

$$\begin{array}{r} \overset{1}{1}73 \\ 102 \\ +\ 328 \\ \hline \boxed{} \end{array}$$

STEP 2 Add the tens. Regroup the tens as hundreds and tens.

$$\begin{array}{r} \overset{1\,1}{1}73 \\ 102 \\ +\ 328 \\ \hline \boxed{}\,3 \end{array}$$

STEP 3 Add the hundreds.

$$\begin{array}{r} \overset{1\,1}{1}73 \\ 102 \\ +\ 328 \\ \hline \boxed{}\,03 \end{array}$$

So, 173 + 102 + 328 = _____.

Name _____

Share and Show

1. Circle the problem in which you need to regroup.
   Use the strategy that is easier to find the sum.

   a. $496 + 284$

   b. $482 + 506$

Estimate. Then find the sum.

2. Estimate: _____
$$\begin{array}{r} 251 \\ +345 \\ \hline \end{array}$$

3. Estimate: _____
$$\begin{array}{r} 479 \\ +395 \\ \hline \end{array}$$

4. Estimate: _____
$$\begin{array}{r} 686 \\ +314 \\ \hline \end{array}$$

5. Estimate: _____
$$\begin{array}{r} 231 \\ 410 \\ +158 \\ \hline \end{array}$$

On Your Own

Estimate. Then find the sum.

Math Talk MATHEMATICAL PRACTICES
Explain how you can compute $403 + 201$ mentally.

6. Estimate: _____
$$\begin{array}{r} 572 \\ +124 \\ \hline \end{array}$$

7. Estimate: _____
$$\begin{array}{r} 163 \\ +205 \\ \hline \end{array}$$

8. Estimate: _____
$$\begin{array}{r} 334 \\ +218 \\ \hline \end{array}$$

9. Estimate: _____
$$\begin{array}{r} 357 \\ 101 \\ +467 \\ \hline \end{array}$$

Practice: Copy and Solve Estimate. Then solve.

10. $253 + 376$

11. $654 + 263$

12. $321 + 439$

13. $482 + 323$

14. $182 + 321$

15. $701 + 108$

16. $543 + 372$

17. $516 + 326$

H.O.T. **Algebra** Find the unknown digits.

18.
$$\begin{array}{r} 1\ \square\ 4 \\ +\ \square\ 3\ \square \\ \hline 2\ 5\ 7 \end{array}$$

19.
$$\begin{array}{r} \square\ 7\ \square \\ +6\ \square\ 4 \\ \hline 9\ 8\ 6 \end{array}$$

20.
$$\begin{array}{r} 2\ \square\ \square \\ +\ \square\ 2\ 9 \\ \hline 6\ 8\ 2 \end{array}$$

21.
$$\begin{array}{r} 3\ \square\ \square \\ +\ \square\ 1\ 7 \\ \hline 9\ 0\ 3 \end{array}$$

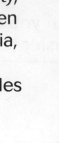

UNLOCK the Problem REAL WORLD

22. A plane flew 187 miles from New York City, New York to Boston, Massachusetts. It then flew 273 miles from Boston to Philadelphia, Pennsylvania. The plane flew the same distance on the return trip. How many miles did the plane fly?

Boston
273 miles
187 miles
New York City
Philadelphia

Ⓐ 460 miles   Ⓒ 900 miles

Ⓑ 820 miles   Ⓓ 920 miles

a. What do you need to find? _____

b. What is an estimate of the total distance?

_____

c. Show the steps you used to solve the problem.

d. Complete the sentences.

The plane flew _____ miles from New York City to Boston.

Then it flew _____ miles from Boston to Philadelphia.

It flew _____ miles from New York City to Boston to Philadelphia.

The total distance is _____ miles round trip.

e. Fill in the bubble for the correct answer choice above.

23. The Colorado River is 119 miles longer than the Kansas River. The Kansas River is 743 miles long. How long is the Colorado River?

Ⓐ 852 miles   Ⓒ 862 miles

Ⓑ 861 miles   Ⓓ 962 miles

24. Mr. Miller drove 568 miles last week. He drove 308 miles this week. What was the number of miles he drove in these two weeks?

Ⓐ 865 miles   Ⓒ 987 miles

Ⓑ 876 miles   Ⓓ 988 miles

Name _____

Module 1 Assessment

▶ Vocabulary

Choose the best term from the box.

1. _____ are numbers that are easy to compute. (p. 7)

2. The _____ states that you can group addends in different ways and still get the same sum. (p. 15)

▶ Concepts and Skills

Use rounding or compatible numbers to estimate the sum. MCC3.NBT.1

3.
$$\begin{array}{r} 56 \\ +32 \\ \hline \end{array}$$
+ _____

4.
$$\begin{array}{r} 271 \\ +425 \\ \hline \end{array}$$
+ _____

5.
$$\begin{array}{r} 328 \\ +127 \\ \hline \end{array}$$
+ _____

Use mental math to find the sum. MCC3.NBT.2

6. 46 + 14 = _____

7. 39 + 243 = _____

8. 326 + 402 = _____

Estimate. Then find the sum. MCC3.NBT.2

9. Estimate: _____

10. Estimate: _____

11. Estimate: _____

12. Estimate: _____

$$\begin{array}{r} 356 \\ +442 \\ \hline \end{array}$$

$$\begin{array}{r} 164 \\ +230 \\ \hline \end{array}$$

$$\begin{array}{r} 545 \\ +139 \\ \hline \end{array}$$

$$\begin{array}{r} 437 \\ +184 \\ \hline \end{array}$$

Fill in the bubble for the correct answer choice.

13. Nancy planted 48 roses and 39 tulips. Which is the best estimate for the number of flowers she planted?
MCC3.NBT.1

   Ⓐ about 50

   Ⓑ about 60

   Ⓒ about 65

   Ⓓ about 90

14. Tomas collected 139 cans for recycling on Monday, and twice that number on Tuesday. How many cans did he collect on Tuesday? MCC3.NBT.2

   Ⓐ 278

   Ⓑ 279

   Ⓒ 280

   Ⓓ 288

15. There are 294 boys and 332 girls in the Hill School. How many students are in the school? MCC3.NBT.2

   Ⓐ 172

   Ⓑ 526

   Ⓒ 626

   Ⓓ 637

16. On Monday, 76 students played soccer. On Tuesday, 62 students played soccer. On Wednesday, 68 students played soccer. How many students played soccer on those three days? MCC3.NBT.2

   Ⓐ 216

   Ⓑ 207

   Ⓒ 206

   Ⓓ 196

Name _____

Estimate Differences

Essential Question How can you use compatible numbers and rounding to estimate differences?

COMMON CORE
Georgia Performance Standard MCC3.NBT.1
Use place value understanding and properties of operations to perform multi-digit arithmetic.

 UNLOCK the Problem REAL WORLD

The largest yellowfin tuna caught by fishers weighed 387 pounds. The largest grouper caught weighed 436 pounds. About how much more did the grouper weigh than the yellowfin tuna?

You can estimate to find *about* how much more.

- Does the question ask for an exact answer? How do you know?

_____

_____

- Circle the numbers you need to use.

🔑 One Way Use compatible numbers.

Think: Compatible numbers are numbers that are easy to compute mentally and are close to the real numbers.

$$
\begin{array}{r} 436 \\ -387 \\ \hline \end{array}
\rightarrow
\begin{array}{r} 425 \\ -375 \\ \hline \end{array}
$$

So, the grouper weighed about

_____ pounds more than the yellowfin tuna.

Yellowfin tuna

Grouper

- What other compatible numbers could you have used?

_____

Try This! Estimate. Use compatible numbers.

Ⓐ
$$
\begin{array}{r} 73 \\ -22 \\ \hline \end{array}
\rightarrow
\begin{array}{r} 75 \\ - \\ \hline \end{array}
$$

Ⓑ
$$
\begin{array}{r} 376 \\ -148 \\ \hline \end{array}
\rightarrow
\begin{array}{r} \\ -150 \\ \hline \end{array}
$$

🔒 Another Way Use place value to round.

$436 - 387 = $ ▪

STEP 1 Round 436 to the nearest ten.

> **Think:** Find the place to which you want to round. Look at the digit to the right.

- Look at the digit in the ones place.
- Since $6 > 5$, the digit 3 increases by one.
- Write a zero for the ones place.

$$4\ 3\ \underset{\uparrow}{6} \qquad \begin{array}{r} 4\ 3\ 6 \\ -\ 3\ 8\ 7 \end{array} \rightarrow \quad -$$

STEP 2 Round 387 to the nearest ten.

- Look at the digit in the ones place.
- Since $7 > 5$, the digit 8 increases by one.
- Write a zero for the ones place.

$$3\ 8\ \underset{\uparrow}{7} \qquad \begin{array}{r} 4\ 3\ 6 \\ -\ 3\ 8\ 7 \end{array} \rightarrow \begin{array}{r} 4\ 4\ 0 \\ - \end{array}$$

STEP 3 Find the difference of the rounded numbers.

$$\begin{array}{r} 4\ 3\ 6 \\ -\ 3\ 8\ 7 \end{array} \rightarrow \begin{array}{r} 4\ 4\ 0 \\ -\ 3\ 9\ 0 \end{array}$$

So, $436 - 387$ is about _____.

Try This! Estimate. Use place value to round.

A
$$\begin{array}{r} 761 \rightarrow 800 \\ -528 \rightarrow - \end{array}$$

> **Think:** Round both numbers to the same place value.

B
$$\begin{array}{r} 642 \rightarrow \\ -287 \rightarrow -300 \end{array}$$

MATHEMATICAL PRACTICES

Math Talk Explain a different way you can round each number in Example B to find another estimate.

Name _____

Share and Show ....

1. Use compatible numbers to complete the problem. Then estimate the difference.

$$546 \rightarrow \quad 550$$
$$-209 \rightarrow - \boxed{}$$
$$\boxed{}$$

Math Talk MATHEMATICAL PRACTICES
Explain another way you can estimate 546 − 209.

Use rounding or compatible numbers to estimate the difference.

2.
$$\begin{array}{r} 57 \\ -21 \\ \hline \end{array}$$

☑ 3.
$$\begin{array}{r} 642 \\ -137 \\ \hline \end{array}$$

☑ 4.
$$\begin{array}{r} 374 \\ -252 \\ \hline \end{array}$$

On Your Own ....

Use rounding or compatible numbers to estimate the difference.

5.
$$\begin{array}{r} 67 \\ -24 \\ \hline \end{array}$$

6.
$$\begin{array}{r} 81 \\ -39 \\ \hline \end{array}$$

7.
$$\begin{array}{r} 936 \\ -421 \\ \hline \end{array}$$

8.
$$\begin{array}{r} 804 \\ -259 \\ \hline \end{array}$$

9.
$$\begin{array}{r} 584 \\ -208 \\ \hline \end{array}$$

10.
$$\begin{array}{r} 442 \\ - 36 \\ \hline \end{array}$$

11.
$$\begin{array}{r} 96 \\ -63 \\ \hline \end{array}$$

12.
$$\begin{array}{r} 528 \\ -274 \\ \hline \end{array}$$

13.
$$\begin{array}{r} 761 \\ -489 \\ \hline \end{array}$$

14. $429 - 51$

$$\boxed{} - \boxed{} = \boxed{}$$

15. $491 - 270$

$$\boxed{} - \boxed{} = \boxed{}$$

Problem Solving REAL WORLD

Use the table for 16–19.

Largest Saltwater Fish Caught

Type of Fish	Weight in Pounds
Pacific Halibut	459
Conger	133
Yellowfin Tuna	387

16. About how many more pounds does the Pacific halibut weigh than the yellowfin tuna? **Explain**.

_____

_____

17. **What's the Question?** The answer is about 500 pounds.

_____

_____

18. Sean said the three fish weigh about 1,000 pounds altogether. **Explain** why you agree or disagree.

_____

_____

SHOW YOUR WORK

19. **H.O.T.** **Write Math** About how much more is the total weight of the Pacific halibut and conger than the weight of the yellowfin tuna? **Explain**.

_____

_____

_____

20. ★ **PARCC Test Prep** A total of 926 people went to a fishing tournament. Of these people, 607 arrived before noon. Which is the best estimate of the number of people who arrived in the afternoon?

(A) 150   (B) 250   (C) 300   (D) 500

Mental Math Strategies for Subtraction

Essential Question What mental math strategies can you use to find differences?

COMMON CORE
Georgia Performance Standard MCC3.NBT.2
Use place value understanding and properties of operations to perform multi-digit arithmetic.

🔑 UNLOCK the Problem REAL WORLD

A sunflower can grow to be very tall. Dylan is 39 inches tall. She watered a sunflower that grew to be 62 inches tall. How many inches shorter was Dylan than the sunflower?

🔒 One Way Use a number line to find 62 − 39.

Ⓐ Count up by tens and then ones.

Think: Start at 39. Count up to 62.

$+10$ $+10$ $+3$

39   49   59   62

Add the lengths of the jumps to find the difference.

$10 + 10 + 3 =$ _____

$62 - 39 =$ _____

So, Dylan was _____ inches shorter than the sunflower.

Ⓑ Take away tens and ones.

Think: Start at 62. Count back 39.

$-7 - 2$ -10 -10 -10

23   30 | 42   52   62

32

Take away lengths of jumps to end on the difference.

MATHEMATICAL PRACTICES

Math Talk Compare the number lines. **Explain** where the answer is on each one.

🔒 Other Ways

Ⓐ Use friendly numbers and adjust to find 74 − 28.

STEP 1 Make the number you subtract a friendly number. $28 + 2 =$ _____

Think: Add to 28 to make a number with 0 ones.

_____

STEP 2 Since you added 2 to 28, you have to add 2 to 74. $74 + 2 =$ _____

_____

STEP 3 Find the difference.   _____ − _____ = _____

So, $74 - 28 =$ _____.

Try This! Use friendly numbers to subtract 9 and 99.

- **Find 36 − 9.**

  Think: 9 is 1 less than 10.

  Subtract 10.   36 − 10 = _____

  Then add 1.   _____ + 1 = _____

  So, 36 − 9 = _____.

- **Find 423 − 99.**

  Think: 99 is 1 less than 100.

  Subtract 100.   423 − 100 = _____

  Then add 1.   _____ + 1 = _____

  So, 423 − 99 = _____.

B Use the break apart strategy to find 458 − 136.

STEP 1 Subtract the hundreds.   400 − 100 = _____
_____

STEP 2 Subtract the tens.   50 − 30 = _____
_____

STEP 3 Subtract the ones.   8 − 6 = _____
_____

STEP 4 Add the differences.   _____ + _____ + _____ = _____

So, 458 − 136 = _____.

Share and Show ·

1. Find 61 − 24. Draw jumps and label the number line to show your thinking.

   Think: Take away tens and ones.

   ⟵——————————————————————————┼——⟶
                                                                    61

   61 − 24 = _____

2. Use friendly numbers to find the difference.

   86 − 42 = _____   **Think:** 42 − 2 = 40
                                                    86 − 2 = 84

MATHEMATICAL PRACTICES

Math Talk **Explain** how you can use the break apart strategy to find 86 − 42.

Name _____

Use mental math to find the difference.
Draw or describe the strategy you use.

☑ 3. $56 - 38 =$ _____ | ☑ 4. $435 - 121 =$ _____

On Your Own ....

Use mental math to find the difference.
Draw or describe the strategy you use.

5. $82 - 49 =$ _____ | 6. $152 - 99 =$ _____

7. $367 - 225 =$ _____ | 8. $96 - 47 =$ _____

Problem Solving REAL WORLD

9. **H.O.T.** **What's the Error?** Erica used friendly numbers to
find $43 - 19$. She added 1 to 19 and subtracted 1 from
43. What is Erica's error? **Explain.**

_____

_____

10. ★ **PARCC Test Prep** There were 87 sunflowers at the
flower shop in the morning. There were 56 sunflowers left
at the end of the day. How many sunflowers were sold?

Ⓐ 13   Ⓑ 31   Ⓒ 41   Ⓓ 143

Compare and Contrast

Emus and ostriches are the world's largest birds. They are alike in many ways and different in others.

When you compare things, you decide how they are alike. When you contrast things, you decide how they are different.

The table shows some facts about emus and ostriches. Use the information on this page to compare and contrast the birds.

Facts About Emus and Ostriches		
	Emus	Ostriches
Can they fly?	No	No
Where do they live?	Australia	Africa
How much do they weigh?	About 120 pounds	About 300 pounds
How tall are they?	About 72 inches	About 108 inches
How fast can they run?	About 40 miles per hour	About 40 miles per hour

11. How are emus and ostriches alike?
    How are they different?

    Alike: 1._____

                2._____

    Different: 1._____

                2._____

                3._____

12. How much taller is an ostrich than an emu?

    _____

13. **What if** an emu weighs 117 pounds and
    an ostrich weighs 274 pounds? How much
    more does the ostrich weigh?

    _____

Ostrich

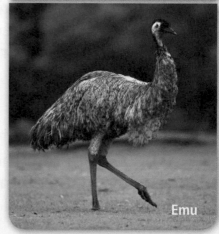

Emu

Name _____

Use Place Value to Subtract

Essential Question How can you use place value to subtract 3-digit numbers?

COMMON CORE
Georgia Performance Standard MCC3.NBT.2
Use place value understanding and properties of operations to perform multi-digit arithmetic.

 UNLOCK the Problem REAL WORLD

Ava sold 473 tickets for the school play. Kim sold 294 tickets. How many more tickets did Ava sell than Kim?

 Use place value to subtract.

Subtract. 473 − 294

Estimate. 475 − 300 = _____

- Do you need to combine or compare the number of tickets sold?

_____

- Circle the numbers you will need to use.

STEP 1

Subtract the ones.
3 < 4, so regroup.

7 tens 3 ones =

6 tens _____ ones

$$
\begin{array}{r}
^{6\ 13} \\
4\,\cancel{7}\,\cancel{3} \\
-2\,9\,4 \\
\hline

\end{array}
$$

STEP 2

Subtract the tens.
6 < 9, so regroup.

4 hundreds 6 tens =

3 hundreds _____ tens

$$
\begin{array}{r}
^{16} \\
3\ \cancel{6}\ ^{13} \\
4\,\cancel{7}\,\cancel{3} \\
-2\,9\,4 \\
\hline
9
\end{array}
$$

STEP 3

Subtract the hundreds.
Add to check your answer.

$$
\begin{array}{r}
^{16} \\
3\ \cancel{6}\ ^{13} \\
4\,\cancel{7}\,\cancel{3} \\
-2\,9\,4 \\
\hline
7\,9
\end{array}
\qquad
\begin{array}{r}
^{1\ 1} \\
1\,7\,9 \\
+2\,9\,4 \\
\hline
4\,7\,3
\end{array}
$$

So, Ava sold _____ more tickets than Kim.

Since _____ is close to the estimate of _____, the answer is reasonable.

Math Idea
Addition and subtraction undo each other. So you can use addition to check subtraction.

Try This! Use place value to subtract. Use addition to check your work.

$$
\begin{array}{r}
6\,3\,1 \\
-2\,5\,8 \\
\hline

\end{array}
$$

🔒 Example Use place value to find 890 − 765.

Estimate. 900 − 750 = _____

STEP 1	**STEP 2**	**STEP 3**
Subtract the ones. Regroup the tens as tens and ones.	Subtract the tens.	Subtract the hundreds. Add to check your answer.

STEP 1

$$
\begin{array}{r}
\overset{8\ 10}{8\cancel{9}\cancel{0}} \\
-\ 7\ 6\ 5 \\
\hline

\end{array}
$$

STEP 2

$$
\begin{array}{r}
\overset{8\ 10}{8\cancel{9}\cancel{0}} \\
-\ 7\ 6\ 5 \\
\hline
5
\end{array}
$$

STEP 3

$$
\begin{array}{r}
\overset{8\ 10}{8\cancel{9}\cancel{0}} \\
-\ 7\ 6\ 5 \\
\hline
2\ 5
\end{array}
\qquad
\begin{array}{r}
1\ 2\ 5 \\
+\ 7\ 6\ 5 \\
\hline

\end{array}
$$

So, 890 − 765 = _____.

> **Math Talk**   MATHEMATICAL PRACTICES
> **Explain** how you know your answer is reasonable.

Try This! Circle the problem in which you need to regroup. Find the difference.

A

$$
\begin{array}{r}
8\ 9\ 4 \\
-\ 5\ 8\ 3 \\
\hline

\end{array}
$$

B

$$
\begin{array}{r}
5\ 2\ 1 \\
-\ 3\ 0\ 1 \\
\hline

\end{array}
$$

C

$$
\begin{array}{r}
9\ 1\ 8 \\
-\ 4\ 2\ 7 \\
\hline

\end{array}
$$

Share and Show ....

1. Estimate. Then use place value to find 627 − 384. Add to check your answer.

   Estimate. _____ − _____ = _____

$$
\begin{array}{r}
6\ 2\ 7 \\
-\ 3\ 8\ 4 \\
\hline

\end{array}
\qquad
\begin{array}{r}
 \\
+\ 3\ 8\ 4 \\
\hline

\end{array}
$$

> **Math Talk**   MATHEMATICAL PRACTICES
> Did you need to regroup to find the difference? **Explain**.

Since _____ is close to the estimate of _____, the answer is reasonable.

38

© Houghton Mifflin Harcourt Publishing Company

Name _____

Estimate. Then find the difference.

2. Estimate: _____
$$\begin{array}{r} 386 \\ -123 \\ \hline \end{array}$$

3. Estimate: _____
$$\begin{array}{r} 519 \\ -205 \\ \hline \end{array}$$

4. Estimate: _____
$$\begin{array}{r} 456 \\ -217 \\ \hline \end{array}$$

☑5. Estimate: _____
$$\begin{array}{r} 642 \\ -159 \\ \hline \end{array}$$

☑6. Estimate: _____
$$\begin{array}{r} 242 \\ -220 \\ \hline \end{array}$$

7. Estimate: _____
$$\begin{array}{r} 870 \\ -492 \\ \hline \end{array}$$

8. Estimate: _____
$$\begin{array}{r} 654 \\ -263 \\ \hline \end{array}$$

9. Estimate: _____
$$\begin{array}{r} 937 \\ -618 \\ \hline \end{array}$$

Math Talk — MATHEMATICAL PRACTICES
Which exercises can you compute mentally? **Explain** why.

On Your Own ....

Estimate. Then find the difference.

10. Estimate: _____
$$\begin{array}{r} 435 \\ -312 \\ \hline \end{array}$$

11. Estimate: _____
$$\begin{array}{r} 617 \\ -501 \\ \hline \end{array}$$

12. Estimate: _____
$$\begin{array}{r} 893 \\ -268 \\ \hline \end{array}$$

13. Estimate: _____
$$\begin{array}{r} 750 \\ -276 \\ \hline \end{array}$$

Practice: Copy and Solve **Estimate. Then solve.**

14. $568 - 276$

15. $761 - 435$

16. $829 - 765$

17. $974 - 285$

 Algebra **Find the unknown number.**

18.
$$\begin{array}{r} 86 \\ -\ \boxed{} \\ \hline 62 \end{array}$$

19.
$$\begin{array}{r} 372 \\ -\ \boxed{} \\ \hline 240 \end{array}$$

20.
$$\begin{array}{r} 537 \\ -\ \boxed{} \\ \hline 172 \end{array}$$

21.
$$\begin{array}{r} 629 \\ -\ \boxed{} \\ \hline 335 \end{array}$$

Problem Solving REAL WORLD

Use the table for 22–24.

22. About how many tickets did Jenna, Matt, and Sonja sell altogether?

_____

23. How many more tickets did Sonja sell than Matt?

_____

24. Alicia sold 59 fewer tickets than Jenna and Matt sold together. How many tickets did Alicia sell?

_____

School Play Tickets Sold	
Student	**Number of Tickets**
Jenna	282
Matt	178
Sonja	331

··· **SHOW YOUR WORK** ···

25. H.O.T. **Sense or Nonsense?** Nina says to check subtraction, add the difference to the number you started with. Does this statement make sense? **Explain.**

_____

_____

_____

26. **Write Math** Do you have to regroup to find 523−141? **Explain.** Then solve.

_____

_____

_____

_____

27. ⭐ **PARCC Test Prep** There are 842 seats in the school auditorium. 138 seats need repairs. How many seats do not need repairs?

Ⓐ 980 Ⓑ 804 Ⓒ 716 Ⓓ 704

FOR MORE PRACTICE:
Standards Practice Book

Combine Place Values to Subtract

Essential Question How can you use the combine place values strategy to subtract 3-digit numbers?

COMMON CORE
Georgia Performance Standard MCC3.NBT.2
Use place value understanding and properties of operations to perform multi-digit arithmetic.

UNLOCK the Problem REAL WORLD

Elena collected 431 bottles for recycling. Pete collected 227 fewer bottles than Elena. How many bottles did Pete collect?

- What do you need to find?

_____

- Circle the numbers you need to use.

Combine place values to find the difference.

A Subtract. 431 − 227

Estimate. 400 − 200 = _____

STEP 1 Look at the ones place. Since 7 > 1, combine place values. Combine the tens and ones places. There are 31 ones and 27 ones. Subtract the ones. Write 0 for the tens.

$$\begin{array}{r} 4\boxed{3\;1} \\ -\;2\boxed{2\;7} \\ \hline \end{array}$$

Think: 31 − 27

STEP 2 Subtract the hundreds.

$$\begin{array}{r} 4\;3\;1 \\ -\;2\;2\;7 \\ \hline 0\;4 \end{array}$$

So, Pete collected _____ bottles.

Since _____ is close to the estimate

of _____, the answer is reasonable.

MATHEMATICAL PRACTICES

Math Talk Explain why there is a zero in the tens place.

B Subtract. 513 − 482

Estimate. 510 − 480 = _____

STEP 1 Subtract the ones.

$$\begin{array}{r} 5\;1\;3 \\ -\;4\;8\;2 \\ \hline \end{array}$$

STEP 2 Look at the tens place. Since 8 > 1, combine place values. Combine the hundreds and tens places. There are 51 tens and 48 tens. Subtract the tens.

$$\begin{array}{r} \boxed{5\;1}3 \\ -\boxed{4\;8}2 \\ \hline 1 \end{array}$$

Think: 51 − 48

So, 513 − 482 = _____.

🔑 Example Combine place values to find 500 − 173.

Estimate. 500 − 175 = _____

STEP 1 Look at the ones and tens places. Since 3 > 0 and 7 > 0, combine the hundreds and tens.	**STEP 2** Subtract the ones.	**STEP 3** Subtract the tens.
There are 50 tens. Regroup 50 tens as 49 tens 10 ones.	Think: 10 − 3	Think: 49 − 17
$$\begin{array}{r} {\scriptstyle 4\ 9\ 10} \\ 5\,0\,0 \\ -\ 1\,7\,3 \\ \hline \end{array}$$	$$\begin{array}{r} {\scriptstyle 4\ 9\ 10} \\ 5\,0\,0 \\ -\ 1\,7\,3 \\ \hline \end{array}$$	$$\begin{array}{r} {\scriptstyle 4\ 9\ 10} \\ 5\,0\,0 \\ -\ 1\,7\,3 \\ \hline 7 \end{array}$$

So, 500 − 173 = _____ .

Math Talk Explain why you combined the hundreds and tens.

Try This! Find 851 − 448 in two ways.

Estimate. 850 − 450 = _____

A Use place value.	**B** Combine place values.
$$\begin{array}{r} 8\,5\,1 \\ -4\,4\,8 \\ \hline \end{array}$$	$$\begin{array}{r} 8\,5\,1 \\ -4\,4\,8 \\ \hline \end{array}$$ Think: Combine tens and ones.

1. When does the combine place values strategy make it easier to find the difference? **Explain**.

_____

_____

_____

2. Which strategy would you use to find 431 − 249? **Explain**.

_____

_____

Name _____

Share and Show

1. Combine place values to find 406 − 274.

$$406$$
$$-274$$

Think: Subtract the ones. Then combine the hundreds and tens places.

MATHEMATICAL PRACTICES

Math Talk Explain how to combine place values.

Estimate. Then find the difference.

☑ 2. Estimate: _____

$$595$$
$$-286$$

3. Estimate: _____

$$728$$
$$-515$$

4. Estimate: _____

$$543$$
$$-307$$

☑ 5. Estimate: _____

$$600$$
$$-453$$

On Your Own

Estimate. Then find the difference.

6. Estimate: _____

$$438$$
$$-257$$

7. Estimate: _____

$$706$$
$$-681$$

8. Estimate: _____

$$839$$
$$-754$$

9. Estimate: _____

$$916$$
$$-558$$

10. Estimate: _____

$$537$$
$$-428$$

11. Estimate: _____

$$528$$
$$-297$$

12. Estimate: _____

$$734$$
$$-327$$

13. Estimate: _____

$$800$$
$$-789$$

Practice: Copy and Solve Estimate. Then solve.

14. 457 − 364

15. 652 − 341

16. 700 − 648

17. 963 − 256

Problem Solving

REAL WORLD

MATHEMATICAL PRACTICES
Model • Reason • Make Sense

Use the table for 18–22.

Roller Coaster Heights		
Roller Coaster	**State**	**Height in Feet**
Titan	Texas	245
Kingda Ka	New Jersey	456
Intimidator 305	Virginia	305
Top Thrill Dragster	Ohio	420

18. The table shows the heights of some roller coasters in the United States. How much taller is Kingda Ka than Titan?

_____

19. How many feet shorter is Intimidator 305 than Top Thrill Dragster?

_____

· · · · SHOW YOUR WORK · · · ·

20. How much shorter is Top Thrill Dragster than the heights of Titan and Kingda Ka together?

_____

21. **What if** a roller coaster was 500 feet tall? Which roller coaster would be 195 feet shorter?

_____

22. **H.O.T.** **Write Math** ▶ **Pose a Problem** Look back at Problem 21. Write and solve a similar problem by using different numbers.

_____

_____

23. ⭐ **PARCC Test Prep** The Goliath roller coaster is 235 feet tall. The Steel Dragon roller coaster is 318 feet tall. How many feet taller is Steel Dragon than Goliath?

Ⓐ 73 feet   Ⓒ 123 feet

Ⓑ 83 feet   Ⓓ 183 feet

Name _____

Module 2 Assessment

▶ Concepts and Skills

Use rounding or compatible numbers to estimate the difference. ◥ MCC3.NBT .1

1. 47
   −31

2. 462
   −125

3. 836
   −208

Use mental math to find the difference. ◥ MCC3.NBT.2

4. 96 − 52 = _____

5. 43 − 9 = _____

6. 457 − 325 = _____

Estimate. Then find the difference. ◥ MCC3.NBT.2

7. Estimate: _____

8. Estimate: _____

9. Estimate: _____

10. Estimate: _____

    536
   −411

    718
   −603

    987
   −459

    850
   −389

Estimate. Then find the difference. ◥ MCC3.NBT.2

11. Estimate: _____

12. Estimate: _____

13. Estimate: _____

14. Estimate: _____

    358
   −264

    562
   −261

    800
   −548

    807
   −182

Fill in the bubble for the correct answer choice.

15. Jana has 47 rose bushes in her garden. She moves 19 of them to another garden. Which is the best estimate for the number of rose bushes she has left?

     MCC3.NBT.1

    Ⓐ about 50

    Ⓑ about 60

    Ⓒ about 40

    Ⓓ about 30

16. Lee is going to visit his grandmother. The car trip takes 56 minutes. If he stops for a snack after 17 minutes, about how much time is left for the trip?

    MCC3.NBT.2

    Ⓐ 40 minutes

    Ⓑ 30 minutes

    Ⓒ 20 minutes

    Ⓓ 10 minutes

17. There are 395 boys and 352 girls at Jerrod's school. About how many more boys than girls are there?

    MCC3.NBT.2

    Ⓐ about 100

    Ⓑ about 90

    Ⓒ about 50

    Ⓓ about 20

18. The tallest tree in the forest is 363 feet tall. The second tallest tree is 329 feet tall. Rounded to the nearest ten what is the difference in heights?

    MCC3.NBT.1

    Ⓐ 50 feet

    Ⓑ 40 feet

    Ⓒ 30 feet

    Ⓓ 20 feet

Name _____

Problem Solving • Organize Data

Essential Question How can you use the strategy *make a table* to organize data and solve problems?

COMMON CORE
Georgia Performance Standard MCC3.MD.3
Represent and interpret data.

🔑 UNLOCK the Problem REAL WORLD

The students in Alicia's class voted for their favorite ice cream flavor. They organized the data in this tally table. How many more students chose chocolate than strawberry?

Another way to show the data is in a frequency table. A **frequency table** uses numbers to record data.

Favorite Ice Cream Flavor	
Flavor	**Tally**
Vanilla	卌 ||
Chocolate	卌 |||
Strawberry	||||

Read the Problem

What do I need to find?

How many more students chose

_____ than _____ ice cream as their favorite?

What information do I need to use?

the data about favorite _____ in the tally table

How will I use the information?

I will count the _____. Then I will put the numbers in a frequency table and compare the number of students

who chose _____ to the number

of students who chose _____.

Solve the Problem

Favorite Ice Cream Flavor	
Flavor	**Number**
Vanilla	

Count the tally marks. Record _____ for vanilla. Write the other flavors and record the number of tally marks.

To compare the number of students who chose strawberry and the number of students who chose chocolate, subtract.

_____ − _____ = _____

So, _____ more students chose chocolate as their favorite flavor.

MATHEMATICAL PRACTICES

Math Talk Explain why you would record data in a frequency table.

🔑 Try Another Problem

Two classes in Carter's school grew bean plants for a science project. The heights of the plants after six weeks are shown in the tally table. The plants were measured to the nearest inch. How many fewer bean plants were 9 inches tall than 7 inches and 8 inches combined?

Bean Plant Heights	
Height in Inches	Tally
7	卌 IIII
8	卌 III
9	卌 卌 II
10	卌 IIII

Read the Problem

What do I need to find?

What information do I need to use?

How will I use the information?

Solve the Problem

Record the steps you used to solve the problem.

- Suppose the number of 3-inch plants was half the number of 8-inch plants. How many 3-inch bean plants were there?

_____

© Houghton Mifflin Harcourt Publishing Company

Math Talk MATHEMATICAL PRACTICES
Explain another strategy you could use to solve the problem.

Share and Show

Use the Shoe Lengths table for 1–4.

1. The students in three third-grade classes recorded the lengths of their shoes to the nearest centimeter. The data are in the tally table. How many more shoes were 18 or 22 centimeters long combined than 20 centimeters long?

   You can put the data in a table and compare the lengths of the shoes to solve the problem.

   First, count the tally marks and put the data in a frequency table.

   To find the number of shoes that were 18 or 22 centimeters long, add

   6 + _____ + _____ + _____ = _____.

   To find the number of shoes that were 20

   centimeters long, add _____ + _____ = _____.

   To find the difference between the shoes that were 18 or 22 centimeters long and the shoes that were 20 centimeters long, subtract the sums.

   _____ – _____ = _____.

   So, _____ more shoes were 18 or 22 centimeters long than 20 centimeters long.

Shoe Lengths		
Length in Centimeters	Tally	
	Boys	Girls
18	JHH I	IIII
19	JHH	IIII
20	JHH III	JHH IIII
21	JHH II	JHH
22	JHH IIII	JHH II

Shoe Lengths		
Length in Centimeters	Number	
	Boys	Girls
18		
19		
20		
21		
22		

2. How many fewer girls' shoes than boys' shoes were measured? _____

3. The length of the least number of shoes was _____ centimeters long.

4. **H.O.T.** **What if** the length of 5 more boys' shoes measured 21 centimeters? **Describe** how the table would look.

_____

_____

On Your Own.....................

5. Isabel is thinking of an even number between 234 and 250. The sum of the digits is double the digit in the ones place. What is Isabel's number?

_____

6. Ben needs 400 points to win a prize at the arcade. He has 237 points. How many more points does he need?

_____

7. There were 428 visitors at the pet show on Saturday and 395 visitors on Sunday. How many visitors in all went to the pet show?

_____

8. Write Math ▸ Heather has 6 dimes and 10 pennies. Jason has 3 quarters. Who has more money? **Explain** your answer.

_____

_____

9. H.O.T. Andrew has 10 more goldfish than Todd. Together, they have 50 goldfish. How many goldfish does each boy have?

_____

10. ★ **PARCC Test Prep** Jade made a tally table to record how many people have dogs. Her table shows

Dog IIII IIII IIII

How many people have dogs?

Ⓐ 4   Ⓒ 14

Ⓑ 9   Ⓓ 15

Choose a
STRATEGY

Act It Out
Draw a Diagram
Find a Pattern
Make a Table

· · · · · · · SHOW YOUR WORK · · · · · · ·

Use Picture Graphs

Essential Question How can you read and interpret data in a picture graph?

COMMON CORE
Georgia Performance Standard MCC3.MD.3
Represent and interpret data.

 UNLOCK the Problem REAL WORLD

A **picture graph** uses small pictures or symbols to show and compare information.

Nick has a picture graph that shows how some students get to school. How many students ride the bus?

- Underline the words that tell you where to find the information to answer the question.
- How many ☺ are shown for bus?

_____

Each row has a label that names one way students get to school.

How We Get to School	
Walk	☺ ☺ ☺
Bike	☺ ☺ ☺ ☺
Bus	☺ ☺ ☺ ☺ ☺ ☺ ☺ ☺
Car	☺ ☺ ☺ ☺ ☺ ☺

Key: Each ☺ = 10 students.

The title says that the picture graph is about how some students get to school.

The key tells that each picture or symbol stands for the way 10 students get to school.

🔑 To find the number of students who ride the bus, count each ☺ as 10 students.

10, 20, _____, _____, _____, _____, _____, _____

So, _____ students ride the bus to school.

1. How many fewer students walk than ride the bus? _____

2. How many students were surveyed? _____

3. **What if** the symbol stands for 5 students? How many symbols will you need to show the number of students who walk to school? _____

Use a Half Symbol

🔒 How many students chose a cupcake as their favorite dessert?

Our Favorite Dessert	
Ice Cream	☺ ☺ ☺ ☺ ☺
Cake	☺ ☺ ☺
Pie	☺ ☺
Cupcake	☺ ☺ ☺ ☺ ◖

Key: Each ☺ = 2 students.

Math Idea

Half of the picture stands for half the value of the whole picture.

☺ = 2 students

◖ = 1 student

Count the ☺ in the cupcake row by twos. Then add 1 for the half symbol.

2, 4, ____, ____   ____ + ____ = ____

So, ____ students chose a cupcake as their favorite dessert.

Share and Show 📋

Use the Number of Books Students Read picture graph for 1–3.

Number of Books Students Read	
September	📖 📖 📖 📗
October	📖 📖 📖 📖 📖 📖 📖
November	📖 📖 📖 📖

Key: Each 📖 = 2 books.

1. What does 📗 stand for?

   Think: Half of 2 is 1.

   _____

✓ 2. How many books did the students read in September?

   _____

✓ 3. How many more books did the students read in October than in November?

   _____

MATHEMATICAL PRACTICES
Math Talk Explain how to find the number of books the students read.

Name _____

On Your Own . . . .

Use the Favorite Game picture graph for 4–10.

4. How many students chose puzzles?

_____

5. How many fewer students chose card games than board games?

_____

Favorite Game	
Puzzles	
Card Games	
Board Games	

Key: Each = 4 students.

6. Which two types of games did a total of 34 students choose?

_____

7. How many students were surveyed?

_____

8. How many students did not choose card games?

_____

9. **Write Math** ➤ **What's the Error?** Jacob said one more student chose board games than puzzles. **Explain** his error.

_____

_____

10. **H.O.T.** **What if** computer games were added as a choice and more students chose it than puzzles, but fewer students chose it than board games? How many students would choose computer games?

_____

UNLOCK the Problem · REAL WORLD

Use the picture graph for 11–13.

11. The students who went to summer camp voted for their favorite activity. Which two activities received a total of 39 votes?

    Ⓐ biking and hiking   Ⓒ biking and boating

    Ⓑ hiking and boating   Ⓓ fishing and hiking

Favorite Camp Activity	
Activity	**Number**
Biking	☀ ☀ ☀ ☼
Hiking	☀ ☀ ☀ ☀
Boating	☀ ☀ ☀
Fishing	☀ ☼
Key: Each ☀ = 6 students.	

a. What do you need to find?

_____

b. What steps will you use to solve the problem?

_____

c. Show the steps you used to solve the problem.

d. Complete the sentences.

Each ☀ = _____ students.

Each ☼ = _____ students.

votes for biking + hiking = _____

votes for hiking + boating = _____

votes for biking + boating = _____

votes for fishing + hiking = _____

e. Fill in the bubble for the correct answer.

12. How many students voted for their favorite camp activity?

    Ⓐ 91

    Ⓑ 81

    Ⓒ 72

    Ⓓ 61

13. ★ **PARCC Test Prep** How many fewer students voted for fishing than for hiking?

    Ⓐ 33

    Ⓑ 24

    Ⓒ 15

    Ⓓ 9

Make Picture Graphs

Essential Question How can you draw a picture graph to show data in a table?

COMMON CORE
Georgia Performance Standard MCC3.MD.3
Represent and interpret data.

UNLOCK the Problem REAL WORLD

Delia made the table at the right. She used it to record the places the third grade classes would like to go during a field trip. How can you show the data in a picture graph?

Field Trip Choices

Place	Number
Museum	6
Science Center	15
Aquarium	12
Zoo	9

🔒 **Make a picture graph.**

STEP 1

Write the title at the top of the picture graph. Write the name of a place in each row.

STEP 2

Look at the numbers in the table. Choose a picture for the key, and tell how many students each picture represents. Write the key at the bottom of the graph.

STEP 3

Draw the correct number of pictures for each field trip choice.

Museum	

Key: Each ____ = ____ students.

- How did you decide how many pictures to draw for the Science Center?

_____

_____

Try This! Make a picture graph from data you collect. Take a survey or observe a subject that interests you. Collect and record the data in a frequency table. Then make a picture graph. Decide on a symbol and a key. Include a title and labels.

Key:	

Share and Show

Jeremy pulled marbles from a bag one at a time, recorded their color, and then put them back. Make a picture graph of the data. Use this key:

Each ◯ = 2 marbles.

Jeremy's Marble Experiment

Color	Number
Blue	4
Green	11
Red	8

Key:	

Use your picture graph above for 1–2.

✓ 1. How many more times did Jeremy pull out a red marble than a blue marble?

_____

✓ 2. How many fewer times did Jeremy pull out green marbles than blue and red marbles combined?

_____

Math Talk MATHEMATICAL PRACTICES
Explain how you knew how many pictures to draw for green.

Name _____

On Your Own

3. Two classes from Delia's school visited the Science Center. They recorded their favorite exhibit in the tally table. Use the data in the table to make a picture graph. Use this key:

Each ☼ = 4 votes.

Favorite Exhibit	
Exhibit	**Tally**
Nature	卌 I
Solar System	卌 III
Light and Sound	卌 卌 IIII
Human Body	卌 III

Key:

Use your picture graph above for 4–6.

4. Which exhibits received the same number of votes?

_____

5. **What if** a weather exhibit received 22 votes? **Explain** how many pictures you would draw.

_____

6. H.O.T. **What if** the Solar System exhibit received 15 votes? Would it make sense to use the key Each ☼ = 4 votes to represent 15 votes? **Explain**.

_____

Problem Solving REAL WORLD

Teeth in Mammals	
Animal	**Number**
Hamster	16
Cat	30
Dog	42
Cow	32

7. While at the Science Center, Delia's classmates learned how many teeth some mammals have. Use the data in the table to make a picture graph. Use this key:

Each △ = 4 teeth.

Key:

Use your picture graph above for 8–10.

8. **Pose a Problem** Write a question that can be answered by using the data in your picture graph. Then answer the question.

_____

_____

9. Write Math ➤ **What if** the only data in the table was for the hamster and cow? **Explain** why you may use a different key.

_____

_____

10. ⭐ **PARCC Test Prep** How many pictures would you draw for Cat if each △ = 5 teeth?

Ⓐ 4   Ⓑ 5   Ⓒ 6   Ⓓ 8

Name _____

Use Bar Graphs

Essential Question How can you read and interpret data in a bar graph?

COMMON CORE
Georgia Performance Standard MCC3.MD.3
Represent and interpret data.

 UNLOCK the Problem REAL WORLD

A **bar graph** uses bars to show data. A **scale** of equally spaced numbers helps you read the number each bar shows.

The students in the reading group made a bar graph to record the number of books they read in October. How many books did Seth read?

• Underline the words that tell you where to find the information to answer the question.

The title tells what the bar graph is about.

Each bar is labeled with a student's name.

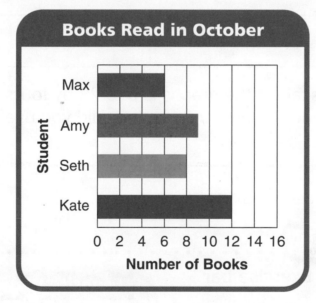

Books Read in October

The length of a bar tells how many books each student read.

The scale is 0–16 by twos.

Math Talk MATHEMATICAL PRACTICES **Explain** how to read the bar that tells how many books Amy read.

🔑 Find the bar for Seth. It ends at _____.

So, Seth read _____ books in October.

1. How many books did Max read? _____

2. Who read 4 fewer books than Kate? _____

3. **What if** Amy read 5 more books? How many books did Amy read? _____ Shade the graph to show how many she read.

More Examples These bar graphs show the same data.

Favorite Winter Activity

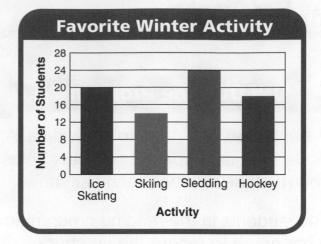

Favorite Winter Activity

In a **horizontal bar graph**, the bars go across from left to right. The length of the bar shows the number.

In a **vertical bar graph**, the bars go up from the bottom. The height of the bar shows the number.

4. What does each space between the numbers represent?

_____

5. Why do you think the scale in the graphs is 0 to 28 by fours instead of 0 to 28 by ones? What other scale could you use?

_____

_____

Share and Show   ·······································

Use the Favorite Way to Exercise bar graph for 1–3.

1. Which activity did the most students choose?

   Think: Which bar is the longest?

   _____

☑ **2.** How many students answered the survey? _____

☑ **3.** Which activity received 7 fewer votes than soccer? _____

Favorite Way to Exercise

MATHEMATICAL PRACTICES

Math Talk What can you tell just by comparing the lengths of the bars in the graph? **Explain.**

Name _____

On Your Own . . . .

Use the Favorite Kind of Book bar graph for 4–5.

4. Which kind of book was chosen by half the number of students as books about animals?

_____

5. Did more students choose books about sports or books about animals and nature together? **Explain**.

_____

_____

Favorite Kind of Book

Kind of Book

Problem Solving REAL WORLD

Use the Favorite Kind of Book bar graph for 6–9.

6. Which two kinds of books together did students choose as often as books about sports?

_____

7. **Write Math** ▸ **Pose a Problem** Write and solve a problem that matches the data in the graph.

_____

_____

8. **H.O.T.** **What if** 10 more students were asked and they chose books about animals? Describe what the bar graph would look like.

_____

_____

9. ⭐**PARCC Test Prep** Which kind of book did 15 fewer students choose than books about sports?

(A) space   (B) animals   (C) nature   (D) puzzles

HOT Sense or Nonsense?

10. The table shows data about some students' favorite amusement park rides. Four students graphed the data. Which student's bar graph makes sense?

Favorite Amusement Ride	
Ride	Number of Students
Super Slide	11
Ferris Wheel	14
Bumper Cars	18
Roller Coaster	23

_____

Alicia

Spencer

Tyler

Kate

• **Explain** why the other bar graphs do not make sense.

_____

_____

_____

Name _____

Make Bar Graphs

Essential Question How can you draw a bar graph to show data in a table or picture graph?

COMMON CORE
Georgia Performance Standard MCC3.MD.3
Represent and interpret data.

 UNLOCK the Problem REAL WORLD

Jordan took a survey of his classmates' favorite team sports. He recorded the results in the table at the right. How can he show the results in a bar graph?

Favorite Team Sport	
Sport	**Tally**
Soccer ⚽	~~IIII~~ ~~IIII~~ II
Basketball 🏀	IIII
Baseball ⚾	~~IIII~~ ~~IIII~~ IIII
Football 🏈	~~IIII~~ IIII

🔑 **Make a bar graph.**

STEP 1

Write a title at the top to tell what the graph is about. Label the side of the graph to tell about the bars. Label the bottom of the graph to explain what the numbers tell.

STEP 2

Choose numbers for the bottom of the graph so that most of the bars will end on a line. Since the least number is 4 and the greatest number is 14, make the scale 0–16. Mark the scale by twos.

STEP 3

Draw and shade a bar to show the number for each sport.

MATHEMATICAL PRACTICES

Math Talk How did you know how long to draw the bar for football?

© Houghton Mifflin Harcourt Publishing Company

Share and Show

Matt's school is having a walk-a-thon to raise money for the school library. Matt made a picture graph to show the number of miles some students walked. Make a bar graph of Matt's data. Use a scale of

0–_____, and mark the scale by _____.

School Walk-a-Thon

Sam	👕 👕 👕 👕 👕
Matt	👕 👕 🁢
Ben	👕
Erica	👕 👕 👕 👕

Key: Each 👕 = 2 miles.

Use your bar graph for 1–4.

1. Which student walked the most miles? _____

   Think: Which student's bar is the tallest?

☑ 2. How many more miles would Matt have had to walk to equal the number of miles Erica walked? _____

☑ 3. How many miles did the students walk? _____

4. Write the number of miles the students walked in order from greatest to least. _____

MATHEMATICAL PRACTICES

Math Talk Explain how the graph would have to change if another student, Daniel, walked double the number of miles Erica walked.

Name _____

On Your Own ....

5. Lydia and Joey did an experiment with a spinner. Lydia recorded the result of each spin in the table at the right. Use the data in the table to make a bar graph. Choose numbers and a scale and decide how to mark your graph.

Spinner Results	
Color	**Tally**
Red	☰☰☰ ☰☰☰ ☰☰☰ I
Yellow	☰☰☰ III
Blue	☰☰☰ ☰☰☰ II
Green	☰☰☰ ☰☰☰

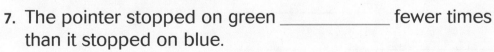

> **! ERROR Alert**
>
> Be sure to draw the bars correctly when you transfer data from a table.

Use your bar graph for 6–8.

6. The pointer stopped on _____ half the number

    of times that it stopped on _____.

7. The pointer stopped on green _____ fewer times than it stopped on blue.

8. **Explain** why you chose the scale you did.

_____

_____

Problem Solving REAL WORLD

Points Scored	
Player	Number of Points
Billy	10
Dwight	30
James	15
Raul	25
Sean	10

9. Susie recorded the number of points some basketball players scored. Use the data in the table to make a bar graph. Choose numbers so that most of the bars will end on a line.

Use your bar graph for 10–12.

10. Which player scored more points than James but fewer points than Dwight? _____

11. H.O.T. **Write Math** ► Write and solve a new question that matches the data in your bar graph.

_____

_____

12. ★ **PARCC Test Prep** Which player scored 10 more points than James?

(A) Billy   (B) Dwight   (C) Raul   (D) Sean

Module 3 Assessment

▶ Vocabulary

Choose the best term from the box.

Vocabulary
bar graph
frequency table
horizontal bar graph
key
picture graph
scale
vertical bar graph

1. A _____ uses numbers to record data. (p. 47)

2. A _____ uses small pictures or symbols to show and compare information. (p. 51)

▶ Concepts and Skills

Use the Favorite Season table for 3–6. ◣ MCC3.MD.3

3. Which season got the most votes?

   _____

4. Which season got 3 fewer votes than winter?

   _____

Favorite Season	
Season	**Number**
Spring	19
Summer	28
Fall	14
Winter	22

5. How many more students chose summer than fall?

   _____

6. How many students were surveyed?

   _____

Use the Our Pets picture graph for 7–9. ◣ MCC3.MD.3

7. How many students have cats as pets?

   _____

Our Pets	
Bird	🐾 🐾 🐾
Cat	🐾 🐾 🐾 🐾
Dog	🐾 🐾 🐾 🐾 🐾 🐾 ◖
Fish	🐾 🐾 🐾
Key: Each 🐾 = 2 students.	

8. Five more students have dogs than which

   other pet? _____

9. How many pets in all do students have?

   _____

Fill in the bubble for the correct answer choice.

Use the Favorite Summer Activity picture graph for 10–14.

10. Some students in Brooke's school chose their favorite summer activity. The results are in the picture graph at the right. How many students chose camping? MCC3.MD.3

   Ⓐ 5

   Ⓑ 10

   Ⓒ 40

   Ⓓ 50

Favorite Summer Activity	
Camping	☀☀☀☀☀
Biking	☀☀☀☀
Swimming	☀☀☀☀☀☀
Canoeing	☀☀☀
Key: Each ☀ = 10 students.	

11. How many more students chose swimming than canoeing? MCC3.MD.3

   Ⓐ 3

   Ⓑ 20

   Ⓒ 30

   Ⓓ 60

12. Which activity did 15 fewer students choose than camping? MCC3.MD.3

   Ⓐ biking

   Ⓑ swimming

   Ⓒ canoeing

   Ⓓ hiking

13. How many pictures would you draw for biking if each ☀ = 5 students? MCC3.MD.3

   Ⓐ 3   Ⓒ 5

   Ⓑ 4   Ⓓ 7

14. How many more students chose biking or canoeing combined than swimming? MCC3.MD.3

   Ⓐ 3   Ⓒ 5

   Ⓑ 4   Ⓓ 7

Name _____

Solve Problems Using Data

Essential Question How can you solve problems using data represented in bar graphs?

COMMON CORE
Georgia Performance Standard MCC3.MD.3
Represent and interpret data.

🔑 UNLOCK the Problem REAL WORLD

CONNECT Answering questions about data helps you better understand the information.

Derek's class voted on a topic for the school bulletin board. The bar graph shows the results. How many more votes did computers receive than space?

🔑 One Way Use a model.

Count back along the scale to find the difference between the bars.

Count back from 10 to 3.

The difference is _____ votes.

🔑 Another Way Write a number sentence.

Think: There are 10 votes for computers. There are 3 votes for space. Subtract to compare the number of votes.

_____

So, computers received _____ more votes than space.

• How do you know you need to subtract?

_____

_____

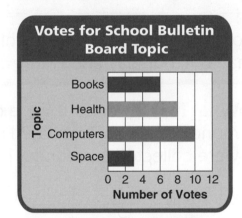

Votes for School Bulletin Board Topic

Topic: Books, Health, Computers, Space
Number of Votes: 0 2 4 6 8 10 12

MATHEMATICAL PRACTICES

Math Talk Explain another way you can skip count to find the difference.

Example

Brooke's school collected cans of food. The bar graph at the right shows the number of cans. How many fewer cans were collected on Tuesday than on Thursday and Friday combined?

Cans of Food Collected

STEP 1 Find the total for Thursday and Friday.

_____

_____

STEP 2 Subtract to compare the total for Thursday and Friday to Tuesday and to find the difference.

_____

So, _____ fewer cans were collected on Tuesday than on Thursday and Friday combined.

- **What if** 4 fewer cans were collected on Monday than on Tuesday? How many cans were collected on Monday? **Explain**.

_____

Share and Show

Use the Spinner Results bar graph for 1–3.

1. How many more times did the pointer stop on green than on purple?

   _____ more times

2. How many fewer times did the pointer stop on blue than on red and green combined?

   _____ fewer times

3. **What if** there were 15 more spins and the pointer stopped 10 more times on green and 5 more times on blue? How many more times did the pointer stop on green than blue?

_____

Spinner Results

MATHEMATICAL PRACTICES

Math Talk What can you tell just by comparing the lengths of the bars in the graphs? **Explain**.

Name _____

On Your Own . . . .

Use the Diego's DVDs bar graph for 4–6.

4. Diego has 5 fewer of this kind of DVD than comedy. Which kind of DVD is this?

_____

5. How many more animated than action DVDs does Diego have?

_____

6. Is the number of comedy and action DVDs greater than or less than the number of animated and drama DVDs? **Explain**.

_____

_____

Problem Solving

Use the Science Fair Projects bar graph for 7–9.

7. How many more students would have to do a project on plants to equal the number of projects on space?

_____

8. ▌**Write Math** ▶ **What's the Question?** The answer is animals, space, rocks, oceans, and plants.

_____

_____

9. ☼**H.O.T.** **What if** 3 fewer students did a project on weather than did a project on rocks? **Describe** what the bar graph would look like.

_____

_____

UNLOCK the Problem REAL WORLD

Use the November Weather bar graph for 10–12.

10. Lacey's class recorded the kinds of weather during the month of November in a bar graph. Were there more cloudy and sunny days or more rainy and snowy days?

November Weather

(Bar graph — x-axis: Kind of Weather; y-axis: Number of Days, scale 0 to 14 by 2s. Cloudy = 9, Rainy = 10, Snowy = 7, Sunny = 4.)

   a. What do you need to find?

   _____

   _____

   b. What operation will you use to find the answer?

   _____

   c. Show the steps you used to find the answer.

   d. Complete the sentences.

   _____ cloudy days +

   _____ sunny days = _____ days

   _____ rainy days +

   _____ snowy days = _____ days

   _____ > _____

   So, there were more _____ days.

11. How many days in November were NOT cloudy?

   Think: There are 30 days in November.

   _____

12. ⭐ **PARCC Test Prep** How many fewer snowy and sunny days were there than cloudy and rainy days?

   Ⓐ 3 days

   Ⓑ 4 days

   Ⓒ 8 days

   Ⓓ 30 days

Name _____

Use and Make Line Plots

Essential Question How can you read and interpret data in a line plot and use data to make a line plot?

COMMON CORE
Georgia Performance Standard MCC3.MD.4
Represent and interpret data.

UNLOCK the Problem REAL WORLD

A **line plot** uses marks to record each piece of data above a number line. It helps you see groups in the data.

Some students took a survey of the number of letters in their first names. Then they recorded the data in a line plot.

How many students have 6 letters in their first names?

Each **X** stands for 1 student. →

Number of Letters in Our First Names

The numbers show the number of letters in a name. ←

🔑 Find 6 on the number line. The 6 stands for 6 _____.

There are _____ **X**s above the 6.

So, _____ students have 6 letters in their first names.

1. Which number of letters was found most often? _____

2. Write a sentence to describe the data. _____

_____

3. How many letters are in your first name? _____

4. Put an **X** above the number of letters in your first name.

Math Talk MATHEMATICAL PRACTICES
What does the shape of the data show you?

🔑 Activity Make a line plot.

Materials ■ ruler ■ measuring tape

Measure the height of four classmates to the nearest inch. Combine your data with other groups. Make a line plot to show the data you collected.

STEP 1 Record the heights in the table.

STEP 2 Write a title below the number line to describe your line plot.

STEP 3 Write the number of inches in order from left to right above the title.

STEP 4 Draw **X**s above the number line to show each student's height.

| Heights in Inches ||
Number of Inches	Tally

———————————————————————————

5. Which height appears most often? _____

   Think: Which height has the most **X**s?

6. Which height appears least often? _____

7. Complete the sentence. Most of the students in the

   class are _____ inches tall or taller.

8. 🔆 **H.O.T.** Is there any height for which there are no data?

   Explain. _____

   _____

© Houghton Mifflin Harcourt Publishing Company

> **MATHEMATICAL PRACTICES**
> **Math Talk** Explain what the shape of the data tells you.

Name _____

Share and Show

Use the Number of Pets line plot for 1–3.

1. How many students have 1 pet?

   Think: How many Xs are above 1?

   _____

✓ 2. What number of pets do no students have?

   _____

✓ 3. Do more students have more than 2 or fewer than 2 pets?

   _____

```
              X
        X  X  X
  X  X  X  X           X
  X  X  X  X           X
  +--+--+--+--+--+--+
  0  1  2  3  4  5
```
Number of Pets

MATHEMATICAL PRACTICES

Math Talk Explain why you think the line plot stops at 5.

On Your Own

4. Use the data in the table to make a line plot.

```
  +----+----+----+----+----+
```
___ ___ ___ ___ ___

How Many Years Have You Owned Your Pet?

How Many Years Have You Owned Your Pet?	
Number of Years	Students
1	5
2	6
3	5
4	3
5	2

5. How many students have owned a pet 1 year? _____

6. Which number of years is found most often? _____

7. ⭐ **PARCC Test Prep** How many students have owned a pet 2 years or more?

   Ⓐ 21   Ⓑ 16   Ⓒ 10   Ⓓ 5

Connect to Reading

Make an Inference

Addison made the line plot below to show the high temperature every day for one month. What *inference* can you make about what season this is?

Daily High Temperatures (in Degrees F)

When you combine what you see with what you already know to come up with an idea, you are making an inference.

You can use what you know about weather and the data on the line plot to make an inference about the season.

You know that the numbers on the line plot are the high temperatures recorded during the month.

The highest temperature recorded was _____.

The lowest temperature recorded was _____.

The temperature recorded most often was _____.

Since all the high temperatures are greater than 100, you know the days were hot. This will help you make an inference about the season.

So, you can infer that the season is _____.

Remember

The Four Seasons

spring

summer

fall

winter

Name _____

Problem Solving •
Use the Distributive Property

Essential Question How can you use the strategy *draw a diagram* to multiply with multiples of 10?

COMMON CORE
Georgia Performance Standard MCC3.NBT.3
Use place value understanding and properties of operations to perform multi-digit arithmetic.

UNLOCK the Problem   REAL WORLD

The school assembly room has 5 rows of chairs with 20 chairs in each row. If the third-grade classes fill 3 rows of chairs, how many third graders are at the assembly?

Read the Problem	Solve the Problem
What do I need to find? I need to find how many _____ are at the assembly.	Draw a diagram. Finish the shading to show 3 rows of 20 chairs. 10 + ____ 3 [30] I can use the sum of the products of the smaller rectangles to find how many third graders are at the assembly.
What information do I need to use? There are _____ chairs in each row. The third graders fill _____ rows of chairs.	$3 \times 10 =$ _____ $3 \times 10 =$ _____ _____ + _____ = _____
How will I use the information? The Distributive Property tells me I can _____ the factor 20 to multiply. $3 \times 20 = 3 \times (10 +$ ____$)$	$3 \times 20 =$ _____ So, _____ third graders are at the assembly.

1. **Explain** how breaking apart the factor 20 makes finding the

   product easier. _____

🔒 Try Another Problem

Megan is watching a marching band practice. The band marches by with 4 rows of people playing instruments. She counts 30 people in each row. How many people march in the band?

Read the Problem	Solve the Problem
What do I need to find?	**Record the steps you used to solve the problem.**
What information do I need to use?	
How will I use the information?	

2. How can you check to see if your answer is reasonable?

_____

_____

3. **Explain** how you can use the Distributive Property to help you find a product.

_____

_____

Name _____

Share and Show MATH BOARD

UNLOCK the Problem **Tips**

✓ Circle the numbers you will use.
✓ Use the Distributive Property and break apart a greater factor to use facts you know.
✓ Draw a diagram to help you solve the problem.

1. People filled all the seats in the front section of the theater. The front section has 6 rows with 40 seats in each row. How many people are in the front section of the theater?

First, write the problem you need to solve. _____

Next, draw and label a diagram to break apart the problem into easier parts to solve.

| 10 | + ___ | + ___ | + ___ |

| 6 | 60 | | | |

Then, find the products of the smaller rectangles.

6 × 10 = _____   _____ × _____ = _____

_____ × _____ = _____   _____ × _____ = _____

Last, find the sum of the products.

_____ + _____ + _____ + _____ = _____

So, there are _____ people in the front section of the theater.

• • • • SHOW YOUR WORK • • • •

2. **H.O.T.** **What if** seats are added to the front section of the theater so that there are 6 rows with 50 seats in each row? How many seats are in the front section?

_____

3. Tova sewed 60 pieces of ribbon together to make a costume. Each piece of ribbon was 2 meters long. How many meters of ribbon did Tova use to make the costume?

_____

On Your Own. . . . .

Choose a STRATEGY

Act It Out
Draw a Diagram
Find a Pattern
Make a Table

4. **H.O.T.** **What's the Error?** Carina draws this diagram to show that $8 \times 30 = 210$. **Explain** her error.

SHOW YOUR WORK

_____

_____

_____

_____

5. **H.O.T.** **Algebra** Mr. Chang orders 160 pencils. The pencils come in packs of 40. How many packs does Mr. Chang order?

_____

6. **Write Math** Tamika wants to display 10 trophies on a table in a rectangular array. How many different ways can Tamika arrange the trophies? **Explain** your answer.

_____

_____

7. The drama club has 350 tickets to sell. They sell 124 tickets on Monday and 98 tickets on Tuesday. How many tickets does the drama club have left to sell?

_____

8. ★**PARCC Test Prep** Steffen orders shirts for each of the 5 members in his family. If each shirt costs $20, what is the total cost for the shirts?

Ⓐ $25   Ⓑ $30   Ⓒ $70   Ⓓ $100

Name _____

Multiplication Strategies with Multiples of 10

Essential Question What strategies can you use to multiply with multiples of 10?

COMMON CORE
Georgia Performance Standard MCC3.NBT.3
Use place value understanding and properties of operations to perform multi-digit arithmetic.

 UNLOCK the Problem REAL WORLD

You can use models and place value to multiply with multiples of 10.

• What is a product of 10 and the counting numbers 1, 2, 3, and so on?

_____

Activity Model multiples of 10.

Materials ■ base-ten blocks

Model the first nine multiples of 10.

1×10	
1×1 ten	
1 ten	
10	

| 2×10 |
| 2×1 ten |
| 2 tens |
| 20 |

| 3×10 |
| 3×1 ten |
| 3 tens |
| 30 |

What are the first nine multiples of 10?

10, 20, 30, _____, _____, _____, _____, _____, _____

Best Care Veterinary Clinic offered free pet care classes for 5 days. Erin attended the pet care class for 30 minutes each day. How many minutes did Erin attend the class?

One Way Use a number line.

$5 \times 30 = $ ■   **Think:** $30 = 3$ tens

STEP 1 Complete the number line. Write the labels for the multiples of 10.

STEP 2 Draw jumps on the number line to show 5 groups of 3 tens.

0   10   100 110   160

$5 \times 30 = $ _____

So, Erin attended the pet care class for _____ minutes.

🔒 Another Way Use place value.

MODEL

THINK

$5 \times 30 = 5 \times$ _____ tens

= _____ tens = _____

So, $5 \times 30 =$ _____.

Try This!

$4 \times 50 =$ _____ $\times$ _____ tens

= _____ tens = _____

Math Talk **MATHEMATICAL PRACTICES** Explain why 5×30 has one zero in the product and 4×50 has two zeros in the product.

Share and Show ·

1. Use a number line to find the product.

   $3 \times 40 =$ _____   Think: There are 3 jumps of 40.

0   10   20   30   40   50   60   70   80   90   100   110   120   130   140   150   160   170   180

Use a number line to find the product.

✓ **2.** $8 \times 20 =$ _____

0   10   20   30   40   50   60   70   80   90   100   110   120   130   140   150   160   170   180

Use place value to find the product.

✓ **3.** $3 \times 70 = 3 \times$ _____ tens

   = _____ tens = _____

4. $50 \times 2 =$ _____ tens $\times 2$

   = _____ tens = _____

Math Talk **MATHEMATICAL PRACTICES** Will the product of 50×2 be the same as the product of 2×50? Explain.

© Houghton Mifflin Harcourt Publishing Company

Name _____

On Your Own ....

Use a number line to find the product.

5. $7 \times 20 =$ _____

6. $3 \times 50 =$ _____

Use place value to find the product.

7. $6 \times 60 = 6 \times$ _____ tens

    $=$ _____ tens $=$ _____

8. $50 \times 7 =$ _____ tens $\times 7$

    $=$ _____ tens $=$ _____

Problem Solving REAL WORLD

Use the table for 9–11.

9. The cost of a bottle of shampoo is $9. If the clinic sells their entire supply of shampoo, how much money will they receive?

_____

10. **What's the Question?** Each bag of treats has 30 treats. The answer is 240.

_____

11. **H.O.T.** There are 4 bottles of vitamins in each box of vitamins. Each bottle of vitamins has 20 vitamins. If the clinic wants to have a supply of 400 vitamins, how many more boxes should they order?

_____

Best Care Clinic Pet Supplies	
Item	**Amount**
Cat toys	10 packs
Treats	8 bags
Shampoo	20 bottles
Vitamins	3 boxes

UNLOCK the Problem REAL WORLD

12. Hiromi needs to set up chairs for 155 people to attend the school career day program. So far she has set up 6 rows with 20 chairs in each row. How many more chairs does Hiromi need to set up?

Ⓐ 25   Ⓑ 35   Ⓒ 75   Ⓓ 95

a. What do you need to find?

_____

b. What operations will you use to find how many more chairs Hiromi needs to set up?

_____

c. Write the steps you will use to solve the problem.

d. Complete the sentences.

Hiromi needs to set up _____ chairs for people to attend the program.

She has set up _____ rows with

_____ chairs in each row.

So, Hiromi needs to set up _____ more chairs.

e. Fill in the bubble for the correct answer above.

13. Last week, Dr. Newman examined the paws of 30 dogs at her clinic. She examined the paws on 20 cats. What is the total number of paws Dr. Newman examined last week?

Ⓐ   50

Ⓑ   80

Ⓒ 120

Ⓓ 200

14. For the career day program, 8 people give presentations. If each person answers 10 questions during the presentations, how many questions are answered?

Ⓐ 18

Ⓑ 80

Ⓒ 88

Ⓓ 90

Multiply Multiples of 10 by 1-Digit Numbers

Essential Question How can you model and record multiplying multiples of 10 by 1-digit whole numbers?

COMMON CORE
Georgia Performance Standard MCC3.NBT.3
Use place value understanding and properties of operations to perform multi-digit arithmetic.

🔑 UNLOCK the Problem

The community center offers 4 dance classes. If 30 students sign up for each class, how many students sign up for dance class altogether?

• How many equal groups are there? _____
• How many are in each group? _____

🔒 Activity Use base-ten blocks to model 4 × 30.

Materials ■ base-ten blocks

STEP 1 Model 4 groups of 30.

STEP 2 Combine the tens. Regroup 12 tens as 1 hundred 2 tens.

4 × 30 = _____

So, _____ students sign up for dance class altogether.

Math Idea
If one factor is a multiple of 10, then the product will also be a multiple of 10.

Try This! Find 7 × 40.

Use a quick picture to record your model. Draw a stick for each ten. Draw a square for each hundred.

STEP 1 Model _____ groups of _____.

STEP 2 Combine the tens. Regroup 28 tens as _____ hundreds _____ tens.

So, 7 × 40 = _____.

Math Talk
MATHEMATICAL PRACTICES
Will the product of 7 × 40 be the same as 4 × 70? **Explain.**

Example Use place value and regrouping.

Find 9×50.

	MODEL	THINK	RECORD
STEP 1		Multiply the ones.	5 0
		9×0 ones = _____ ones	$\times$ 9
			0

	MODEL	THINK	RECORD
STEP 2		Multiply the tens.	5 0
		9×5 tens = 45 tens	$\times$ 9
		Regroup the _____ tens	4 5 0
		as _____ hundreds	
		_____ tens.	

So, $9 \times 50 =$ _____ .

Share and Show

1. Use the quick picture to find 5×40.

    $5 \times 40 =$ _____

Find the product. Use base-ten blocks or draw a quick picture on your MathBoard.

2. $7 \times 30 =$ _____   3. _____ $= 2 \times 90$ 4. $8 \times 40 =$ _____   5. _____ $= 4 \times 60$

Find the product.

6. $\begin{array}{r} 80 \\ \times\ 9 \\ \hline \end{array}$ 7. $\begin{array}{r} 70 \\ \times\ 7 \\ \hline \end{array}$ 8. $\begin{array}{r} 90 \\ \times\ 4 \\ \hline \end{array}$ 9. $\begin{array}{r} 60 \\ \times\ 8 \\ \hline \end{array}$

MATHEMATICAL PRACTICES

Math Talk Explain how you can use place value to solve Exercise 9.

Name _____

On Your Own ....

**Find the product. Use base-ten blocks or draw a
quick picture on your MathBoard.**

10. $2 \times 70 =$ ____   11. $8 \times 50 =$ ____   12. ____ $= 3 \times 90$ 13. $2 \times 80 =$ ____

Find the product.

14.
$$\begin{array}{r} 80 \\ \times\ 3 \\ \hline \end{array}$$

15.
$$\begin{array}{r} 60 \\ \times\ 9 \\ \hline \end{array}$$

16.
$$\begin{array}{r} 90 \\ \times\ 8 \\ \hline \end{array}$$

17.
$$\begin{array}{r} 80 \\ \times\ 8 \\ \hline \end{array}$$

Practice: Copy and Solve Find the product.

18. 6×70 19. 9×90 20. 70×8 21. 90×7

H.O.T. Algebra Find the unknown factor.

22. $a \times 80 = 480$ 23. $b \times 30 = 30$ 24. $7 \times \blacksquare = 420$ 25. $50 \times \blacktriangle = 0$

$a =$ ____ $b =$ ____ $\blacksquare =$ ____ $\blacktriangle =$ ____

Problem Solving REAL WORLD

26. Ben writes the product of 7 and 50. Then he
subtracts the least 3-digit multiple of 10 from
the product. What is the difference?

_____

27. **H.O.T. Sense or Nonsense?** Lori says that 8 is
not a factor of 80 because 8 does not end in
zero. Does Lori's statement make sense? **Explain.**

_____

28. **H.O.T.** The book club members read 200 books in
all. Each member read 5 books. Write an equation
to find the number of members in the book club.
Use a letter to stand for the unknown factor.

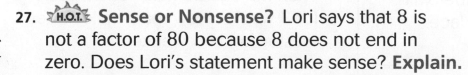

SHOW YOUR WORK

🔑 UNLOCK the Problem REAL WORLD

29. Frank has a 2-digit number on his baseball uniform. The number is a multiple of 10 and has 3 for one of its factors. What three numbers could Frank have on his uniform?

a. What do you need to find?

_____

_____

b. What information do you need to use?

_____

_____

c. How can you solve the problem?

d. Complete the sentences.

Frank has a _____ on his uniform.

The number is a multiple of _____.

One factor of the number is _____.

Frank could have _____, _____, or

_____ on his uniform.

30. Use a property to explain why the product of a multiple of 10 and a number will have a zero in the ones place.

_____

_____

_____

_____

31. ⭐ **PARCC Test Prep** Wesley jogs 10 miles each week for 2 weeks. Then he jogs 20 miles each week for 3 weeks. How many miles does Wesley jog in 5 weeks?

Ⓐ 20 miles

Ⓑ 30 miles

Ⓒ 60 miles

Ⓓ 80 miles

Name _____

▶ Vocabulary

Choose the best term from the box.

Vocabulary
line plot
picture graph

1. A _____ uses marks to record each piece of data above a number line. (p. 73)

▶ Concepts and Skills

Use the Number of Goals Scored line plot for 2–4.

MCC3.MD.3, MCC3.MD.4

2. Katie recorded the number of goals the players on her team scored during soccer practice. How many players scored 2 goals?

```
        X
        X   X
    X   X   X
    X   X   X   X   X
    +---+---+---+---+
    0   1   2   3   4
```
Number of Goals Scored

_____

3. What does each **X** stand for? _____

4. What was the least number of goals scored?

_____

5. Explain how you know this statement is true: More students play guitar and drums than play flute and piano.

_____

_____

6. How many total number of students play musical instruments?

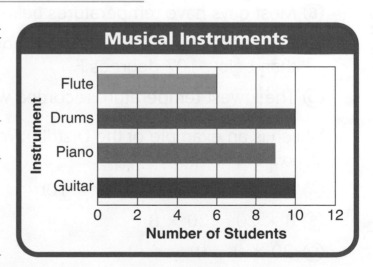

_____

Use place value to find the product. MCC3.NBT.3

7. $6 \times 50 =$ _____

8. $3 \times 70 =$ _____

9. $4 \times 80 =$ _____

10. _____ $= 5 \times 90$

Fill in the bubble for the correct answer choice.

Use the Daily High Temperatures line plot for 11–13.

MCC3.MD.4

11. What temperature was recorded the most? MCC3.MD.4

Ⓐ 115 degrees F

Ⓑ 114 degrees F

Ⓒ 107 degrees F

Ⓓ 102 degrees F

Daily High Temperatures (in Degrees F)

12. How many days has the high temperature been 110 degrees or higher? ▶ MCC3.MD.4

Ⓐ 20

Ⓑ 14

Ⓒ 11

Ⓓ 3

13. Which sentence best describes the data? ▶ MCC3.MD.4

Ⓐ More days have temperatures 107–115 degrees F than temperatures 101–106 degrees F.

Ⓑ Most days have temperatures below 101 degrees F.

Ⓒ Fewer days have temperatures above 107 degrees F than below 107 degrees F.

Ⓓ The lowest temperature recorded was 102 degrees F.

14. Which is an example of the Distributive Property?

▶ MCC3.NBT.3

Ⓐ $8 \times 20 = (8 \times 10) + (8 \times 10)$

Ⓑ $8 \times 20 = 20 \times 8$

Ⓒ $20 \times 0 = 0$

Ⓓ $160 = 8 \times 30$

15. Jacob buys 4 packs of sports cards for $20 each. What is the total cost of the sports cards? ▶ MCC3.NBT.3

Ⓐ $100   Ⓒ $80

Ⓑ $40   Ⓓ $16

Name _____

✓ Unit 1 Assessment

▶ **Vocabulary**

Choose the best term from the box to complete the sentence.

(p. 13)

1. A number close to an exact number is called an

   _____. (p. 13)

2. A _____ uses bars to show data. (p. 47)

Vocabulary
bar graph
compatible numbers
estimate
frequency table
line plot
picture graph
round

▶ **Concepts and Skills**

Estimate. Then find the sum or difference. ▮MCC3.NBT.1, MCC3.NBT.2

3. Estimate: _____
$$218 \\ +342$$

4. Estimate: _____
$$766 \\ +125$$

5. Estimate: _____
$$261 \\ -150$$

6. Estimate: _____
$$948 \\ -532$$

Use the Dolphins Max Saw table for 7–8. ▮MCC3.MD.3

7. Max recorded in a table the number of dolphins he saw. How many dolphins did he see?

   _____

8. If you made a bar graph of the data in the table, what labels would you use? _____

   _____

Dolphins Max Saw	
Day	**Number**
Friday	12
Saturday	15
Sunday	19

Find the product. ▮MCC3.NBT.3

9. $$30 \\ \times 6$$

10. $$20 \\ \times 8$$

11. $$60 \\ \times 7$$

12. $$80 \\ \times 9$$

GO Online Assessment Options Unit Test

Fill in the bubble for the correct answer choice.

13. Spencer sold 363 tickets for the school fair. Bryson sold 289 tickets. How many more tickets did Spencer sell that Bryson? MCC3.NBT.2

   Ⓐ 74
   Ⓑ 84
   Ⓒ 122
   Ⓓ 150

14. Alya planted 20 trays of flowers. Each tray had 6 flowers in it. How many flowers did she plant? MCC3.NBT.3

   Ⓐ 80
   Ⓑ 120
   Ⓒ 160
   Ⓓ 180

15. Use the number line to find 5 × 20. What is the product? MCC3.NBT.3

   Ⓐ 100
   Ⓑ 20
   Ⓒ 10
   Ⓓ   5

16. Katie recorded the number of goals the players on her team scored during soccer practice. How many players scored 2 goals? MCC.MD.4

   Ⓐ 0   Ⓒ 3
   Ⓑ 1   Ⓓ 4

Number of Goals Scored

Name _____

Fill in the bubble for the correct answer choice.

Use the Musical Instruments bar graph for 17–21.

MCC3.MD.3

17. Three more students play piano than which other instrument?

Ⓐ flute   Ⓒ violin

Ⓑ drums   Ⓓ guitar

18. The same number of students play which two instruments?

Ⓐ guitar and drums

Ⓑ piano and drums

Ⓒ drums and flute

Ⓓ flute and piano

19. How many fewer students play flute than play drums?

Ⓐ 2

Ⓑ 3

Ⓒ 4

Ⓓ 5

20. How many more students play piano and guitar combined than play drums?

Ⓐ 29

Ⓑ 19

Ⓒ 10

Ⓓ 9

21. Which of the following statements is true?

Ⓐ All of the students play flute.

Ⓑ None of the students play guitar.

Ⓒ Some of the students play piano.

Ⓓ Most of the students play flute.

22. Ruben is collecting cans for the school recycling contest.

★ Ruben is going to collect 20 cans a week for 8 weeks. How many cans will he collect in all? **Explain** how you found your answer.

_____

_____

_____

★★ Ruben is going to collect cans for 9 weeks. For the first 4 weeks, he plans to collect 30 cans each week. For the last 5 weeks, he plans to collect 20 cans each week. Ruben says he will collect 250 cans. Do you agree? **Explain** your reasoning.

_____

_____

_____

_____

★★★ Ruben has two plans for collecting cans.

Plan A: Collect 20 cans a week for 9 weeks.

Plan B: Collect 30 cans a week for 7 weeks.

Which plan should Ruben choose? **Identify** and **justify** your choice.

_____

_____

_____

_____

Show What You Know ✓

Check your understanding of important skills.

Name _____

▶ **Count On to Add** Use the number line. Write the sum.

1. $6 + 2 =$ _____

2. $3 + 7 =$ _____

▶ **Skip Count by Twos and Fives** Skip count. Write the missing numbers.

3. 2, 4, 6, _____, _____, _____

4. 5, 10, 15, _____, _____, _____

▶ **Model with Arrays** Use the array. Complete.

5.

_____ + _____ + _____ = _____

6.

_____ + _____ = _____

MATH DETECTIVE WITH CARMEN SANDIEGO™

Ryan's class went on a field trip to a farm. They saw 5 cows and 6 chickens. Be a Math Detective to find how many legs were on all the animals they saw.

Vocabulary Builder

▶ **Visualize It** ••••••••••••••••••••••••••••••••

Complete the tree map by using the review words.

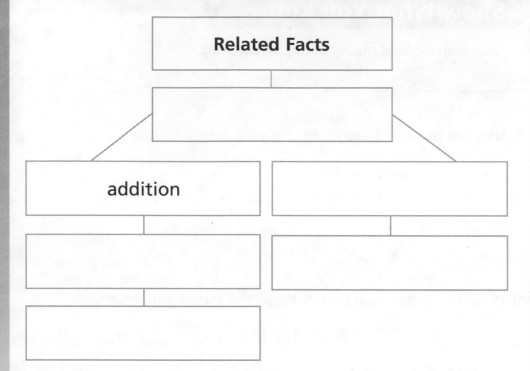

Related Facts

addition

Review Words

addend

addition

difference

number sentences

related facts

subtraction

sum

Preview Words

divide

equation

factor

multiple

multiply

product

quotient

▶ **Understand Vocabulary** •••••••••••••••••••••••••

Read the definition. Write the preview word that matches it.

1. A number sentence that uses the equal sign to show that two amounts are equal. _____

2. The answer in a multiplication problem _____

3. When you combine equal groups to find how many in all _____

4. A number that is multiplied by another number to find a product _____

GO Online • eStudent Edition • Multimedia eGlossary

Name _____

Count Equal Groups

Essential Question How can you use equal groups to find how many in all?

 COMMON CORE
Georgia Performance Standard MCC3.0A.1
Represent and solve problems involving multiplication and division.

🔑 UNLOCK the Problem REAL WORLD

Equal groups have the same number of objects in each group.

Matchbox® cars were invented in 1952. Tim has 6 Matchbox cars. Each car has 4 wheels. How many wheels are there in all?

- How many wheels are on each car?

  _____

- How many equal groups of wheels are there?

  _____

- How can you find how many wheels in all?

  _____

🔒 Activity Use counters to model the equal groups.

Materials ■ counters

STEP 1 Draw 4 counters in each group.

STEP 2 Skip count to find how many wheels in all.
Skip count by 4s until you say 6 numbers.

number of
equal groups →   1   2   3   4   5   6

4, _____, 12, _____, _____, _____

There are _____ groups with _____ wheels in each group.

So, there are _____ wheels in all.

Math Talk

MATHEMATICAL PRACTICES
What if Tim had 8 cars? How could you find the total number of wheels?

🔑 Example Count equal groups to find the total.

Sam, Kyla, and Tia each have 5 pennies.
How many pennies do they have in all?

How many pennies does each person have? _____

How many equal groups of pennies are there? _____

Draw 5 counters in each group.

Think: There are _____ groups of 5 pennies.

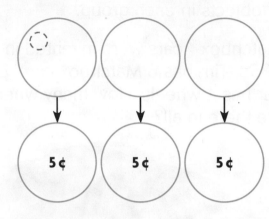

Think: There are _____ fives.

Skip count to find how many pennies in all.   _____ , _____ , _____

So, they have _____ pennies in all.

- ⚡H.O.T. **Explain** why you can skip count by 5s to find how many in all.

_____

_____

Share and Show 📝 MATH BOARD ....

1. Complete. Use the picture. Skip count to find
   how many wheels in all.

_____ groups of 2

_____ twos

Skip count by 2s.   2, 4, _____ , _____

So, there are _____ wheels in all.

Math Talk   What if there were 2
groups of 4 wheels? Would your
answers change? If so, how?

Name _____

Draw equal groups. Skip count to find how many.

2. 2 groups of 6 _____

 3. 3 groups of 2 _____

Count equal groups to find how many.

 4.

_____ groups of _____

_____ in all

5.

_____ groups of _____

_____ in all

On Your Own ....

Draw equal groups. Skip count to find how many.

6. 3 groups of 3 _____

7. 2 groups of 9 _____

Count equal groups to find how many.

8.

_____ groups of _____

_____ in all

9.

_____ groups of _____

_____ in all

UNLOCK the Problem REAL WORLD

★ PARCC TEST PREP

10. Tina, Charlie, and Amber have Matchbox cars. Each car has 4 wheels. How many wheels do their cars have altogether?

Ⓐ 10 Ⓒ 40

Ⓑ 22 Ⓓ 44

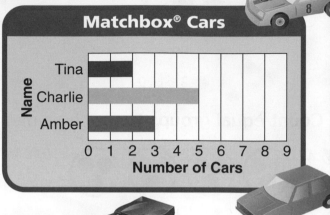

Matchbox® Cars

Name:
Tina
Charlie
Amber

0 1 2 3 4 5 6 7 8 9
Number of Cars

a. What do you need to find?

_____

b. What information will you use from the graph to solve the problem?

_____

c. Show the steps you used to solve the problem.

d. Complete the sentences.

Tina has _____ cars.

Charlie has _____ cars.

Amber has _____ cars.

There are _____ groups of 4 wheels.

The cars have _____ wheels altogether.

e. Fill in the bubble for the correct answer choice.

11. A Matchbox car costs $3. What is the price of 4 Matchbox® cars?

Ⓐ $7

Ⓑ $12

Ⓒ $14

Ⓓ $20

12. Nita has 7 Matchbox cars. Each car has 4 wheels. How many wheels do Nita's cars have altogether?

Ⓐ 4

Ⓑ 7

Ⓒ 11

Ⓓ 28

Name _____

Relate Addition and Multiplication

Essential Question How is multiplication like addition? How is it different?

ALGEBRA
Lesson 5.2

COMMON CORE
Georgia Performance Standard MCC3.OA.1
Represent and solve problems involving multiplication and division.

🔑 UNLOCK the Problem REAL WORLD

Tomeka needs 3 apples to make one apple cake. Each cake has the same number of apples. How many apples does Tomeka need to make 4 cakes?

- How many cakes is Tomeka making?
  _____
- How many apples are in each cake?
  _____
- How can you solve the problem?
  _____

🔒 One Way Add equal groups.

Use the 4 circles to show the 4 cakes.

Draw 3 counters in each circle to show the apples Tomeka needs for each cake.

Find the number of counters in all. Complete the addition sentence.

3 + _____ + _____ + _____ = _____

So, Tomeka needs _____ apples to

make _____ cakes.

Math Talk MATHEMATICAL PRACTICES How is the picture you drew like the addition sentence you wrote?

© Houghton Mifflin Harcourt Publishing Company

🔑 Another Way Multiply.

When you combine equal groups, you can **multiply** to find how many in all.

Think: 4 groups of 3

Draw 3 counters in each circle.

Since there are the same number of counters in each circle, you can multiply to find how many in all.

Multiplication is another way to find how many there are altogether in equal groups.

Write:

$$4 \times 3 = 12$$

    ↑   ↑   ↑

  factor   factor   product

or

$$\begin{array}{r} 3 \leftarrow \text{factor} \\ \times\, 4 \leftarrow \text{factor} \\ \hline 12 \leftarrow \text{product} \end{array}$$

Read: Four times three equals twelve.

The **factors** are the numbers multiplied.
The **product** is the answer to a multiplication problem.

Share and Show . . . .

1. Write related addition and multiplication sentences for the model.

_____ + _____ + _____ + _____ = _____

_____ × _____ = _____

Math Talk How would you change this model so you could write a multiplication sentence to match it?

Name _____

Draw a quick picture to show the equal groups. Then write related addition and multiplication sentences.

2. 3 groups of 6

___ + ___ + ___ = ___

___ × ___ = ___

3. 2 groups of 3

___ + ___ = ___

___ × ___ = ___

On Your Own ....

Draw a quick picture to show the equal groups. Then write related addition and multiplication sentences.

4. 4 groups of 2

___ + ___ + ___ + ___ = ___

___ × ___ = ___

5. 5 groups of 4

___ + ___ + ___ + ___ + ___ = ___

___ × ___ = ___

Complete. Write a multiplication sentence.

6.

___ × ___ = ___

7.

___ × ___ = ___

8.

___ × ___ = ___

9. 2 + 2 + 2 + 2 = ____

___ × ___ = ___

10. 4 + 4 + 4 + 4 = ____

___ × ___ = ___

11. 9 + 9 + 9 = ___

___ × ___ = ___

Problem Solving REAL WORLD

Use the table for 12–13.

12. Morris bought 4 peaches. How much do the peaches weigh in all? Write a multiplication sentence to find the weight of the peaches.

    _____ × _____ = _____ ounces

13. **H.O.T.** Thomas bought 2 apples. Sydney bought 4 bananas. Which weighed more— the 2 apples or the 4 bananas? How much more? **Explain** how you know.

    _____

    _____

    _____

Average Weight of Fruits	
Fruit	Weight in Ounces
Apple	6
Orange	5
Peach	3
Banana	4

SHOW YOUR WORK

14. **Sense or Nonsense?** Shane said that he could write related multiplication and addition sentences for $6 + 4 + 3$. Does Shane's statement make sense? **Explain**.

    _____

    _____

    _____

15. **Write Math** Write a word problem that can be solved using 3×4. Solve the problem.

    _____

    _____

    _____

16. ⭐ **PARCC Test Prep** Which is another way to show $2 + 2 + 2 + 2$?

    Ⓐ 2×2 Ⓒ 4×2

    Ⓑ 5×2 Ⓓ 2×8

Skip Count on a Number Line

Essential Question How can you use a number line to skip count and find how many in all?

COMMON CORE
Georgia Performance Standard MCC3.OA.3
Represent and solve problems involving multiplication and division.

 UNLOCK the Problem REAL WORLD

Caleb wants to make 3 balls of yarn for his cat to play with. He uses 6 feet of yarn to make each ball. How many feet of yarn does Caleb need in all?

- How many equal groups of yarn will Caleb make?

  _____

- How many feet of yarn will be in each group?

  _____

- What do you need to find?

  _____

🔑 **Use a number line to count equal groups.**

How many feet of yarn does Caleb

need for each ball? _____

How many equal lengths of yarn does he need? _____

Begin at 0. Skip count by 6s by drawing jumps on the number line.

0 1 2 3 4 5 6 7 8 9 10 11 12 13 14 15 16 17 18 19 20

How many jumps did you make? _____

How long is each jump? _____

Multiply. $3 \times 6 =$ _____

So, Caleb needs _____ feet of yarn in all.

Math Talk MATHEMATICAL PRACTICES

What if Caleb made 4 balls of yarn with 5 feet of yarn in each ball? What would you do differently to find the total number of feet of yarn?

- Why did you jump by 6s on the number line?

  _____

Share and Show

1. Skip count by drawing jumps on the number line. Find how many in 5 jumps of 4. Then write the product.

Think: 1 jump of 4 shows 1 group of 4.

0 1 2 3 4 5 6 7 8 9 10 11 12 13 14 15 16 17 18 19 20 21 22 23 24 25

$5 \times 4 =$ _____

Draw jumps on the number line to show equal groups. Find the product.

✓ 2. 3 groups of 8

0 1 2 3 4 5 6 7 8 9 10 11 12 13 14 15 16 17 18 19 20 21 22 23 24 25

$3 \times 8 =$ _____.

_____

3. 8 groups of 3

0 1 2 3 4 5 6 7 8 9 10 11 12 13 14 15 16 17 18 19 20 21 22 23 24 25

$8 \times 3 =$ _____

Write the multiplication sentence the number line shows.

✓ 4.

0 1 2 3 4 5 6 7 8 9 10 11 12 13 14 15 16 17 18 19 20 21 22 23 24 25

_____ $\times$ _____ = _____

Math Talk MATHEMATICAL PRACTICES
How do equal jumps on the number line show equal groups?

Name _____

On Your Own ....

Draw jumps on the number line to show equal groups.
Find the product.

5. 6 groups of 4

$6 \times 4 =$ _____

6. 7 groups of 3

$7 \times 3 =$ _____

7. 2 groups of 10

$2 \times 10 =$ _____

Write the multiplication sentence the number line shows.

8.

_____ × _____ = _____

9.

_____ × _____ = _____

© Houghton Mifflin Harcourt Publishing Company

Problem Solving REAL WORLD

10. Erin displays her toy cat collection on 3 shelves. She puts 8 cats on each shelf. If she collects 3 more cats, how many cats will she have?

_____

11. **H.O.T.** Write two multiplication sentences that have a product of 12. Draw jumps on the number line to show the multiplication.

_____ × _____ = _____

_____ × _____ = _____

12. **Write Math** ▶ **Pose a Problem** Write a problem that can be solved by finding 8 groups of 5. Write a multiplication sentence to solve the problem. Then solve.

_____

_____

_____

_____

13. ⭐**PARCC Test Prep** Brooke needs 4 lengths of string, each 2 inches long. How much string does she need altogether?

(A) 2   (C) 6

(B) 4   (D) 8

Name _____

Model with Arrays

Essential Question How can you use arrays to model multiplication and find factors?

COMMON CORE
Georgia Performance Standard MCC3.OA.3
Represent and solve problems involving multiplication and division.

UNLOCK the Problem REAL WORLD

Many people grow tomatoes in their gardens. Lee plants 3 rows of tomato plants with 6 plants in each row. How many tomato plants are there?

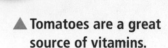 Activity 1

Materials ■ square tiles ■ MathBoard

- You make an **array** by placing the same number of tiles in each row. Make an array with 3 rows of 6 tiles to show the tomato plants.

- Now draw the array you made.

▲ Tomatoes are a great source of vitamins.

- Find the total number of tiles.

  Multiply.   3   ×   6 = _____
              ↑   ↑
         number   number
         of rows   in each row

So, there are _____ tomato plants.

Math Talk Does the number of tiles change if you turn the array to show 6 rows of 3? **Explain.**

MATHEMATICAL PRACTICES

🔒 Activity 2 Materials ■ square tiles ■ MathBoard

Use 8 tiles. Make as many different arrays as you can, using all 8 tiles. Draw the arrays. The first one is done for you.

A

1 row of 8

$1 \times 8 = 8$

B

8 rows of _____

$8 \times$ _____ $= 8$

C

_____ rows of _____

_____ $\times$ _____ $= 8$

D

_____ rows of _____

_____ $\times$ _____ $= 8$

You can make _____ different arrays using 8 tiles.

Share and Show ....

1. Complete. Use the array.

_____ rows of _____ = _____

_____ $\times$ _____ = _____

Write a multiplication sentence for the array.

✓ 2.

_____

✓ 3.

_____

© Houghton Mifflin Harcourt Publishing Company

MATHEMATICAL PRACTICES

Math Talk Suppose you make an array with 12 tiles and you want to put 3 tiles in each row. How do you decide how many rows you need to make?

Name _____

On Your Own......................................

Write a multiplication sentence for the array.

4. ![5×5 array] _____

5. _____

Draw an array to find the product.

6. $3 \times 6 =$ _____

7. $4 \times 7 =$ _____

8. $3 \times 5 =$ _____

9. $4 \times 4 =$ _____

10. Use 6 tiles. Make as many different arrays as you can using all the tiles. Draw the arrays. Then write a multiplication sentence for each array.

_____

_____

Problem Solving REAL WORLD

Use the table to solve 11–12.

11. Mr. Bloom grows vegetables in his garden. Draw an array and write the multiplication sentence to show how many corn plants Mr. Bloom has in his garden.

Mr. Bloom's Garden	
Vegetable	**Planted In**
Beans	4 rows of 6
Carrots	2 rows of 8
Corn	5 rows of 9
Beets	4 rows of 7

_____

12. Write Math ▸ Could Mr. Bloom have planted his carrots in equal rows of 4? If so, how many rows could he have planted? **Explain.**

· · · · · · · · · SHOW YOUR WORK · · · · · · · ·

_____

_____

_____

_____

13. H.O.T. Mr. Bloom has 12 strawberry plants. Describe all of the different arrays that Mr. Bloom could make using all of his strawberry plants. The first one is done for you.

2 rows of 6; _____

_____

14. ⭐ **PARCC Test Prep** What multiplication sentence does this array show?

(A) $2 \times 3 = 6$ (C) $2 \times 5 = 10$

(B) $4 \times 1 = 4$ (D) $2 \times 4 = 8$

Module 5 Assessment

▶ Vocabulary

Choose the best term from the box.

Vocabulary
equal groups
factors
multiply
product

1. When you combine equal groups, you can

   _____ to find how many in all. (p. 102)

2. The answer in a multiplication problem is called the

   _____. (p. 102)

3. The numbers you multiply are called the _____. (p. 102)

▶ Concepts and Skills

Count equal groups to find how many. MCC3.OA.1

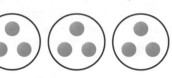

4.

_____ groups of _____

_____ in all

5.

_____ groups of _____

_____ in all

6.

_____ groups of _____

_____ in all

Write related addition and multiplication sentences. MCC3.OA.1

7. 3 groups of 9

   ___ + ___ + ___ = ___

   ___ × ___ = ___

8. 5 groups of 7

   ___ + ___ + ___ + ___ + ___ = ___

   ___ × ___ = ___

Draw jumps on the number line to show equal groups.
Find the product. MCC3.OA.3

9. 6 groups of 3

_____ × _____ = _____

Fill in the bubble for the correct answer choice.

10. Beth's mother made some cookies. She put 4 cookies on each of 8 plates. Which multiplication sentence can be used to find the number of cookies Beth's mother made? MCC3.OA.1

    Ⓐ $8 + 4 = \blacksquare$ Ⓒ $8 \times 4 = \blacksquare$

    Ⓑ $4 \times 4 = \blacksquare$ Ⓓ $4 + 4 + 4 + 4 + 4 + 4 + 4 + 4 = \blacksquare$

11. Avery gave 5 animal stickers to each of 10 friends. Which number sentence can be used to find the number of stickers she gave away? MCC3.OA.3

    Ⓐ $10 + 5 = \blacksquare$

    Ⓑ $10 - 5 = \blacksquare$

    Ⓒ $10 \times 5 = \blacksquare$

    Ⓓ $10 \times 10 = \blacksquare$

12. Matt made 2 equal groups of marbles. Which multiplication sentence shows the total number of marbles? MCC3.OA.1

    Ⓐ $2 \times 2 = 4$

    Ⓑ $2 \times 8 = 16$

    Ⓒ $3 \times 8 = 24$

    Ⓓ $8 \times 8 = 64$

13. Lindsey needs 3 lengths of ribbon each 5 inches long. How much ribbon does she need altogether? MCC3.OA.3

    Ⓐ   3 inches

    Ⓑ   5 inches

    Ⓒ   15 inches

    Ⓓ   20 inches

Name _____

Multiply with 2 and 4

Essential Question How can you multiply with 2 and 4?

COMMON CORE
Georgia Performance Standard MCC3.OA.3
Represent and solve problems involving
multiplication and division.

🔑 UNLOCK the Problem REAL WORLD

Two students are in a play. Each of the students has 3 costumes. How many costumes do they have in all?

Multiplying when there are two equal groups is like adding doubles.

- What does the word "each" tell you?

  _____

- How can you find the number of costumes the 2 students have?

  _____

 Find 2 × 3.

MODEL	THINK	RECORD
Draw counters to show the costumes.	2 groups of 3 3 + 3 6	2 × 3 = 6 ↑ ↑ ↑ how many groups how many in each group how many in all

So, the 2 students have _____ costumes in all.

Try This!

$2 \times 1 = 1 + 1 = 2$

$2 \times 2 = 2 + 2 = 4$

$2 \times \underline{\quad} = 3 + \underline{\quad} = 6$

$2 \times \underline{\quad} = 4 + \underline{\quad} = 8$

$2 \times \underline{\quad} = 5 + \underline{\quad} = \underline{\quad}$

$2 \times \underline{\quad} = 6 + \underline{\quad} = \underline{\quad}$

$2 \times \underline{\quad} = 7 + \underline{\quad} = \underline{\quad}$

$2 \times \underline{\quad} = 8 + \underline{\quad} = \underline{\quad}$

$2 \times \underline{\quad} = 9 + \underline{\quad} = \underline{\quad}$

MATHEMATICAL PRACTICES

Math Talk What do you notice about the product when you multiply by 2?

🔑 **Count by 2s.**

When there are 2 in each group, you can count by 2s to find how many there are in all.

There are 4 students with 2 costumes each. How many costumes do they have in all?

Skip count by drawing the jumps on the number line.

So, the 4 students have _____ in all.

• How can you decide whether to count by 2s or double?

_____

🔑 **Example** Use doubles to find 4×5.

When you multiply with 4, you can multiply with 2 and then double the product.

	MULTIPLY WITH 2	**DOUBLE THE PRODUCT**
4×5	$2 \times 5 = 10$	$10 + 10 = 20$

So, $4 \times 5 =$ _____.

Share and Show 📝

1. Double 2×7 to find 4×7.

   Multiply with 2. $2 \times 7 =$ _____

   Double the product. $14 + 14 =$ _____

   So, $4 \times 7 =$ _____.

© Houghton Mifflin Harcourt Publishing Company

MATHEMATICAL PRACTICES

Math Talk **Explain** how knowing the product for 2×8 helps you find the product for 4×8.

Name _____

Write a multiplication sentence for the model.

2.

____ × ____ = ____

 ✓ 3.

____ × ____ = ____

Find the product.

4.	6	5.	9	6.	2	7.	8	✓ 8.	5
	×2		×4		×7		×4		×2

On Your Own..

Write a multiplication sentence for the model.

9.

____ × ____ = ____

10.

____ × ____ = ____

Find the product. Use your MathBoard.

11.	10	12.	2	13.	4	14.	7	15.	2
	× 4		×9		×6		×2		×0

16.	4	17.	2	18.	4	19.	10	20.	4
	×3		×8		×4		× 2		×5

Algebra Complete the table for the factors 2 and 4.

×	1	2	3	4	5	6	7	8	9	10
21. 2										
22. 4										

 Algebra Write the unknown number.

23. $4 \times 8 = 16 +$ _____   24. $20 = 2 \times$ _____   25. $8 \times 2 = 10 +$ _____

🔑 UNLOCK the Problem — REAL WORLD

26. Ms. Peterson's class sold tickets for the class play. How many tickets in all did Brandon and Haylie sell?

Play Tickets	
Name	**Tickets Sold**
Brandon	🎟🎟🎟🎟
Haylie	🎟🎟🎟🎟🎟🎟
Elizabeth	🎟🎟🎟🎟🎟🎟🎟

Key: Each 🎟 = 2 tickets sold.

a. What do you need to find? _____

_____

b. Why can you multiply to find the number of tickets shown? **Explain**.

_____

_____

c. Show the steps you used to solve the problem.

d. Complete the sentences.

Brandon sold _____ tickets.

Haylie sold _____ tickets.

Together, Brandon and Haylie sold

_____ tickets.

---

27. 🔶**H.O.T.** Suppose Sam sold 20 tickets to the school play. How many tickets should be on the picture graph above to show his sales? **Explain**.

_____

_____

_____

28. ⭐**PARCC Test Prep** Lindsey, Louis, Sally, and Matt each brought 5 guests to the school play. Which number sentence shows their total number of guests?

Ⓐ $4 + 5 = 9$ Ⓒ $4 \times 4 = 16$

Ⓑ $5 + 4 = 9$ Ⓓ $4 \times 5 = 20$

Name _____

Multiply with 5 and 10

Essential Question How can you multiply with 5 and 10?

Lesson 6.2

COMMON CORE
Georgia Performance Standard MCC3.OA.3
Represent and solve problems involving multiplication and division.

🔑 UNLOCK the Problem REAL WORLD

Marcel is making 6 doll-sized banjos. He needs 5 strings for each banjo. How many strings does he need in all?

🔑 **Use skip counting.**

Skip count by 5s until you say 6 numbers.

5, _____, _____, _____, _____, _____

$6 \times 5 =$ _____

So, Marcel needs _____ strings in all.

- How many banjos is Marcel making? _____
- How many strings does each banjo have? _____

🔑 Example 1 Use a number line.

Each string is 10 inches long. How many inches of string will Marcel use for each banjo?

Think: 1 jump = 10 inches

0   5   10   15   20   25   30   35   40   45   50

- Draw 5 jumps for the 5 strings. Jump 10 spaces at a time for the length of each string.

- You land on 10, _____, _____, _____, and _____. $5 \times 10 =$ _____

The numbers 10, 20, 30, 40, and 50 are multiples of 10.

So, Marcel will use _____ inches of string for each banjo.

A **multiple** of 10 is any product that has 10 as one of its factors.

Math Talk

MATHEMATICAL PRACTICES

What do you notice about the multiples of 10?

© Houghton Mifflin Harcourt Publishing Company

Module 6   119

🔒 Example 2 Use a bar model.

Marcel bought 3 packages of strings. Each package cost 10¢. How much did the packages cost in all?

MODEL	THINK	RECORD
	1 unit → 10¢	
10¢ | 10¢ | 10¢	3 units → ____ × ____	____ × ____ = ____

So, the packages of strings cost _____ in all.

Share and Show MATH BOARD •

1. How can you use this number line to find 8 × 5?

```
0     5     10     15     20     25     30     35     40
```

_____

_____

Math Talk MATHEMATICAL PRACTICES
Explain how knowing 4 × 5 can help you find 4 × 10.

Find the product.

2. 2 × 5 = ____   3. ____ = 6 × 10   4. ____ = 5 × 5   ✓5. 10 × 7 = ____

6. 10   7.   5   8. 10   ✓9.   5
   × 4   ×6   × 0   ×3

10.   7   11.   5   12.   4   13.   9
    ×5   ×10   ×5   ×10

© Houghton Mifflin Harcourt Publishing Company

Name _____

On Your Own ....

Find the product.

14. $5 \times 1 =$ _____

15. _____ $= 10 \times 2$

16. _____ $= 4 \times 5$

17. $10 \times 10 =$ _____

18. $10 \times 0 =$ _____

19. $10 \times 5 =$ _____

20. _____ $= 1 \times 5$

21. _____ $= 5 \times 9$

22. $\begin{array}{r} 3 \\ \times 4 \\ \hline \end{array}$

23. $\begin{array}{r} 5 \\ \times 0 \\ \hline \end{array}$

24. $\begin{array}{r} 4 \\ \times 8 \\ \hline \end{array}$

25. $\begin{array}{r} 10 \\ \times 5 \\ \hline \end{array}$

26. $\begin{array}{r} 10 \\ \times 9 \\ \hline \end{array}$

27. $\begin{array}{r} 10 \\ \times 1 \\ \hline \end{array}$

28. $\begin{array}{r} 10 \\ \times 8 \\ \hline \end{array}$

29. $\begin{array}{r} 9 \\ \times 2 \\ \hline \end{array}$

30. $\begin{array}{r} 4 \\ \times 10 \\ \hline \end{array}$

31. $\begin{array}{r} 5 \\ \times 9 \\ \hline \end{array}$

32. $\begin{array}{r} 5 \\ \times 0 \\ \hline \end{array}$

33. $\begin{array}{r} 5 \\ \times 7 \\ \hline \end{array}$

H.O.T. **Algebra** Use the pictures to find the unknown numbers.

34.

$3 \times$ _____ $=$ _____

35.

_____ $\times 3 =$ _____ _____

Complete the bar model to solve.

36. Marcel played 5 songs on the banjo. If each song lasted 8 minutes, how long did he play?

_____ minutes

37. There are 6 banjo players. If each player needs 10 sheets of music, how many sheets of music are needed?

_____ sheets

Problem Solving REAL WORLD

Use the table for 38–39.

38. John and his dad own 7 banjos. They want to replace the strings on all of them. How many strings should they buy? Write a multiplication sentence to solve.

39. **H.O.T.** Mr. Lemke has 5 guitars, 4 banjos, and 2 mandolins. What is the total number of strings on Mr. Lemke's instruments?

40. Mrs. Thompson has 4 shelves with 5 violins on each shelf. How many violins does Mrs. Thompson have? Complete the bar model to solve.

violins

41. **Write Math** **What's the Error?** Mr. James has 3 banjos. Mr. Lewis has 5 times the number of banjos Mr. James has. Riley says Mr. Lewis has 12 banjos. Describe her error.

42. ⭐ **PARCC Test Prep** There are 5 guitars on each of 5 shelves at a music store. How many guitars are there?

Ⓐ 10   Ⓒ 20

Ⓑ 15   Ⓓ 25

Stringed Instruments	
Instrument	Strings
Guitar	6
Banjo	5
Mandolin	8
Violin	4

················ **SHOW YOUR WORK** ················

Name _____

Multiply with 3 and 6

Essential Question What are some ways to multiply with 3 and 6?

 COMMON CORE
Georgia Performance Standard MCC3.OA.3
Represent and solve problems involving multiplication and division.

UNLOCK the Problem REAL WORLD

Sabrina is making triangles with toothpicks. She uses 3 toothpicks for each triangle. She makes 4 triangles. How many toothpicks does Sabrina use?

> • Why does Sabrina need 3 toothpicks for each triangle?
>
> _____
>
> _____

🔒 **Draw a picture.**

STEP 1

Complete the 4 triangles.

STEP 2

Skip count by the number of sides. _____, _____, _____, _____

How many triangles are there in all? _____

How many toothpicks are in each triangle? _____

How many toothpicks are there in all?

4 × _____ = _____

4 triangles have _____ toothpicks.

So, Sabrina uses _____ toothpicks.

Math Talk MATHEMATICAL PRACTICES How can you use what you know about the number of toothpicks needed for 4 triangles to find the number of toothpicks needed for 8 triangles? **Explain.**

Try This! Find the number of toothpicks needed for 6 triangles.

Draw a quick picture to help you. How did you find the answer?

_____

_____

_____

Jessica is using craft sticks to make 6 octagons.
How many craft sticks will she use in all?

🔑 One Way Use 5s facts and addition.

▲ An octagon has 8 sides.

To multiply a factor by 6, multiply the factor
by 5, and then add the factor.

$6 \times 7 = 5 \times 7 + 7 = 42$

$6 \times 6 = 5 \times 6 + \underline{\hspace{1cm}} = \underline{\hspace{1cm}}$

$6 \times 8 = 5 \times \underline{\hspace{1cm}} + \underline{\hspace{1cm}} = \underline{\hspace{1cm}}$

$6 \times 9 = \underline{\hspace{1cm}} \times \underline{\hspace{1cm}} + \underline{\hspace{1cm}} = \underline{\hspace{1cm}}$

So, Jessica will use _____ craft sticks.

5×8

$+ 8$

🔑 Other Ways

Ⓐ Use doubles.

When at least one factor is an even number, you can use doubles.

$6 \times 8 = \blacksquare$

First multiply with half of an even number.

$3 \times 8 = \underline{\hspace{1cm}}$

After you multiply, double the product.

$\underline{\hspace{1cm}} + 24 = \underline{\hspace{1cm}}$

$6 \times 8 = \underline{\hspace{1cm}}$

Ⓑ Use a multiplication table.

Find the product 6×8 where
row 6 and column 8 meet.

$6 \times 8 = \underline{\hspace{1cm}}$

• Shade the row for 3 in the table. Then,
compare the rows for 3 and 6. What do
you notice about their products?

_____

_____

×	0	1	2	3	4	5	6	7	8	9	10
0	0	0	0	0	0	0	0	0	0	0	0
1	0	1	2	3	4	5	6	7	8	9	10
2	0	2	4	6	8	10	12	14	16	18	20
3	0	3	6	9	12	15	18	21	24	27	30
4	0	4	8	12	16	20	24	28	32	36	40
5	0	5	10	15	20	25	30	35	40	45	50
6	0	6	12	18	24	30	36	42	48	54	60
7	0	7	14	21	28	35	42	49	56	63	70
8	0	8	16	24	32	40	48	56	64	72	80
9	0	9	18	27	36	45	54	63	72	81	90
10	0	10	20	30	40	50	60	70	80	90	100

Name _____

Share and Show

1. Use 5s facts and addition to find $6 \times 4 = $ ■.

$6 \times 4 = $ _____ $\times$ _____ $+$ _____ $= $ _____

$6 \times 4 = $ _____

Math Talk **Explain** how you would use 5s facts and addition to find 6×3.

Find the product.

2. $6 \times 1 = $ _____   3. _____ $= 3 \times 7$ ✓ 4. _____ $= 6 \times 5$ ✓ 5. $3 \times 9 = $ _____

On Your Own

Find the product.

6. $2 \times 3 = $ _____   7. _____ $= 3 \times 6$ 8. _____ $= 3 \times 0$ 9. $1 \times 6 = $ _____

10. $\begin{array}{r} 3 \\ \times 6 \\ \hline \end{array}$ 11. $\begin{array}{r} 8 \\ \times 3 \\ \hline \end{array}$ 12. $\begin{array}{r} 6 \\ \times 7 \\ \hline \end{array}$ 13. $\begin{array}{r} 3 \\ \times 3 \\ \hline \end{array}$ 14. $\begin{array}{r} 10 \\ \times 6 \\ \hline \end{array}$

H.O.T. Algebra Complete the table.

	Multiply by 3.	
	Factor	Product
15.	4	
16.		18

	Multiply by 6.	
	Factor	Product
17.	5	
18.	7	

19.	Multiply by ☐.	
	Factor	Product
	3	15
20.	2	

Problem Solving

REAL WORLD

Use the table for 21–22.

21. The table tells about quilt pieces Jenna has made. How many squares are there in 6 of Jenna's quilt pieces?

_____

22. How many more squares than triangles are in 3 of Jenna's quilt pieces?

_____

Quilt Pieces	
Shape	Number in One Quilt Piece
Square	6
Triangle	4
Circle	4

SHOW YOUR WORK

23. **Write Math** ▶ **What if** you used craft sticks to make shapes? If you used one craft stick for each side, would you use more craft sticks for 5 squares or 6 triangles? **Explain**.

_____

_____

_____

_____

24. **H.O.T.** Draw a picture and use words to explain the Commutative Property of Multiplication with the factors 3 and 4.

_____

_____

_____

25. ⭐ **PARCC Test Prep** There are 8 crayons in each of 6 packages. How many crayons are there?

Ⓐ 2   Ⓑ 14   Ⓒ 24   Ⓓ 48

Name _____

Find Unknown Factors

Essential Question How can you use an array or a multiplication table to find an unknown factor?

COMMON CORE
Georgia Performance Standard MCC3.OA.4
Represent and solve problems involving multiplication and division.

🔑 UNLOCK the Problem   REAL WORLD

Tanisha plans to invite 24 people to a picnic. The invitations come in packs of 8. How many packs of invitations does Tanisha need to buy?

An **equation** is a number sentence that uses the equal sign to show that two amounts are equal.

A symbol or letter can stand for an unknown factor. You can write the equation, $n \times 8 = 24$, to find how many packs of invitations Tanisha needs. Find the number, n, that makes the equation true.

- How many people is Tanisha inviting? _____
- How many invitations are in 1 pack? _____

🔒 One Way Use an array.

- Show an array with 24 tiles with 8 tiles in each row by completing the drawing.

$$
\begin{array}{ccccc}
n & \times & 8 & = & 24 \\
\uparrow & & \uparrow & & \uparrow \\
\text{factor} & & \text{factor} & & \text{product} \\
\text{number of} & & \text{number in} & & \text{total} \\
\text{rows} & & \text{each row} & & \text{number}
\end{array}
$$

Math Talk **MATHEMATICAL PRACTICES**
Explain how the array represents the problem. How do the factors relate to the array?

- Count how many rows of 8 tiles there are.   **Think:** What number times 8 equals 24?

There are _____ rows of 8 tiles. The unknown factor is _____. $n =$ _____

_____ $\times 8 = 24$ Check.

_____ $= 24$ ✓ The equation is true.

So, Tanisha needs _____ packs of invitations.

🔑 Another Way Use a multiplication table.

■ × 8 = 24

Think: The symbol, ■, stands for the unknown factor.

×	0	1	2	3	4	5	6	7	8	9	10
0	0	0	0	0	0	0	0	0	0	0	0
1	0	1	2	3	4	5	6	7	8	9	10
2	0	2	4	6	8	10	12	14	16	18	20
3	0	3	6	9	12	15	18	21	24	27	30
4	0	4	8	12	16	20	24	28	32	36	40
5	0	5	10	15	20	25	30	35	40	45	50
6	0	6	12	18	24	30	36	42	48	54	60
7	0	7	14	21	28	35	42	49	56	63	70
8	0	8	16	24	32	40	48	56	64	72	80
9	0	9	18	27	36	45	54	63	72	81	90
10	0	10	20	30	40	50	60	70	80	90	100

Start at the column for the factor 8, since 8 is the second factor.

Look down to find the product, 24.

Look left across the row from 24.

The unknown factor is _____.

■ = _____

_____ × 8 = 24   Check.

_____ = 24 ✓ The equation is true.

Math Talk MATHEMATICAL PRACTICES
How can you use the Commutative Property to check your answer?

Share and Show ....

1. What is the unknown factor shown by this array?

5 × ■ = 35

■ = _____

Find the unknown factor.

2. $d × 3 = 27$

$d =$ _____

3. $6 × ▲ = 30$

$▲ =$ _____

✓4. $20 = c × 5$

$c =$ _____

✓5. $■ × 2 = 14$

$■ =$ _____

6. $36 = b × 9$

$b =$ _____

7. $8 × e = 64$

$e =$ _____

8. $7 × ★ = 42$

$★ =$ _____

9. $z × 9 = 72$

$z =$ _____

Math Talk MATHEMATICAL PRACTICES
Explain how you know if you are looking for the number of rows or the number in each row when you make an array to find an unknown factor.

On Your Own ....

Find the unknown factor.

10. $\blacksquare \times 2 = 18$

$\blacksquare =$ _____

11. $28 = 4 \times m$

$m =$ _____

12. $y \times 3 = 9$

$y =$ _____

13. $7 \times g = 63$

$g =$ _____

14. $5 \times p = 40$

$p =$ _____

15. $8 \times w = 56$

$w =$ _____

16. $36 = \blacklozenge \times 6$

$\blacklozenge =$ _____

17. $8 \times e = 72$

$e =$ _____

18. $9 \times \bigstar = 27$

$\bigstar =$ _____

19. $6 \times a = 60$

$a =$ _____

20. $d \times 5 = 10$

$d =$ _____

21. $32 = 8 \times n$

$n =$ _____

22. $a \times 4 = 24$

$a =$ _____

23. $7 = 7 \times n$

$n =$ _____

24. $w \times 3 = 15$

$w =$ _____

25. $\bigstar \times 8 = 48$

$\bigstar =$ _____

26. $35 = h \times 5$

$h =$ _____

27. $54 = \blacktriangle \times 6$

$\blacktriangle =$ _____

28. $7 \times p = 49$

$p =$ _____

29. $y \times 4 = 36$

$y =$ _____

H.O.T. **Algebra** Find the unknown factor.

30. $3 \times 6 = k \times 9$

$k =$ _____

31. $4 \times y = 2 \times 6$

$y =$ _____

32. $5 \times g = 36 - 6$

$g =$ _____

33. $6 \times 4 = \blacksquare \times 3$

$\blacksquare =$ _____

34. $9 \times d = 70 + 2$

$d =$ _____

35. $8 \times h = 60 - 4$

$h =$ _____

Problem Solving REAL WORLD

Use the table for 36–40.

Picnic Supplies

Item	Number in 1 Pack	Cost
Bowls	6	$10
Cups	8	$3
Tablecloth	1	$2
Napkins	36	$2
Forks	50	$3

36. Tanisha needs 40 cups for the picnic. How many packs of cups should she buy?

_____

37. **H.O.T.** **Write Math** **What if** Tanisha needs 40 bowls for the picnic? **Explain** how to write an equation with a letter for an unknown factor to find the number of packs she should buy. Then find the unknown factor.

_____

_____

_____

38. Ms. Hill buys 3 tablecloths and 2 packs of napkins. How much does she spend?

_____

39. **H.O.T.** **What if** Randy needs an equal number of bowls and cups for his picnic? How many packs of each will he need to buy?

_____

_____

40. **H.O.T.** Lori buys 200 forks. She gives the cashier $20. How much change should she get?

_____

41. ★ **PARCC Test Prep** What is the unknown factor?

$$m \times 6 = 48$$

Ⓐ 8   Ⓑ 7   Ⓒ 6   Ⓓ 5

SHOW YOUR WORK

Name _____

▶ **Vocabulary**

Choose the term from the box to complete the sentence.

Vocabulary
equation
multiple
multiply

1. An _____ is a number sentence that uses the equal sign to show that two amounts are equal. (p. 127)

2. A _____ of 4 is any product that has 4 as one of its factors. (p. 119)

▶ **Concepts and Skills**

Find the product. MCC3.OA.3

3. $3 \times 1 =$ _____

4. $5 \times 6 =$ _____

5. $5 \times 5 =$ _____

6. $2 \times 10 =$ _____

7. $2 \times 5 =$ _____

8. $4 \times 10 =$ _____

9. $6 \times 4 =$ _____

10. $3 \times 7 =$ _____

11. $\begin{array}{r} 2 \\ \times 1 \\ \hline \end{array}$

12. $\begin{array}{r} 6 \\ \times 6 \\ \hline \end{array}$

13. $\begin{array}{r} 4 \\ \times 4 \\ \hline \end{array}$

14. $\begin{array}{r} 6 \\ \times 0 \\ \hline \end{array}$

15. $\begin{array}{r} 3 \\ \times 8 \\ \hline \end{array}$

Find the unknown factor. MCC3.OA.4

16. $m \times 5 = 30$

   $m =$ _____

17. $\blacksquare \times 6 = 48$

   $\blacksquare =$ _____

18. $20 = 2 \times n$

   $n =$ _____

Fill in the bubble for the correct answer choice.

19. Lori saw 6 lightning bugs. They each had 6 legs. How many legs did the lightning bugs have in all?

 MCC3.OA.3

Ⓐ 36

Ⓑ 24

Ⓒ 12

Ⓓ 6

20. Zach gave his dog 2 dog biscuits a day, for 5 days. How many biscuits did Zach give to his dog?

MCC3.OA.3

Ⓐ 3

Ⓑ 7

Ⓒ 10

Ⓓ 30

21. Annette buys 4 boxes of pencils. If there are 8 pencils in each box, how many pencils does she have? MCC3.OA.3

Ⓐ 32

Ⓑ 24

Ⓒ 16

Ⓓ 12

22. What is the unknown factor? MCC3.OA.4
$$f \times 5 = 30$$

Ⓐ 8

Ⓑ 7

Ⓒ 6

Ⓓ 5

Name _____

Problem Solving • Model Division

Essential Question How can you use the strategy *act it out* to solve problems with equal groups?

COMMON CORE
Georgia Performance Standard MCC3.OA.3
Represent and solve problems involving multiplication and division.

 UNLOCK the Problem REAL WORLD

Stacy has 16 flowers. She puts an equal number of flowers in each of 4 vases. How many flowers does Stacy put in each vase?

Use the graphic organizer below to solve the problem.

Read the Problem

What do I need to find?

I need to find the number

of _____ Stacy puts in

each _____ .

What information do I need to use?

Stacy has _____ flowers. She puts an equal number of flowers in each of

_____ vases.

How will I use the information?

I will act out the problem

by making equal _____ with counters.

Solve the Problem

Describe how to act out the problem to solve.

First, count out _____ counters.

Next, make _____ equal groups. Place 1 counter at a time in each group until all 16 counters are used.

Last, draw the equal groups by completing the picture below.

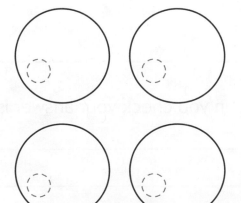

So, Stacy puts _____ flowers in each vase.

© Houghton Mifflin Harcourt Publishing Company

🔑 Try Another Problem

Hayden is planning a party. He bakes 21 cookies. If he plans to give each person 3 cookies, how many people will be at his party?

Read the Problem	Solve the Problem
What do I need to find?	**Describe how to act out the problem to solve.**
What information do I need to use?	
How will I use the information?	

• How can you check your answer is reasonable? _____

_____

_____

© Houghton Mifflin Harcourt Publishing Company

Math Talk **Explain** how acting out a problem helps you solve it.

Name _____

Share and Show

♀ UNLOCK the Problem Tips

✓ Circle the question.
✓ Underline important facts.
✓ Act out the problem with counters.

1. Sue is having a party. She has 16 cups. She puts them in 2 equal stacks. How many cups are in each stack?

   First, decide how to act out the problem.

   You can use counters to represent the _____.

   You can draw _____ to represent the stacks.

   Then, draw to find the number of _____ in each stack.

SHOW YOUR WORK

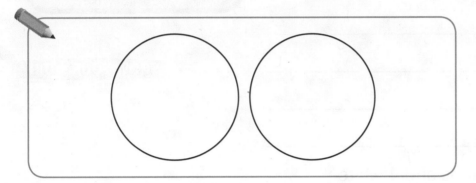

   There are _____ groups. There are _____ counters in each group.

   So, there are _____ cups in each stack.

2. **H.O.T.** **What if** Sue has 24 cups and puts 4 cups in each stack? If she already made 4 stacks, how many more stacks can she make with the remaining cups?

   _____

3. At Luke's school party, the children get into teams to play a game. If there are 35 children and they make teams of 5, how many teams are there?

   _____

4. Anne put 20 cupcakes on 4 plates. If she put the same number of cupcakes on each one, how many cupcakes did she put on each plate?

   _____

© Houghton Mifflin Harcourt Publishing Company

On Your Own

Use the table for 5–6.

Choose a
STRATEGY

Act It Out
Draw a Diagram
Find a Pattern
Make a Table

MATHEMATICAL PRACTICES

Model • Reason • Make Sense

5. Sadie's plates came in packages of 5. How many packages of plates did she buy?

_____

6. **Write Math** ▶ Sadie bought 4 packages of napkins and 3 packages of cups. Which item had more in each package? How many more? **Explain** how you found your answer.

_____

_____

_____

_____

Sadie's Party Supplies

Item	Number
Plates	30
Napkins	28
Cups	24

SHOW YOUR WORK

7. Megan put 3 red balloons and 4 white balloons at each of 4 tables. How many balloons are at the tables altogether?

_____

8. **H.O.T.** There are 12 cookies on plates. List all the ways the cookies could be put equally on the plates.

_____

_____

_____

9. ★ **PARCC Test Prep** Miguel bought 18 party favors. He gave 2 party favors to each of the children at his party. How many children were at Miguel's party?

Ⓐ 20   Ⓑ 16   Ⓒ 9   Ⓓ 8

Size of Equal Groups

Essential Question How can you model a division problem to find how many in each group?

COMMON CORE
Georgia Performance Standard MCC3.OA.2
Represent and solve problems involving multiplication and division.

🔑 **UNLOCK the Problem** REAL WORLD

Hector has 12 rocks from Onondaga Cave State Park. He puts an equal number of his rocks in each of 3 boxes. How many rocks are in each box?

When you multiply, you put equal groups together. When you **divide**, you separate into equal groups.

You can divide to find the number in each group.

• What do you need to find?

_____

• Circle the numbers you need to use.

🔓 **Activity** Use counters to model the problem.

Materials ■ counters ■ MathBoard

STEP 1

Use 12 counters.

▲ Onondaga Cave is located in Leasburg, Missouri. Over the years, water has formed flowstones and other colorful deposits.

STEP 2

Draw 3 circles on your MathBoard. Place 1 counter at a time in each circle until all 12 counters are used. Draw the rest of the counters to show your work.

There are _____ counters in each group.

So, there are _____ rocks in each box.

Try This!

Madison has 15 rocks. She puts an equal number of rocks in each of 5 boxes. How many rocks are in each box?

STEP 1

Draw 5 squares to show 5 boxes.

_____

STEP 2

Draw 1 counter in each square to show the rocks. Continue drawing 1 counter at a time in each box until all 15 counters are drawn.

There are _____ counters in each group.

So, there are _____ rocks in each box.

MATHEMATICAL PRACTICES

Math Talk **Describe** another way to arrange 15 counters to make equal groups.

1. How many counters did you draw? _____

2. How many equal groups did you make? _____

3. How many counters are in each group? _____

Name _____

Share and Show

1. Jon has 8 counters. He makes 4 equal groups.
   Draw a picture to show the number of counters
   in each group.

Math Talk MATHEMATICAL PRACTICES

Explain how you made the groups equal.

Use counters or draw a quick picture on your
MathBoard. Make equal groups. Complete the table.

	Counters	Number of Equal Groups	Number in Each Group
✓ 2.	10	2	
✓ 3.	24	6	
4.	12	4	

On Your Own

Use counters or draw a quick picture on your
MathBoard. Make equal groups. Complete the table.

	Counters	Number of Equal Groups	Number in Each Group
5.	14	7	
6.	21	3	
7.	20	5	
8.	12	6	
9.	36	9	

© Houghton Mifflin Harcourt Publishing Company

Problem Solving REAL WORLD

Use the table for 10–11.

10. Madison puts all of her photos in a photo album. She puts an equal number of photos on each of 4 pages in her album. How many photos are on each page?

Photos	
Name	**Number of Photos**
Madison	28
Joe	25
Ella	15

_____

11. **H.O.T.** Joe and Ella combine their photos. Then they put an equal number on each page of an 8-page photo album. How many photos are on each page?

_____

SHOW YOUR WORK

12. **Write Math** ➤ Rebekah's family found 30 sand dollars. **Explain** how to share the sand dollars equally among the 6 people in her family.

_____

_____

_____

_____

13. ⭐ **PARCC Test Prep** Zana has 9 rocks from a trip. She puts an equal number of rocks in each of 3 bags. How many rocks are in each bag?

Ⓐ 27   Ⓒ 6

Ⓑ 12   Ⓓ 3

© Houghton Mifflin Harcourt Publishing Company

Name _____

Number of Equal Groups

Essential Question How can you model a division problem to find how many equal groups?

COMMON CORE
Georgia Performance Standard MCC3.OA.2
Represent and solve problems involving multiplication and division.

CONNECT You have learned how to divide to find the number in each group. Now you will learn how to divide to find the number of equal groups.

🔑🗝 UNLOCK the Problem REAL WORLD

William has 12 shells and some boxes. He wants to put his shells in groups of 3. How many boxes does he need for his shells?

- Underline what you need to find.
- How many shells does William want in each group? _____

🔑 **Make equal groups.**

- Look at the 12 counters.
- Circle a group of 3 counters.
- Continue circling groups of 3 until all 12 counters are in groups.

There are _____ groups of counters.

So, William needs _____ boxes for his shells.

Math Talk MATHEMATICAL PRACTICES
Explain how the drawing would change if William wanted to put his shells in groups of 4.

▲ The horse conch can grow to a length of 24 inches!

Try This!

Sarah has 15 shells. She wants to put each group of 5 shells in a box. How many boxes does she need for her shells?

STEP 1

Draw 15 counters.

STEP 2

Make a group of 5 counters by drawing a circle around them. Continue circling groups of 5 until all 15 counters are in groups.

There are _____ groups of 5 counters.

So, Sarah needs _____ boxes for her shells.

- **H.O.T.** **What if** Sarah puts her 15 shells in groups of 3?

How many boxes does she need? _____
Draw a quick picture to show your work.

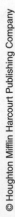

Name _____

Share and Show ....

1. Emily has 12 counters. She puts them in groups of 2. Draw a picture to show the number of groups.

MATHEMATICAL PRACTICES

Math Talk Explain how you find the number of equal groups when you divide.

Draw counters on your MathBoard. Then circle equal groups. Complete the table.

	Counters	Number of Equal Groups	Number in Each Group
✓ 2.	20		4
✓ 3.	24		3
4.	18		2

On Your Own ....

Draw counters on your MathBoard. Then circle equal groups. Complete the table.

	Counters	Number of Equal Groups	Number in Each Group
5.	16		8
6.	25		5
7.	27		9
8.	32		4

UNLOCK the Problem   REAL WORLD

9. A store has 24 beach towels in stacks of 6 towels each. How many stacks of beach towels are at the store?

a. What do you need to find? _____

_____

b. How will you use what you know about making equal groups

to solve the problem? _____

_____

c. Draw equal groups to find how many stacks of beach towels there are at the store.

d. Complete the sentences.

The store has _____ beach towels.

There are _____ towels in each stack.

So, there are _____ stacks of beach towels at the store.

10. Some friends share 35 beach toys equally. If each friend gets 5 beach toys, how many friends are there?

_____

11. ★ **PARCC Test Prep** Dan's train is 27 inches long. If each train car is 3 inches long, how many train cars are there?

- (A) 9
- (B) 8
- (C) 7
- (D) 6

Name _____

Model with Bar Models

Essential Question How can you use bar models to solve division problems?

COMMON CORE
Georgia Performance Standard MCC3.OA.2
Represent and solve problems involving multiplication and division.

UNLOCK the Problem

A dog trainer has 20 dog treats for 5 dogs in his class. If each dog gets the same number of treats, how many treats will each dog get?

• What do you need to find?

_____

Activity 1 Use counters to find how many in each group.

Materials ■ counters ■ MathBoard

• Use 20 counters.

• Draw 5 circles on your MathBoard.

• Place 1 counter at a time in each circle until all 20 counters are used.

• Draw the rest of the counters to show your work.

There are _____ counters in each of the 5 groups.

A bar model can show how the parts of a problem are related.

• Complete the bar model to show 20 dog treats divided into 5 equal groups.

20 dog treats

So, each dog will get _____ treats.

🔑 Activity 2 Draw to find how many equal groups.

A dog trainer has 20 dog treats. If he gives 5 treats to each dog in his class, how many dogs are in the class?

- Look at the 20 counters.
- Circle a group of 5 counters.
- Continue circling groups of 5 until all 20 counters are in groups.

There are _____ groups of 5 counters.

- Complete the bar model to show 20 treats divided into groups of 5 treats.

So, there are _____ dogs in the class.

____ dogs

| 5 | | 5 |

20 dog treats

Here are two ways to record division.

Write: 20 ÷ 5 = 4
↑   ↑   ↑
dividend   **divisor**   **quotient**

$$4 \leftarrow \text{quotient}$$
divisor → $5\overline{)20}$
↑
dividend

Read: Twenty divided by five equals four.

Math Talk   MATHEMATICAL PRACTICES
Describe how you solved the problem. Use the terms *dividend*, *divisor*, and *quotient* in your explanation.

Share and Show . . . .

1. Complete the picture to find 12 ÷ 4. _____

Math Talk   MATHEMATICAL PRACTICES
Explain how you know how many groups to make.

146

Name _____

Write a division equation for the picture.

2.

_____

3.

_____

On Your Own ....

Write a division equation for the picture.

4.

_____

5.

_____

Practice: Copy and Solve Make equal groups to find the quotient. Draw a quick picture to show your work.

6. $20 \div 2$ 7. $27 \div 9$

8. $20 \div 5$ 9. $18 \div 3$

Complete the bar model to solve. Then write a division equation for the bar model.

10. There are 24 books in 4 equal stacks. How many books are in each stack?

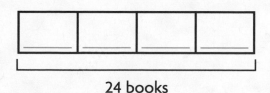

24 books

_____

11. There are 8 matching socks. How many pairs of socks can you make?

_____ pairs

2			2

8 socks

_____

Problem Solving REAL WORLD

Use the table for 12–13.

12. Kevin bought a box of Puppy Chips for his dog. If he gives his dog 5 treats each day, for how many days will one box of treats last?

_____

13. **H.O.T.** Pat bought one box of Chew Sticks to share equally between his 2 dogs. Mia bought one box of Chewies to share equally among her 5 dogs. How many more treats will each of Pat's dogs get than each of Mia's dogs? **Explain**.

_____

_____

_____

_____

Dog Treats

Type	Number in Box
Chew Sticks	14
Chewies	25
Dog Bites	30
Puppy Chips	45

SHOW YOUR WORK

14. **Write Math** **Pose a Problem** Write and solve a problem for $42 \div 7$ in which the quotient is the number of groups.

_____

_____

_____

15. ⭐ **PARCC Test Prep** Ed buys 5 bags of treats. He buys 15 treats in all. How many treats are in each bag?

15 treats

(A) 2   (B) 3   (C) 4   (D) 5

Relate Subtraction and Division

Essential Question How is division related to subtraction?

 COMMON CORE
Georgia Performance Standard MCC3.OA.3
Represent and solve problems involving multiplication and division.

 UNLOCK the Problem REAL WORLD

Serena and Mandy brought a total of 12 newspapers to school for the recycling program. Each girl brought in one newspaper each day. For how many days did the girls bring in newspapers?

- How many newspapers were brought in altogether?

  _____

- How many newspapers did the two girls bring in altogether each day?

  _____

 One Way Use repeated subtraction.

- Start with 12.

- Subtract 2 until you reach 0.

- Count the number of times you subtract 2.

Number of times you subtract 2:

$$\begin{array}{cccccc} 12 & 10 & 8 & 6 & 4 & 2 \\ -\,2 & -\,2 & -2 & -2 & -2 & -2 \\ \hline 10 & 8 & \quad & \quad & \quad & \quad \end{array}$$

       1   2   3   4   5   6

Since you subtract 2 six times, there are _____ groups of 2 in 12.

So, Serena and Mandy brought in newspapers for _____ days.

Write: $12 \div 2 = 6$ or $2\overline{)12}$ (with 6 above)

Read: Twelve divided by two equals six.

⚠ **ERROR Alert**
Be sure to keep subtracting 2 until you are unable to subtract 2 anymore.

🔑 Another Way Count back on a number line.

- Start at 12.
- Count back by 2s as many times as you can. Draw the rest of the jumps on the number line.
- Count the number of times you jumped back 2.

You jumped back by 2 six times.

There are _____ jumps of 2 in 12.

$12 \div 2 =$ _____

> **Math Talk** MATHEMATICAL PRACTICES
> **Explain** in your own words how you found the answer.

- What do your jumps of 2 represent? _____

_____

Share and Show ....

1. Draw the rest of the jumps on the number line to complete the division equation. $12 \div 4 =$ _____

> **Math Talk** MATHEMATICAL PRACTICES
> **Explain** how counting back on a number line is like using repeated subtraction.

Write a division equation.

✓2.
$$\begin{array}{r} 10 \\ -\ 5 \\ \hline 5 \end{array} \qquad \begin{array}{r} 5 \\ -\ 5 \\ \hline 0 \end{array}$$

✓3.

Name _____

On Your Own ....

Write a division equation.

4.

$$\begin{array}{r} 28 \\ -\ 7 \\ \hline 21 \end{array} \nearrow \begin{array}{r} 21 \\ -\ 7 \\ \hline 14 \end{array} \nearrow \begin{array}{r} 14 \\ -\ 7 \\ \hline 7 \end{array} \nearrow \begin{array}{r} 7 \\ -\ 7 \\ \hline 0 \end{array}$$

_____

5.

_____

6.

$$\begin{array}{r} 24 \\ -\ 8 \\ \hline 16 \end{array} \nearrow \begin{array}{r} 16 \\ -\ 8 \\ \hline 8 \end{array} \nearrow \begin{array}{r} 8 \\ -\ 8 \\ \hline 0 \end{array}$$

_____

7.

_____

8. **H.O.T.** Write a word problem that can be solved by
using one of the division equations above.

_____

_____

Use repeated subtraction or a number line to solve.

9. $18 \div 6 =$ _____

10. $14 \div 7 =$ _____

11. $9\overline{)27}$

12. $3\overline{)24}$

Problem Solving REAL WORLD

Use the graph for 13–15.

Box Top Collections

13. Matt puts his box tops in 2 equal piles. How many box tops are in each pile?

_____

14. **H.O.T.** Paige brought an equal number of box tops to school each day for 5 days. Alma also brought an equal number of box tops each day for 5 days. How many box tops did the two students bring in altogether each day? **Explain**.

_____

_____

_____

_____

.....SHOW YOUR WORK.....

15. **Write Math** ▶ **What's the Question?** Dwayne puts all his box tops into bins. He puts an equal number in each bin. The answer is 5. What's the question?

_____

_____

16. ⭐ **PARCC Test Prep** Maya collected 7 box tops each day. She collected 21 box tops in all. For how many days did Maya collect box tops?

  Ⓐ 2 days   Ⓒ 4 days

  Ⓑ 3 days   Ⓓ 6 days

Name _____

Model with Arrays

Essential Question How can you use arrays to solve division problems?

COMMON CORE
Georgia Performance Standard MCC3.OA.3
Represent and solve problems involving multiplication and division.

Investigate

Materials ■ square tiles

You can use arrays to model division and find equal groups.

A. Count out 30 tiles. Make an array to find how many rows of 5 are in 30.

B. Make a row of 5 tiles.

C. Continue to make as many rows of 5 tiles as you can.

How many rows of 5 did you make? _____

Draw Conclusions . . . .

1. **Explain** how you used the tiles to find the number of rows of 5 in 30.

_____

_____

2. What multiplication equation could you write for the array? **Explain**.

_____

_____

3. 🌟**H.O.T.** **Apply** Tell how to use an array to find how many rows of 6 are in 30.

_____

_____

Make Connections ....

You can write a division equation to show how
many rows of 5 are in 30. Show the array you made
in Investigate by completing the drawing below.

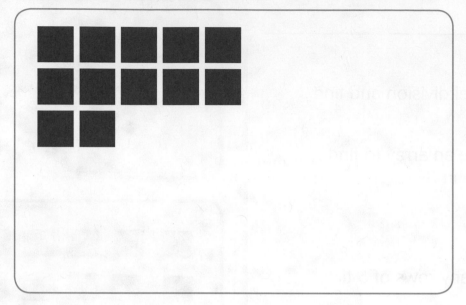

$30 \div 5 = $ ■

There are _____ rows of 5 tiles in 30.

So, $30 \div 5 = $ _____.

Try This!

Count out 24 tiles. Make an array with the same number of tiles in
4 rows. Place 1 tile in each of the 4 rows. Then continue placing
1 tile in each row until you use all the tiles. Draw your array below.

MATHEMATICAL PRACTICES

Math Talk Explain how making
an array helps you divide.

- How many tiles are in each row? _____

- What division equation can you write for your array? _____

Name _____

Share and Show ....

Use square tiles to make an array. Solve.

1. How many rows of 3 are in 18?

   _____

☑ 2. How many rows of 6 are in 12?

   _____

3. How many rows of 7 are in 21?

   _____

4. How many rows of 8 are in 32?

   _____

Make an array. Then write a division equation.

5. 25 tiles in 5 rows

   _____

☑ 6. 14 tiles in 2 rows

   _____

7. 28 tiles in 4 rows

   _____

8. 27 tiles in 9 rows

   _____

9. How many rows of 3 are in 15?

   _____

10. How many rows of 8 are in 24?

    _____

MATHEMATICAL PRACTICES

Math Talk Explain when you count the number of rows to find the answer and when you count the number of tiles in each row to find the answer.

11. **Write Math** ➤ **Show** two ways you could make an array with tiles for 18 ÷ 6. Shade squares on the grid to record the arrays.

© Houghton Mifflin Harcourt Publishing Company

UNLOCK the Problem REAL WORLD

12. Thomas has 28 tomato seedlings to plant in his garden. He wants to plant 4 seedlings in each row. How many rows of tomato seedlings will Thomas plant?

(A) 5   (B) 6   (C) 7   (D) 8

a. What do you need to find? _____

_____

b. What operation could you use to solve the problem? _____

_____

c. Draw an array to find the number of rows of tomato seedlings.

d. What is another way you could have solved the problem?

_____

_____

e. Complete the sentences.

Thomas has _____ tomato seedlings.

He wants to plant _____

seedlings in each _____.

So, Thomas will plant _____ rows of tomato seedlings.

f. Fill in the bubble for the correct answer choice above.

13. Faith plants 36 flowers in 6 equal rows. How many flowers are in each row?

(A) 42   (B) 30   (C) 7   (D) 6

14. There were 20 plants sold at a store on Saturday. Customers bought 5 plants each. How many customers bought the plants?

(A) 3   (B) 4   (C) 5   (D) 6

Name _____

▶ **Vocabulary**

Choose the best term from the box to complete the sentence.

Vocabulary
divide
divisor

1. You _____ when you separate into equal groups. (p. 137)

▶ **Concepts and Skills**

Use counters or draw a quick picture on your MathBoard. Make or circle equal groups. Complete the table. ▌MCC3.OA.2

	Counters	Number of Equal Groups	Number in Each Group
2.	6	2	
3.	30		5
4.	28	7	

Write a division equation for the picture. ▌MCC3.OA.2

5.

_____

6.

_____

Write a division equation. ▌MCC.3.OA.3

7. $\begin{array}{r} 36 \\ -9 \\ \hline 27 \end{array}$ $\begin{array}{r} 27 \\ -9 \\ \hline 18 \end{array}$ $\begin{array}{r} 18 \\ -9 \\ \hline 9 \end{array}$ $\begin{array}{r} 9 \\ -9 \\ \hline 0 \end{array}$

_____

8.

_____

© Houghton Mifflin Harcourt Publishing Company

Fill in the bubble for the correct answer choice.

9. Adam plants 14 seeds in some flowerpots. If he puts 2 seeds in each pot, how many flowerpots does he use? MCC3.OA.2

Ⓐ 7   Ⓒ 12

Ⓑ 8   Ⓓ 16

10. Desiree has 20 stickers. She gives the same number of stickers to each of 5 friends. Which equation can be used to find the number of stickers each friend receives? MCC3.OA.3

Ⓐ $20 + 5 = \blacksquare$

Ⓑ $20 - 5 = \blacksquare$

Ⓒ $20 \times 5 = \blacksquare$

Ⓓ $20 \div 5 = \blacksquare$

11. Jayden modeled a division equation with some counters. Which division equation matches the model? MCC3.OA.2

Ⓐ $12 \div 2 = 6$ Ⓒ $16 \div 2 = 8$

Ⓑ $14 \div 2 = 7$ Ⓓ $18 \div 2 = 9$

12. Lillian bought 24 cans of cat food. There were 4 cans in each pack. How many packs of cat food did Lillian buy? MCC3.OA.2

Ⓐ 5   Ⓑ 6   Ⓒ 7   Ⓓ 8

158

Name _____

Divide by 2

Essential Question What does dividing by 2 mean?

COMMON CORE
Georgia Performance Standard MCC3.OA.3
Represent and solve problems involving
multiplication and division.

🔑 UNLOCK the Problem — REAL WORLD

There are 10 hummingbirds and 2 feeders in Marissa's backyard. If there are an equal number of birds at each feeder, how many birds are at each one?

- What do you need to find?

  _____

- Circle the numbers you need to use.

- What can you use to help solve the

  problem? _____

🔒 Activity 1

Use counters to find how many in each group.

Materials ■ counters ■ MathBoard

MODEL

- Use 10 counters.
- Draw 2 circles on your MathBoard.
- Place 1 counter at a time in each circle until all 10 counters are used.
- Draw the rest of the counters to show your work.

THINK

_____ in all

_____ equal groups

_____ in each group

RECORD

$$10 \div 2 = 5 \text{ or } 2\overline{)10}^{\,5}$$

Read: Ten divided by two equals five.

There are _____ counters in each of the 2 groups.

So, there are _____ hummingbirds at each feeder.

A hummingbird can fly right, left, up, down, ▶ forward, backward, and even upside down!

Math Talk **MATHEMATICAL PRACTICES**

Explain what each number in $10 \div 2 = 5$ represents from the word problem.

🔑 Activity 2 Draw to find how many equal groups.

There are 10 hummingbirds in Tyler's backyard. If there are 2 hummingbirds at each feeder, how many feeders are there?

Math Idea

You can divide to find the number in each group or to find the number of equal groups.

MODEL

- Look at the 10 counters.
- Circle a group of 2 counters.
- Continue circling groups of 2 until all 10 counters are in groups.

THINK

_____ in all

_____ in each group

_____ equal groups

RECORD

$$10 \div 2 = 5 \text{ or } 2\overline{)10}^{\,5}$$

Read: Ten divided by two equals five.

There are _____ groups of 2 counters.

So, there are _____ feeders.

Share and Show 📝 MATH BOARD ....

1. Complete the picture to find $6 \div 2$. _____

Math Talk MATHEMATICAL PRACTICES
Describe another division equation that could be written for the picture you drew.

Write a division equation for the picture.

2.

_____

☑3.

_____

☑4.

_____

160

Name _____

On Your Own ....

Write a division equation for the picture.

5.

_____

6.

_____

7.

_____

Find the quotient. You may want to draw a quick picture to help.

8. $2 \div 2 =$ _____

9. _____ $= 10 \div 2$

10. _____ $= 14 \div 2$

11. _____ $= 18 \div 2$

12. $16 \div 2 =$ _____

13. _____ $= 0 \div 2$

14. $2\overline{)8}$

15. $2\overline{)12}$

16. $2\overline{)20}$

 Algebra Find the unknown number.

17. _____ $\div 2 = 5$

18. _____ $\div 2 = 2$

19. _____ $\div 2 = 3$

20. _____ $\div 2 = 8$

Problem Solving REAL WORLD

Use the table for 21–22.

21. Two hummingbirds of the same type have a mass of 10 grams. Which type of hummingbird are they? Write a division equation to show how to find the answer.

_____

Hummingbirds

Type	Mass (in grams)
Magnificent	7
Ruby-throated	3
Violet-crowned	5

22. **H.O.T.** There are 3 ruby-throated hummingbirds and 2 of another type of hummingbird at a feeder. The birds have a mass of 23 grams in all. What other type of hummingbird is at the feeder? **Explain**.

_____

_____

_____

_____

SHOW YOUR WORK

23. **Write Math** There are 12 hummingbird eggs in all. If there are 2 eggs in each nest, how many nests are there? **Explain** how you found your answer.

_____

_____

_____

_____

24. ⭐ **PARCC Test Prep** Jo sees the same number of birds each hour for 2 hours. She sees 16 birds in all. How many birds does Jo see each hour?

Ⓐ 6   Ⓑ 7   Ⓒ 8   Ⓓ 9

Name _____

Divide by 5

Essential Question What does dividing by 5 mean?

COMMON CORE
Georgia Performance Standard MCC3.OA.3
Represent and solve problems involving multiplication and division.

🔑 UNLOCK the Problem REAL WORLD

Kaley wants to buy a new cage for Coconut, her guinea pig. She has saved 35¢. If she saved a nickel each day, for how many days has she been saving?

• How much is a nickel worth?

_____

🔒 One Way Count up by 5s.

- Begin at 0.

- Count up by 5s until you reach 35.   5, 10, _____, _____, _____, _____, _____

- Count the number of times you count up.

　　　　　　1　　2　　3　　4　　5　　6　　7

You counted up by 5 seven times. 35 ÷ 5 = _____

So, Kaley has been saving for _____ days.

🔒 Another Way Count back on a number line.

- Start at 35.

- Count back by 5s until you reach 0. Complete the jumps on the number line.

- Count the number of times you jumped back 5.

0　5　10　15　20　25　30　35

You jumped back by 5 _____ times.

$35 \div 5 =$ _____

Math Talk   MATHEMATICAL PRACTICES
What if Kaley saved 7¢ each day instead of a nickel? What would you do differently to find how many days she has saved?

Strategies for Multiplying and Dividing with 5

You have learned how to use doubles to multiply. Now you will learn how to use doubles to divide by 5.

 Use 10s facts, and then take half to multiply with 5.

When one factor is 5, you can use a 10s fact.

$5 \times 2 = $ ■

First, multiply by 10.

$10 \times 2 = $ _____

After you multiply, take half of the product.

$20 \div 2 = $ _____

So, $5 \times 2 = $ _____.

 Divide by 10, and then double to divide by 5.

When the divisor is 5 and the dividend is even, you can use a 10s fact.

$30 \div 5 = $ ■

First, divide by 10.

$30 \div 10 = $ _____

After you divide, double the quotient.

$3 + $ _____ $ = $ _____

So, $30 \div 5 = $ _____.

Share and Show MATH BOARD ·

1. Count back on the number line to find $15 \div 5$. _____

```
   0        5        10       15
```

MATHEMATICAL PRACTICES

Math Talk Explain how counting up to solve a division problem is like counting back on a number line.

Use count up or count back on a number line to solve.

2. $10 \div 2 = $ _____

```
 0 1 2 3 4 5 6 7 8 9 10
```

☑ 3. $20 \div 5 = $ _____

```
   0        5       10       15       20
```

Find the quotient.

4. $50 \div 5 = $ _____

5. $5 \div 5 = $ _____

☑ 6. $45 \div 5 = $ _____

164

Name _____

On Your Own ·

Use count up or count back on a number line to solve.

7. $30 \div 5 =$ _____

8. $25 \div 5 =$ _____

Find the quotient.

9. ___ $= 20 \div 5$ 10. $40 \div 5 =$ ___ 11. ___ $= 18 \div 2$ 12. $0 \div 5 =$ ___

13. $35 \div 5 =$ ___ 14. ___ $= 10 \div 5$ 15. $40 \div 10 =$ ___ 16. ___ $= 4 \div 2$

17. $10\overline{)30}$ 18. $2\overline{)16}$ 19. $5\overline{)45}$ 20. $5\overline{)15}$

Algebra Complete the table.

21.
×	1	2	3	4	5
10					
5					

22.
÷	10	20	30	40	50
10					
5					

Problem Solving

23. Guinea pigs eat hay, pellets, and vegetables. If Wonder Hay comes in a 5-pound bag and costs $15, how much does 1 pound of hay cost?

_____

24. Guinea pigs sleep about 45 hours every 5 days with their eyes open. About how many hours a day do guinea pigs sleep?

_____

25. ⭐ **PARCC Test Prep** The pet store has 20 guinea pigs and plans to put a pair of guinea pigs in each cage. If the pet store has 8 cages, how many more cages will the pet store need?

Ⓐ 1   Ⓑ 2   Ⓒ 4   Ⓓ 5

H.O.T. Pose a Problem

26. Maddie went to a veterinary clinic. She saw the vet preparing some carrots for the guinea pigs.

Write a division problem that can be solved using the picture of carrots.

Pose a problem.   **Solve your problem.**

_____   _____

_____   _____

_____   _____

_____   _____

_____   _____

_____   _____

- Write a similar problem by exchanging the number of equal groups and number in each group. Then solve the problem.

_____

_____

_____

- **Describe** what the quotient in your problem represents.

_____

_____

FOR MORE PRACTICE:
Standards Practice Book

Name _____

Divide by 8

Essential Question What strategies can you use to divide by 8?

COMMON CORE
Georgia Performance Standard MCC3.OA.4
Represent and solve problems involving
multiplication and division.

🔑 UNLOCK the Problem · REAL WORLD

At Stephen's camping store, firewood is sold in bundles of 8 logs. He has 32 logs to put in bundles. How many bundles of firewood can he make?

- What will Stephen do with the 32 logs?

_____

_____

🔒 One Way Use repeated subtraction.

- Start with 32.
- Subtract 8 until you reach 0.
- Count the number of times you subtract 8.

$$\begin{array}{cccc} 32 & 24 & & \\ -8 & -8 & -8 & -8 \\ \hline 24 & & & \end{array}$$

> ⚠️ **ERROR Alert**
>
> Be sure to keep subtracting the divisor until the difference is less than the divisor.

Number of times
you subtract 8:   1   2   3   4

You subtracted 8 _____ times.

So, Stephen can make _____ bundles of firewood.

You can write $32 \div 8 =$ _____ or $8\overline{)32}$.

🔒 Another Way Use a related multiplication fact.

$32 \div 8 =$ ■   ■ $\times 8 = 32$ **Think:** What number completes the multiplication fact? $32 \div 8 =$ _____ or $8\overline{)32}$

$4 \times 8 = 32$

> **Math Talk** · MATHEMATICAL PRACTICES
> How does knowing $4 \times 8 = 32$ help you find $32 \div 8$?

Example Find the unknown divisor.

Stephen has a log that is 16 feet long. If he cuts the log into pieces that are 2 feet long, how many pieces will Stephen have?

Divide. $16 \div \blacksquare = 2$

You can also use a multiplication table to find the divisor in a division problem.

Think: $\blacksquare \times 2 = 16$

STEP 1 Find the factor, 2, in the top row.

STEP 2 Look down to find the product, 16.

STEP 3 Look left to find the unknown factor.

The unknown factor is _____.

$\blacksquare = $ _____

_____ $\times 2 = 16$ **Check.**

_____ $= 16$ ✓   The equation is true.

So, Stephen will have _____ pieces.

×	0	1	2	3	4	5	6	7	8	9	10
0	0	0	0	0	0	0	0	0	0	0	0
1	0	1	2	3	4	5	6	7	8	9	10
2	0	2	4	6	8	10	12	14	16	18	20
3	0	3	6	9	12	15	18	21	24	27	30
4	0	4	8	12	16	20	24	28	32	36	40
5	0	5	10	15	20	25	30	35	40	45	50
6	0	6	12	18	24	30	36	42	48	54	60
7	0	7	14	21	28	35	42	49	56	63	70
8	0	8	16	24	32	40	48	56	64	72	80
9	0	9	18	27	36	45	54	63	72	81	90
10	0	10	20	30	40	50	60	70	80	90	100

Math Talk MATHEMATICAL PRACTICES
Explain how to use the multiplication table to find the unknown dividend for $\blacksquare \div 8 = 5$.

Share and Show ·

1. Use repeated subtraction to find $24 \div 8$. _____

Think: How many times do you subtract 8?

Math Talk MATHEMATICAL PRACTICES
Explain why you subtract 8 from 24 to find $24 \div 8$.

Find the unknown factor and quotient.

2. $8 \times$ _____ $= 56$ $56 \div 8 =$ _____

✓3. _____ $\times 8 = 40$ $40 \div 8 =$ _____

Find the quotient.

4. $18 \div 3 =$ _____   5. _____ $= 48 \div 8$ 6. $56 \div 7 =$ _____   ✓7. _____ $= 32 \div 8$

Name _____

On Your Own ....

Find the unknown factor and quotient.

8. $8 \times$ _____ $= 8$ $8 \div 8 =$ _____   9. _____ $\times 5 = 35$ _____ $= 35 \div 5$

10. $6 \times$ _____ $= 18$ $18 \div 6 =$ _____   11. $8 \times$ _____ $= 72$ _____ $= 72 \div 8$

Find the quotient.

12. $28 \div 4 =$ _____   13. $42 \div 7 =$ _____   14. _____ $= 3 \div 3$ 15. _____ $= 28 \div 7$

16. $8\overline{)0}$ 17. $6\overline{)24}$ 18. $8\overline{)64}$ 19. $1\overline{)8}$

Find the unknown number.

20. $72 \div \bigstar = 9$ 21. $t \div 8 = 2$ 22. $64 \div \blacktriangle = 8$ 23. $m \div 8 = 10$

    $\bigstar =$ _____ $t =$ _____ $\blacktriangle =$ _____ $m =$ _____

24. $\blacktriangle \div 2 = 10$ 25. $40 \div \blacksquare = 8$ 26. $25 \div k = 5$ 27. $54 \div n = 9$

    $\blacktriangle =$ _____ $\blacksquare =$ _____ $k =$ _____ $n =$ _____

28. **H.O.T.** Write a word problem that can be solved by using one of the division facts above.

_____

_____

H.O.T. Algebra Write $+$, $-$, $\times$, or $\div$.

29. $6 \times 6 = 32 \bigcirc 4$ 30. $12 \bigcirc 3 = 19 - 15$ 31. $40 \div 8 = 35 \bigcirc 7$

Problem Solving REAL WORLD

Use the table for 32–33.

Tent Sizes	
Type	**Number of People**
Cabin	10
Vista	8
Trail	4

32. **H.O.T.** There are 36 people camping at Max's family reunion. They have cabin tents and vista tents. How many of each type of tent do they need to sleep exactly 36 people if each tent is filled? **Explain**.

_____

_____

_____

_____

 SHOW YOUR WORK

33. **Write Math** There are 32 people who plan to camp over the weekend. What is the least number of trail tents they need? **Explain**.

_____

_____

_____

34. Josh is dividing 64 marshmallows equally among 8 campers. How many marshmallows will each camper get?

_____

35. ⭐**PARCC Test Prep** Grace set 8 plates at each picnic table so 24 campers could eat dinner. How many picnic tables did Grace have to set?

Ⓐ 3

Ⓑ 4

Ⓒ 5

Ⓓ 6

Module 8 Assessment

▶ **Concepts and Skills**

Find the quotient. MCC3.OA.3, MCC3.OA.4

1. $12 \div 2 =$ _____   **2.** $35 \div 5 =$ _____   **3.** _____ $= 0 \div 2$ **4.** _____ $= 20 \div 5$

5. _____ $= 48 \div 8$ **6.** _____ $= 8 \div 8$ **7.** $64 \div 8 =$ _____   **8.** $45 \div 5 =$ _____

9. $2\overline{)12}$ **10.** $2\overline{)2}$ **11.** $8\overline{)56}$ **12.** $8\overline{)72}$

13. $2\overline{)8}$ **14.** $5\overline{)40}$ **15.** $3\overline{)18}$ **16.** $8\overline{)32}$

Find the unknown factor and quotient. MCC3.OA.4

17. $5 \times$ _____ $= 30$ $30 \div 5 =$ _____   **18.** $8 \times$ _____ $= 72$ _____ $= 72 \div 8$

19. _____ $\times 8 = 16$ $16 \div 8 =$ _____   **20.** $2 \times$ _____ $= 20$ _____ $= 20 \div 2$

Fill in the bubble for the correct answer choice.

21. Jana counts butterflies in her garden. She sees the same number of butterflies each hour for 8 hours. She sees 64 butterflies in all. How many butterflies does Jana see each hour? MCC3.OA.3

    Ⓐ 9
    Ⓑ 8
    Ⓒ 6
    Ⓓ 5

22. Gabriella made 5 waffles for breakfast. She has 30 berries to put on top of the waffles. She will put an equal number of berries on each waffle. How many berries will Gabriella put on each waffle?

    MCC3.OA.3

    Ⓐ 4
    Ⓑ 5
    Ⓒ 6
    Ⓓ 7

23. There are 48 students at basketball camp. The coaches put 8 players on a team. How many teams did they make? MCC3.OA.4

    Ⓐ 2
    Ⓑ 6
    Ⓒ 8
    Ⓓ 16

24. Alyssa has 4 cupcakes. She gives 2 cupcakes to each of her cousins. How many cousins does Alyssa have?

     MCC3.OA.3

    Ⓐ 8
    Ⓑ 6
    Ⓒ 4
    Ⓓ 2

Unit 2 Assessment

▶ **Vocabulary**

Choose the best term from the box to complete the sentence.

Vocabulary
dividend
factors
quotient

1. The numbers you multiply are called the

   _____. (p. 102)

2. The answer in a division problem is called the

   _____. (p. 146)

▶ **Concepts and Skills**

Find the product. ▌MCC3.OA.3

3. $5 \times 2 = $_____   **4.** $4 \times 7 = $_____   **5.** $8 \times 2 = $_____   **6.** $2 \times 0 = $_____

7. $2 \times 1 = $_____   **8.** $5 \times 0 = $_____   **9.** $9 \times 6 = $_____   **10.** $7 \times 3 = $_____

Complete the equations. ▌MCC3.OA.3

11. $\begin{array}{r} 6 \\ \times 8 \\ \hline \end{array}$ **12.** $\begin{array}{r} 10 \\ \times 4 \\ \hline \end{array}$ **13.** $\begin{array}{r} 5 \\ \times 9 \\ \hline \end{array}$ **14.** $\begin{array}{r} 6 \\ \times 3 \\ \hline \end{array}$ **15.** $\begin{array}{r} 5 \\ \times 8 \\ \hline \end{array}$ **16.** $\begin{array}{r} 8 \\ \times 2 \\ \hline \end{array}$

Find the unknown factor and quotient. ▌MCC3.OA.4

17. $6 \times$ _____ $= 42$ $42 \div 6 = $ _____   **18.** $7 \times$ _____ $= 28$ _____ $= 28 \div 7$

19. _____ $\times 8 = 16$ $16 \div 8 = $ _____   **20.** $6 \times$ _____ $= 60$ _____ $= 60 \div 6$

GO Online Assessment Options Unit Test

Fill in the bubble for the correct answer choice.

21. The camping club rents 4 rafts. Each raft can hold 6 people. How many people can 4 rafts hold? ◢ MCC3.OA.3

   (A) 16
   (B) 20
   (C) 24
   (D) 30

22. Caroline has 24 books. She put an equal number of her books on each of 3 shelves. How many books are on each shelf? ◢ MCC3.OA.2

   (A) 7
   (B) 8
   (C) 9
   (D) 10

23. John made 3 groups of 8 marbles. Which number sentence could be used to find the number of marbles? ◢ MCC3.OA.1

   (A) $3 + 5 = $ ■
   (B) $3 + 8 = $ ■
   (C) $3 \times 5 = $ ■
   (D) $3 \times 8 = $ ■

24. Aidan bought 14 goldfish and 2 fishbowls. He put an equal number of fish in each fishbowl. Which equation can be used to find how many goldfish are in each fishbowl? ◢ MCC3.OA.3

   (A) $14 - 2 = $ ■
   (B) $2 + $ ■ $ = 14$
   (C) $14 \div 2 = $ ■
   (D) $2 \times 14 = $ ■

Fill in the bubble for the correct answer choice.

25. Dan and his dad baked some cookies. They put 5 cookies on each of 4 plates. Which number sentence shows how many cookies they put on plates?
MCC3.OA.1

Ⓐ $4 \times 5 = 20$

Ⓑ $4 \times 4 = 16$

Ⓒ $3 \times 4 = 12$

Ⓓ $2 \times 5 = 10$

26. Jasmine made some cards for her family. She used 16 stickers and put 4 of them on each card. How many cards did Jasmine make? MCC3.OA.2

Ⓐ 2

Ⓑ 3

Ⓒ 4

Ⓓ 5

27. Lacy planted 4 rows of 9 flowers. How many flowers did she plant? MCC3.OA.3

Ⓐ 13

Ⓑ 35

Ⓒ 36

Ⓓ 49

28 . There are 56 students at basketball camp. The coaches put 8 players on each team. How many teams did they make? MCC3.OA.4

Ⓐ 6

Ⓑ 7

Ⓒ 48

Ⓓ 64

29. Mr. Hamilton has 3 music classes. He puts the students in each class in equal groups.

Mr. Hamilton's Classes	
Class	Number of Students
First	24
Second	20
Third	18

★ Mr. Hamilton puts the students in his first class in 6 equal groups. How many students are in each group? **Explain** how you got your answer.

_____

_____

_____

★★ List as many ways as you can to put the students in Mr. Hamilton's second class in equal groups. **Explain** how you got your answer.

_____

_____

_____

_____

★★★ Mr. Hamilton has 4 music books. He will give one music book to each group in his third class. He wants each group to have as few students as possible. How many equal groups of students should Mr. Hamilton make? Will he have any music books left over? **Describe** how you found your answer.

_____

_____

_____

_____

_____

176

Show What You Know ✓

Check your understanding of important skills.

Name _____

▶ **Doubles and Doubles Plus One**

Write the doubles and doubles plus one facts.

1.

____ + ____ = ____   ____ + ____ = ____

2.

____ + ____ = ____   ____ + ____ = ____

▶ **Equal Groups** Complete.

3.

____ groups of ____

____ in all

4.

____ groups of ____

____ in all

MATH DETECTIVE
WITH
CARMEN SANDIEGO™

Stephen needs to use these clues to find a buried time capsule.

• Start with a number that is the product of 3 and 4.

• Double the product and go to that number.

• Add 2 tens and find the number that is 1 less than the sum.

Be a Math Detective to help him find the time capsule.

14	12	22
24	33	15
21	43	32

▶ **Visualize It** •••

Complete the tree map by using the words with a ✓.

Multiplication Properties

Property of Multiplication	Property of Multiplication	Property of Multiplication
$1 \times 4 = 4$	$0 \times 5 = 0$ $6 \times 0 = 0$	$3 \times 2 = 2 \times 3$

▶ **Understand Vocabulary** ••

Complete the sentences by using the preview words.

1. The _____ Property of Multiplication states that when the order of the factors is changed, the product is the same.

2. The _____ Property of Multiplication states that the product of any number and 1 is that number.

3. The _____ Property states that multiplying a sum by a number is the same as multiplying each addend by the number and then adding the products.

    Example: $2 \times 8 = 2 \times (4 + 4)$

               $2 \times 8 = (2 \times 4) + (2 \times 4)$

               $2 \times 8 = 8 + 8$

               $2 \times 8 = 16$

Name _____

Multiply with 1 and 0

Essential Question What happens when you multiply a number by 0 or 1?

COMMON CORE
Georgia Performance Standard MCC3.OA.5
Understand properties of multiplication and the relationship between multiplication and division.

ALGEBRA
Lesson 9.2

🔑 UNLOCK the Problem — REAL WORLD

Luke sees 4 birdbaths. Each birdbath has 2 birds in it. What multiplication sentence tells how many birds there are?

🔑 **Draw a quick picture to show the birds in the birdbaths.**

- How many birdbaths are there?

  _____

- How many birds are in each

  birdbath to start? _____

_____ × _____ = _____

One bird flies away from each birdbath. Cross out 1 bird in each birdbath above. What multiplication sentence shows the total number of birds left?

_____ × _____ = _____
　↑　　　　↑　　　　　↑
birdbaths　bird left　total number
　　　in each birdbath　of birds

Now cross out another bird in each birdbath. What multiplication sentence shows the total number of birds left in the birdbaths?

_____ × _____ = _____
　↑　　　　↑　　　　　↑
birdbaths　birds left　total number
　　　in each birdbath　of birds

MATHEMATICAL PRACTICES
Math Talk **What if** there were 5 birdbaths with 0 birds in each of them? What would be the product? **Explain.**

- How do the birdbaths look now?

© Houghton Mifflin Harcourt Publishing Company

Module 9　**183**

🔒 Example

Jenny has 2 pages of bird stickers. There are 4 stickers on each page. How many stickers does she have in all?

2 × 4 = _____   **Think:** 2 groups of 4

So, Jenny has _____ stickers in all.

Suppose Jenny uses 1 page of the stickers. What fact shows how many stickers are left?

_____ × _____ = _____   **Think:** 1 group of 4

So, Jenny has _____ stickers left.

Now, Jenny uses the rest of the stickers. What fact shows how many stickers Jenny has left?

_____ × _____ = _____   **Think:** 0 groups of 4

So, Jenny has _____ stickers left.

 ERROR Alert

A 0 in a multiplication sentence means 0 groups or 0 things in a group, so the product is always 0.

• What does each number in 0 × 4 = 0 tell you?

_____

_____

1. What pattern do you see when you multiply numbers with 1 as a factor?

Think: 1 × 2 = 2   1 × 3 = 3   1 × 4 = 4

_____

_____

The **Identity Property of Multiplication** states that the product of any number and 1 is that number.

7 × 1 = 7   6 × 1 = 6
1 × 7 = 7   1 × 6 = 6

2. What pattern do you see when you multiply numbers with 0 as a factor?

Think: 0 × 1 = 0   0 × 2 = 0   0 × 5 = 0

_____

_____

The **Zero Property of Multiplication** states that the product of zero and any number is zero.

0 × 5 = 0   0 × 8 = 0
5 × 0 = 0   8 × 0 = 0

Name _____

Share and Show

1. What multiplication sentence matches this picture? Find the product.

_____

Find the product.

2. $5 \times 1 =$ _____   3. $0 \times 2 =$ _____   ☑4. $4 \times 0 =$ _____   ☑5. $1 \times 6 =$ _____

6. $3 \times 0 =$ _____   7. $1 \times 2 =$ _____   8. $0 \times 6 =$ _____   9. $8 \times 1 =$ _____

Math Talk MATHEMATICAL PRACTICES
Explain how 3×1 and $3 + 1$ are different.

On Your Own

Find the product.

10. $3 \times 1 =$ _____   11. $8 \times 0 =$ _____   12. $1 \times 9 =$ _____   13. $0 \times 7 =$ _____

14. $0 \times 4 =$ _____   15. $10 \times 1 =$ _____   16. $1 \times 3 =$ _____   17. $6 \times 1 =$ _____

18. $1 \times 0 =$ _____   19. $1 \times 7 =$ _____   20. $6 \times 0 =$ _____   21. $1 \times 4 =$ _____

22. $0 \times 8 =$ _____   23. $9 \times 1 =$ _____   24. $0 \times 9 =$ _____   25. $1 \times 1 =$ _____

26. $4 \times 1 =$ _____   27. $1 \times 5 =$ _____   28. $0 \times 0 =$ _____   29. $5 \times 0 =$ _____

H.O.T. **Algebra Complete the multiplication sentence.**

30. _____ $\times 1 = 15$ 31. $1 \times 28 =$ _____   32. $0 \times 46 =$ _____   33. $36 \times 0 =$ _____

34. _____ $\times 5 = 5$ 35. $19 \times$ _____ $= 0$ 36. _____ $\times 0 = 0$ 37. $7 \times$ _____ $= 7$

Problem Solving REAL WORLD

Use the table for 38–40.

38. At the circus Jon saw 5 unicycles. How many wheels are on the unicycles in all? Write a multiplication sentence.

Circus Vehicles

Type of Vehicle	Number of Wheels
Car	4
Tricycle	3
Bicycle	2
Unicycle	1

39. **H.O.T.** Brian saw some circus vehicles. He saw 17 wheels in all. If 2 of the vehicles are cars, how many vehicles are bicycles and tricycles?

SHOW YOUR WORK

40. **What's the Question?** Julia used multiplication with 1 and the information in the table. The answer is 3.

41. **Write Math** ▶ Write a word problem that uses multiplying with 1 or 0. Show how to solve your problem.

42. ⭐ **PARCC Test Prep** Eric has 1 pencil box at school. He has 6 pencils in the box. Which number sentence shows how many pencils Eric has in the pencil box?

Ⓐ $6 + 1 = 7$ Ⓒ $6 - 1 = 5$

Ⓑ $0 \times 6 = 0$ Ⓓ $1 \times 6 = 6$

Name _____

Distributive Property

Essential Question How can you use the Distributive Property to find products?

COMMON CORE
Georgia Performance Standard MCC3.OA.5
Understand properties of multiplication and the relationship between multiplication and division.

🔑 UNLOCK the Problem REAL WORLD

Mark bought 6 new fish for his aquarium. He paid $7 for each fish. How much did he spend in all?

Find 6 × $7.

You can use the Distributive Property to solve the problem.

The **Distributive Property** states that multiplying a sum by a number is the same as multiplying each addend by the number and then adding the products.

• Describe the groups in this problem.

_____

• Circle the numbers you will use to solve the problem.

Remember

sum—the answer to an addition problem

addends—the numbers being added

🔑 Activity **Materials** ■ square tiles

Make an array with tiles to show 6 rows of 7.

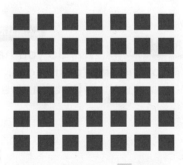

6 × 7 = ■

Break apart the array to make two smaller arrays for facts you know.

6 × 5   6 × 2

6 × 7 = ■

6 × 7 = 6 × (5 + 2)   **Think:** 7 = 5 + 2

6 × 7 = (6 × 5) + (6 × 2)   Multiply each addend by 6.

6 × 7 = _____ + _____   Add the products.

6 × 7 = _____

So, Mark spent $_____ for his new fish.

Math Talk MATHEMATICAL PRACTICES What other ways could you break apart the 6 × 7 array?

Try This!

Suppose Mark bought 9 fish for $6 each.

You can break apart a 9×6 array into two smaller arrays for facts you know. One way is to think of 9 as $5 + 4$. Draw a line to show this way. Then find the product.

_____ × _____

_____ × _____

$9 \times 6 = ($_____ $\times$ _____$) + ($_____ $\times$ _____$)$

$9 \times 6 =$ _____ $+$ _____

So, Mark spent $_____ for 9 fish.

Share and Show

1. Draw a line to show how you could break apart this 6×8 array into two smaller arrays for facts you know.

- What numbers do you multiply? _____ and _____

  _____ and _____

- What numbers do you add? _____ $+$ _____

$6 \times 8 = 6 \times ($_____ $+$ _____$)$

$6 \times 8 = ($_____ $\times$ _____$) + ($_____ $\times$ _____$)$

$6 \times 8 =$ _____ $+$ _____

$6 \times 8 =$ _____

Math Talk MATHEMATICAL PRACTICES

Why do you have to add to find the total product when you use the Distributive Property?

Write one way to break apart the array. Then find the product.

2.

_____

_____

3.

_____

_____

Name _____

On Your Own ·

**Write one way to break apart the array.
Then find the product.**

4.

_____

_____

5.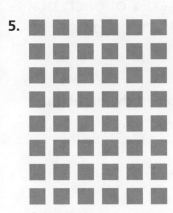

_____

_____

6. Shade tiles to make an array that shows
   a fact with 7, 8, or 9 as a factor. Write the
   fact. **Explain** how you found the product.

   _____

   _____

   _____

7. **H.O.T.** **Sense or Nonsense?** Robin
   says, "I can find 8×7 by multiplying
   3×7 and doubling it." Does her
   statement make sense? **Explain**
   your answer.

   _____

   _____

   _____

8. ★ **PARCC Test Prep** Which number
   sentence below is an example
   of the Distributive Property?

   (A) $6 \times 8 = 40 + 8$

   (B) $(8 \times 2) \times 3 = 8 \times (2 \times 3)$

   (C) $6 \times 8 = 8 \times 6$

   (D) $6 \times 8 = (6 \times 2) + (6 \times 6)$

Problem Solving REAL WORLD

🔆 H.O.T. What's the Error?

9. Brandon needs 8 boxes of spinners for his fishing club. The cost of each box is $9. How much will Brandon pay.

$8 \times \$9 = \blacksquare$

Look at how Brandon solved the problem.
Find and describe his error.

$8 \times 9 = (4 \times 9) + (5 \times 9)$

$8 \times 9 = 36 + 45$

$8 \times 9 = 81$

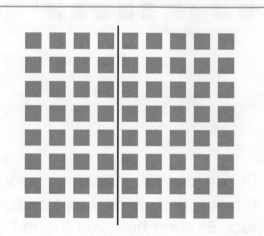

_____

_____

Use the array to help solve the problem
and correct his error.

$8 \times 9 = (4 + 4) \times 9$

$8 \times 9 = (\underline{\quad} \times \underline{\quad}) + (\underline{\quad} \times \underline{\quad})$

$8 \times 9 = \underline{\quad} + \underline{\quad}$

$8 \times 9 = \underline{\quad}$

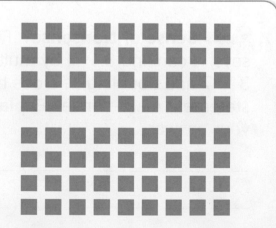

So, Brandon will pay $ _____ for the spinners.

Multiply with 7

Essential Question What strategies can you use to multiply with 7?

COMMON CORE
Georgia Performance Standard MCC3.OA.7
Multiply and divide within 100.

🔑 UNLOCK the Problem REAL WORLD

Jason's family has a new puppy. Jason takes a turn walking the puppy once a day. How many times will Jason walk the puppy in 4 weeks?

Find 4 × 7.

- How often does Jason walk the puppy?
  _____
- How many days are in 1 week?
  _____

🔓 One Way Use the Commutative Property of Multiplication.

If you know 7 × 4, you can use that fact to find 4 × 7.
You can change the order of the factors and the product is the same.

7 × 4 = _____, so 4 × 7 = _____.

So, Jason will walk the puppy _____ times in 4 weeks.

🔓 Other Ways

Ⓐ Use the Distributive Property.

STEP 1 Complete the array to show 4 rows of 7.

STEP 2 Draw a line to break the array into two smaller arrays for facts you know.

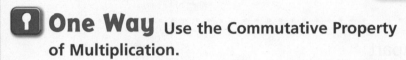

STEP 3 Multiply the facts for the smaller arrays. Add the products.

4 × _____ = _____   4 × _____ = _____

_____ + _____ = _____

So, 4 × 7 = _____.

MATHEMATICAL PRACTICES

Math Talk **Explain** two other ways you can break apart the 4 × 7 array.

B Use a fact you know.

Multiply. $4 \times 7 =$ ■

- Start with a fact you know.

$2 \times 7 =$ _____

- Add a group of 7 for 3×7.

$2 \times 7 + 7 =$ _____

- Then add 7 more for 4×7.

$3 \times 7 + 7 =$ _____

So, $4 \times 7 =$ _____.

Share and Show MATH BOARD ....

1. **Explain** how you could break apart an array to find 6×7. Draw an array to show your work.

_____

_____

MATHEMATICAL PRACTICES

Math Talk How can you use doubles to find 8×7?

Find the product.

2. $9 \times 7 =$ _____   3. _____ $= 5 \times 7$ ✓ 4. _____ $= 7 \times 3$ ✓ 5. $1 \times 7 =$ _____

On Your Own ....

Find the product.

6. _____ $= 7 \times 7$ 7. $6 \times 7 =$ _____   8. _____ $= 7 \times 10$ 9. _____ $= 7 \times 2$

10. $\begin{array}{r} 7 \\ \times 3 \\ \hline \end{array}$
11. $\begin{array}{r} 6 \\ \times 7 \\ \hline \end{array}$
12. $\begin{array}{r} 9 \\ \times 7 \\ \hline \end{array}$
13. $\begin{array}{r} 8 \\ \times 7 \\ \hline \end{array}$
14. $\begin{array}{r} 1 \\ \times 7 \\ \hline \end{array}$
15. $\begin{array}{r} 4 \\ \times 7 \\ \hline \end{array}$

16. $\begin{array}{r} 10 \\ \times 4 \\ \hline \end{array}$
17. $\begin{array}{r} 0 \\ \times 7 \\ \hline \end{array}$
18. $\begin{array}{r} 2 \\ \times 7 \\ \hline \end{array}$
19. $\begin{array}{r} 5 \\ \times 7 \\ \hline \end{array}$
20. $\begin{array}{r} 6 \\ \times 9 \\ \hline \end{array}$
21. $\begin{array}{r} 7 \\ \times 8 \\ \hline \end{array}$

Problem Solving REAL WORLD

Use the table for 22–24.

Rusty's Care	
Food	3 cups a day
Water	4 cups a day
Bath	2 times a month

22. Lori has a dog named Rusty. How many baths will Rusty have in

    7 months? _____

23. How many more cups of water than food will Rusty get in 1 week?

    _____

24. 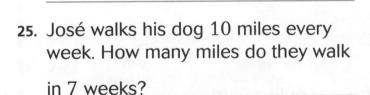 **Write Math** ▸ Tim's dog, Midnight, eats 28 cups of food in a week. Midnight eats the same amount each day. In one day, how many more cups of food will Midnight eat than Rusty? **Explain**.

    _____

    _____

    _____

    _____

··········· **SHOW YOUR WORK** ···············

25. José walks his dog 10 miles every week. How many miles do they walk

    in 7 weeks? _____

26. Dave takes Zoey, his dog, for a 3-mile walk twice a day. How many miles do they walk in one week?

    _____

27. ⭐ **PARCC Test Prep** Sam walks his dog 5 miles a day. How many miles does he walk in one week?

    Ⓐ 5 miles   Ⓒ 35 miles

    Ⓑ 25 miles   Ⓓ 40 miles

Summarize

To help you stay healthy, you should eat a balanced diet and exercise every day.

The table shows the recommended daily servings for third graders. You should eat the right amounts of the food groups.

Suppose you want to share with your friends what you learned about healthy eating. How could you summarize what you learned?

When you *summarize*, you restate the most important information in a shorter way to help you understand what you have read.

Recommended Daily Servings

Food Group	Servings
Whole Grains (bread, cereal)	6 ounces
Vegetables (beans, corn)	2 cups
Fruits (apples, oranges)	1 cup
Dairy Products (milk, cheese)	3 cups
Meat, Beans, Fish, Eggs, Nuts	5 ounces

8 ounces = 1 cup

- To stay healthy, you should eat a balanced

  _____ and _____ every day.

- A third grader should eat 3 cups of _____,
  such as milk and cheese, each day.

- A third grader should eat _____ of
  vegetables and fruits each day.

  How many cups of vegetables and fruits should a third

  grader eat in 1 week? _____

  Remember: 1 week = 7 days

- A third grader should eat _____ of whole
  grains, such as bread and cereal, each day.

  How many ounces of whole grains should a third grader

  eat in 1 week? _____

Name _____

Module 9 Assessment

▶ Vocabulary

Choose the best term from the box to complete the sentence.

Vocabulary
Commutative Property of Multiplication
Distributive Property
Zero Property of Multiplication

1. The _____ Property of Multiplication states that the product of zero and any number is zero. (p. 184)

2. This is an example of the _____ Property.

$$3 \times 8 = (3 \times 6) + (3 \times 2)$$

This property states that multiplying a sum by a number is the same as multiplying each addend by the number and then adding the products. (p. 187)

▶ Concepts and Skills

Write one way to break apart the array.
Then find the product. MCC3.OA.5

3.

_____

_____

4.

_____

_____

Find the product. MCC3.OA.5, MCC3.OA.7

5. $3 \times 1 =$ _____

6. $5 \times 6 =$ _____

7. $7 \times 7 =$ _____

8. $2 \times 10 =$ _____

9.
$$\begin{array}{r} 2 \\ \times 1 \\ \hline \end{array}$$

10.
$$\begin{array}{r} 6 \\ \times 6 \\ \hline \end{array}$$

11.
$$\begin{array}{r} 8 \\ \times 7 \\ \hline \end{array}$$

12.
$$\begin{array}{r} 6 \\ \times 0 \\ \hline \end{array}$$

13.
$$\begin{array}{r} 3 \\ \times 8 \\ \hline \end{array}$$

© Houghton Mifflin Harcourt Publishing Company

Module 9 Assessment   195

Fill in the bubble for the correct answer choice.

14. Which is an example of the Distributive Property?

MCC3.OA.5

(A) $5 \times 7 = (5 \times 5) + (5 \times 2)$

(B) $5 \times 7 = 7 \times 5$

(C) $5 \times 7 = 35$

(D) $5 \times 7 = (5 + 5) + (5 + 2)$

15. Zach gave his dog 2 dog biscuits a day, for 7 days. How many biscuits did Zach give to his dog?

MCC3.OA.7

(A) 3

(B) 7

(C) 14

(D) 30

16. Annette has 1 sticker album at home. She has 8 stickers in her album. Which number sentence shows how many stickers Annette has in her album?

MCC3.OA.5

(A) $1 \times 8 = 8$

(B) $8 - 1 = 7$

(C) $0 \times 8 = 0$

(D) $1 + 8 = 9$

17. Shelly can paint 4 pictures in a day. How many pictures can she paint in 7 days? MCC3.OA.7

(A) 3

(B) 11

(C) 28

(D) 32

Name _____

Associative Property of Multiplication

Essential Question How can you use the Associative Property of Multiplication to find products?

COMMON CORE
Georgia Performance Standard MCC3.OA.5
Understand properties of multiplication and the relationship between multiplication and division.

CONNECT You have learned the Associative Property of Addition. When the grouping of the addends is changed, the sum stays the same.

$$(2 + 3) + 4 = 2 + (3 + 4)$$

The **Associative Property of Multiplication** states that when the grouping of the factors is changed, the product is the same. It is also called the Grouping Property of Multiplication.

> **Math Idea**
> Always multiply the numbers inside the parentheses first.

🔑 UNLOCK the Problem REAL WORLD

Each car on the roller coaster has 2 rows of seats. Each row has 2 seats. There are 3 cars in each train. How many seats are on each train?

- Underline what you need to find.
- Describe the grouping of the seats.

_____

 Use an array.

You can use an array to show $3 \times (2 \times 2)$.

$3 \times (2 \times 2) = $ ▨

$3 \times$ _____ = _____

So, there are 3 cars with 4 seats in each car.

There are _____ seats on each roller coaster train.

You can change the grouping with parentheses and the product is the same.

$(3 \times 2) \times 2 = $ ▨

_____ $\times 2 = $ _____

Math Talk MATHEMATICAL PRACTICES
Explain why the products $3 \times (2 \times 2)$ and $(3 \times 2) \times 2$ are the same.

🔑 Example Use the Commutative and Associative Properties.

You can also change the order of the factors.
The product is the same.

$(4 \times 3) \times 2 = \blacksquare$

$4 \times (3 \times 2) = \blacksquare$ Associative Property

$4 \times \underline{\hspace{2cm}} = \underline{\hspace{2cm}}$

$4 \times (3 \times 2) = \blacksquare$

$4 \times (2 \times 3) = \blacksquare$ Commutative Property

$(4 \times 2) \times 3 = \blacksquare$ Associative Property

$\underline{\hspace{2cm}} \times 3 = \underline{\hspace{2cm}}$

Share and Show ·

1. Find the product of 5, 2, and 3. Write another way to group the factors. Is the product the same? Why?

   _____

   _____

Write another way to group the factors. Then find the product.

2. $(2 \times 1) \times 7$

   _____

   _____

3. $3 \times (3 \times 4)$

   _____

   _____

✓ 4. $5 \times (2 \times 5)$

   _____

   _____

✓ 5. $3 \times (2 \times 6)$

   _____

   _____

6. $2 \times (2 \times 5)$

   _____

   _____

7. $(1 \times 3) \times 6$

   _____

   _____

MATHEMATICAL PRACTICES

Math Talk Choose one answer from Exercises 2–7. **Explain** why you multiplied those factors first.

© Houghton Mifflin Harcourt Publishing Company

Name _____

On Your Own ....

Write another way to group the factors. Then find the product.

8. $(2 \times 3) \times 3$

9. $(8 \times 3) \times 2$

10. $2 \times (5 \times 5)$

11. $(3 \times 2) \times 4$

12. $(6 \times 1) \times 4$

13. $2 \times (2 \times 6)$

14. $2 \times (4 \times 2)$

15. $5 \times (2 \times 4)$

16. $9 \times (1 \times 2)$

Practice: Copy and Solve Use parentheses and multiplication properties. Then, find the product.

17. $6 \times 5 \times 2$

18. $2 \times 3 \times 5$

19. $3 \times 1 \times 6$

20. $2 \times 5 \times 6$

21. $2 \times 0 \times 8$

22. $1 \times 9 \times 4$

23. $2 \times 2 \times 2$

24. $4 \times 2 \times 2$

25. $2 \times 4 \times 5$

26. $2 \times 6 \times 1$

27. $2 \times 9 \times 3$

28. $2 \times 7 \times 2$

H.O.T. **Algebra** Find the unknown factor.

29. $7 \times (2 \times \underline{\quad}) = 56$

30. $30 = 6 \times (5 \times \underline{\quad})$

31. $\underline{\quad} \times (2 \times 2) = 32$

32. $42 = 7 \times (2 \times \underline{\quad})$

33. $8 \times (5 \times \underline{\quad}) = 40$

34. $0 = \underline{\quad} \times (25 \times 1)$

35. $(2 \times 9) \times \underline{\quad} = 18$

36. $60 = (2 \times \underline{\quad}) \times 6$

37. $4 \times (3 \times \underline{\quad}) = 24$

© Houghton Mifflin Harcourt Publishing Company

Module 10 • Lesson 1   199

Problem Solving · REAL WORLD

Use the graph for 38–39.

38. Each car on the Steel Force train has 3 rows with 2 seats in each row. How many seats are on the train? Draw a quick picture.

39. **H.O.T.** A Kingda Ka train has 4 seats per car, but the last car has only 2 seats. How many seats are on one Kingda Ka train?

················ **SHOW YOUR WORK** ···············

40. **Write Math** **Sense or Nonsense?** Each week, Kelly works 2 days for 4 hours each day and earns $5 an hour. Len works 5 days for 2 hours each day and earns $4 an hour. Kelly says they both earn the same amount. Does this statement make sense? **Explain.**

41. ⭐ **PARCC Test Prep** Mark has 2 rows of 3 car models on each of his 3 shelves. How many models does he have?

Ⓐ 8   Ⓒ 11

Ⓑ 9   Ⓓ 18

Name _____

Multiply with 8

Essential Question What strategies can you use to multiply with 8?

COMMON CORE
Georgia Performance Standard MCC3.OA.7
Multiply and divide within 100.

🔑 UNLOCK the Problem REAL WORLD

A scorpion has 8 legs. How many legs do 5 scorpions have?

Find 5×8.

🔓 One Way Use doubles.

$5 \times 8 = $ ▪
       ↙ ↘
     $4 + 4$

Think: The factor 8 is an even number. $4 + 4 = 8$

$5 \times 4 = $ _____

20 doubled is _____.

$5 \times 8 = $ _____

So, 5 scorpions have _____ legs.

🔓 Another Way Use a number line.

Use the number line to show 5 jumps of 8.

• How many legs does one scorpion have?

_____

• What are you asked to find?

_____

_____

0 2 4 6 8 10 12 14 16 18 20 22 24 26 28 30 32 34 36 38 40

So, 5 jumps of 8 is _____. _____ × _____ = _____

⚠ ERROR Alert

Be sure to count the spaces between the tick marks, not the tick marks.

• **Describe** two different ways you can use doubles to find 6×8.

_____

_____

🔒 Example Use the Associative Property of Multiplication.

Scorpions have two eyes on the top of the head, and usually two to five pairs along the front corners of the head. If each scorpion has 6 eyes, how many eyes would 8 scorpions have?

$8 \times 6 = \blacksquare$

$8 \times 6 = (2 \times 4) \times 6$ Think: $8 = 2 \times 4$

$8 \times 6 = 2 \times (4 \times 6)$ Use the Associative Property.

$8 \times 6 = 2 \times \underline{\hspace{1cm}}$ Multiply. 4×6

$8 \times 6 = \underline{\hspace{1cm}} + \underline{\hspace{1cm}}$ Double the product.

$8 \times 6 = \underline{\hspace{1cm}}$

Math Talk MATHEMATICAL PRACTICES
When you multiply with 8, will the product always be even? **Explain.**

Share and Show [MATH BOARD] . . . .

1. **Explain** one way you can find 4×8.

_____

_____

Find the product.

2. $3 \times 8 = \underline{\hspace{1cm}}$ 3. $\underline{\hspace{1cm}} = 8 \times 2$ 🗸 4. $\underline{\hspace{1cm}} = 7 \times 8$ 🗸 5. $9 \times 8 = \underline{\hspace{1cm}}$

Math Talk MATHEMATICAL PRACTICES
Explain why using doubles is a good strategy for finding 8×9.

On Your Own . . . .

Find the product.

6. $\underline{\hspace{1cm}} = 6 \times 8$ 7. $10 \times 8 = \underline{\hspace{1cm}}$ 8. $\underline{\hspace{1cm}} = 8 \times 3$ 9. $1 \times 8 = \underline{\hspace{1cm}}$

10. $4 \times 8 = \underline{\hspace{1cm}}$ 11. $5 \times 8 = \underline{\hspace{1cm}}$ 12. $0 \times 8 = \underline{\hspace{1cm}}$ 13. $8 \times 8 = \underline{\hspace{1cm}}$

14. $\begin{array}{r} 6 \\ \times 8 \\ \hline \end{array}$ 15. $\begin{array}{r} 8 \\ \times 2 \\ \hline \end{array}$ 16. $\begin{array}{r} 5 \\ \times 8 \\ \hline \end{array}$ 17. $\begin{array}{r} 3 \\ \times 8 \\ \hline \end{array}$ 18. $\begin{array}{r} 10 \\ \times 8 \\ \hline \end{array}$ 19. $\begin{array}{r} 7 \\ \times 8 \\ \hline \end{array}$

Name _____

 Algebra Complete the table.

	Multiply by 4.	
20.	8	
21.	5	
22.	10	

	Multiply by 8.	
23.	4	
24.	2	
25.	7	

26.	Multiply by ___.	
	3	9
	6	18
27.	10	

Problem Solving REAL WORLD

Use the table for 28–31.

28. About how much rain falls in the Chihuahuan Desert in 6 years? **Explain** how you can use doubles to find the answer.

_____

_____

Average Yearly Rainfall in North American Deserts	
Desert	**Inches**
Chihuahuan	8
Great Basin	9
Mojave	4
Sonoran	9

29. **Predict** In 2 years, about how many more inches of rain will fall in the Sonoran Desert than in the Chihuahuan Desert? **Explain.**

_____

_____

30. **Write Math** **Pose a Problem** Look back at Exercise 29. Write and show how to solve a similar problem by comparing two different deserts.

_____

_____

_____

31. **H.O.T.** How can you find about how many inches of rain will fall in the Mohave Desert in 20 years?

_____

32. ⭐**PARCC Test Prep** A black widow spider has 8 legs. How many legs do 7 black widow spiders have?

Ⓐ 1   Ⓑ 15   Ⓒ 48   Ⓓ 56

Connect to Science

There are 90 species of scorpions that live in the United States. Only 3 species of scorpions live in Arizona. They are the Arizona bark scorpion, the Desert hairy scorpion, and the Stripe-tailed scorpion.

Facts About Scorpions

Scorpions:
- are between 1 and 4 inches long
- mostly eat insects
- glow under ultraviolet light

They have:
- 8 legs for walking
- 2 long, claw-like pincers used to hold their food
- a curled tail held over their body with a stinger on the tip

▲ Scorpions glow under ultraviolet light.

33. How many species of scorpions do *not* live in Arizona?

_____

34. Students saw 8 scorpions. What multiplication sentences can help you find how many pincers and legs the 8 scorpions had?

_____

35. Three scorpions were in a display with ultraviolet light. Eight groups of 4 students saw the display. How many students saw the glowing scorpions?

_____

Multiply with 9

Essential Question What strategies can you use to multiply with 9?

COMMON CORE
Georgia Performance Standard MCC3.OA.7
Multiply and divide within 100.

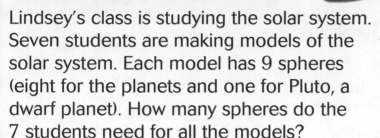 **UNLOCK the Problem** REAL WORLD

Lindsey's class is studying the solar system. Seven students are making models of the solar system. Each model has 9 spheres (eight for the planets and one for Pluto, a dwarf planet). How many spheres do the 7 students need for all the models?

Find 7 × 9.

• What are you asked to find?

_____

_____

• How many students are making

models? _____

🔑 One Way Use the Distributive Property.

Ⓐ With multiplication and addition

$$7 \times 9 = \blacksquare$$

Think: 9 = 3 + 6 $7 \times 9 = 7 \times (3 + 6)$

Multiply each addend by 7. $7 \times 9 = (7 \times 3) + (7 \times 6)$

Add the products. $7 \times 9 = $ _____ + _____

$7 \times 9 = $ _____

Ⓑ With multiplication and subtraction

$$7 \times 9 = \blacksquare$$

Think: 9 = 10 − 1 $7 \times 9 = 7 \times (10 - 1)$

Multiply each number by 7. $7 \times 9 = (7 \times 10) - (7 \times 1)$

Subtract the products. $7 \times 9 = $ _____ − _____

$7 \times 9 = $ _____

So, 7 students need _____ spheres for all the models.

🔒 Another Way Use patterns of 9.

The table shows the 9s facts.

Multiply by 9.	
Factors	**Product**
1 × 9	9
2 × 9	18
3 × 9	27
4 × 9	36
5 × 9	45
6 × 9	54
7 × 9	
8 × 9	
9 × 9	

- What do you notice about the tens digit in the product?

  The tens digit is _____ less than the factor that is multiplied by 9.

- What do you notice about the sum of the digits in the product?

  The sum of the digits in the product is always _____.

  So, to multiply 7 × 9, think the tens digit is _____

  and the ones digit is _____. The product is _____.

Try This! Complete the table above.

Use the patterns to find 8 × 9 and 9 × 9.

Share and Show ....

1. What is the tens digit in the product

   3 × 9? _____

   Think: What number is 1 less than 3?

Find the product.

2. 9 × 8 = _____   3. _____ = 2 × 9   ✓ 4. _____ = 6 × 9   ✓ 5. 9 × 1 = _____

On Your Own ....

Find the product.

6. 4 × 9 = _____   7. 5 × 9 = _____   8. 10 × 9 = _____   9. 1 × 9 = _____

10. 9 × 2 = _____   11. 9 × 9 = _____   12. 8 × 9 = _____   13. 7 × 9 = _____

14. 9   15. 9   16. 6   17. 7   18. 4
    × 5   × 3   × 9   × 9   × 9

Name _____

 H.O.T. **Algebra** Compare. Write <, >, or =.

19. $2 \times 9 \bigcirc 3 \times 6$ **20.** $5 \times 9 \bigcirc 6 \times 7$ **21.** $1 \times 9 \bigcirc 3 \times 3$

22. $9 \times 4 \bigcirc 7 \times 5$ **23.** $9 \times 0 \bigcirc 2 \times 3$ **24.** $5 \times 8 \bigcirc 3 \times 9$

Problem Solving REAL WORLD

Use the table for 25–28.

25. The number of moons for one of the planets can be found by multiplying 7×9. Which planet is it?

_____

26. **H.O.T.** Uranus has 27 moons. What multiplication fact with 9 can be used to find the number of moons Uranus has? **Describe** how you can find the fact.

_____

_____

_____

27. **H.O.T.** This planet has 9 times the number of moons that Mars and Earth have together. Which planet is it? **Explain** your answer.

_____

_____

_____

28. **Write Math** ▶ **What's the Question?** Nine students made models of Mars and its moons. The answer is 18. What's the question?

_____

Moons	
Planet	Number of Moons
Earth	1
Mars	2
Jupiter	63
Saturn	47
Uranus	27
Neptune	13

UNLOCK the Problem REAL WORLD

29. The school library has 97 books about space. John and 3 of his friends each check out 9 books. How many space books are still in the school library?

Ⓐ 27   Ⓑ 36   Ⓒ 61   Ⓓ 70

a. What do you need to find? _____

_____

b. Describe one way you can find the answer. _____

_____

c. Show the steps you used to solve the problem.

d. Complete the sentences.

The library has _____ space books.

Multiply _____ × _____ to find how many books John and his 3 friends check out in all.

After you find the number of books they check out,

_____ to find the number of books still in the library.

So, there are _____ space books still in the library.

e. Fill in the bubble for the answer choice above.

30. Mark read 5 pages of a space book every day for a week. How many pages did he read?

Ⓐ 5   Ⓒ 35

Ⓑ 12   Ⓓ 40

31. Joel has 5 shelves of model airplanes. He has 9 airplanes on each shelf. How many model airplanes does he have?

Ⓐ 45   Ⓒ 9

Ⓑ 36   Ⓓ 5

Module 10 Assessment

▶ **Vocabulary**

Choose the best term from the box to complete
the sentence.

Vocabulary
Associative Property of Multiplication
Commutative Property of Multiplication

1. The _____ Property of
Multiplication states that when the grouping of
factors is changed, the product is the same. (p. 197)

▶ **Concepts and Skills**

Write another way to group the factors.
Then find the product. ▶ MCC3.OA.5

2. $(3 \times 1) \times 6$

_____

_____

3. $2 \times (3 \times 4)$

_____

_____

4. $5 \times (2 \times 4)$

_____

_____

5. $(1 \times 2) \times 7$

_____

_____

Use parentheses and multiplication properties.
Then find the product.

6. $4 \times 5 \times 2$

7. $2 \times 0 \times 6$

8. $2 \times 4 \times 1$

Find the product. ▶ MCC3.OA.7

9. $4 \times 9 =$ _____

10. $5 \times 6 =$ _____

11. $9 \times 3 =$ _____

12. $1 \times 8 =$ _____

13. $\begin{array}{r} 8 \\ \times 1 \\ \hline \end{array}$

14. $\begin{array}{r} 6 \\ \times 8 \\ \hline \end{array}$

15. $\begin{array}{r} 8 \\ \times 9 \\ \hline \end{array}$

16. $\begin{array}{r} 9 \\ \times 0 \\ \hline \end{array}$

17. $\begin{array}{r} 3 \\ \times 8 \\ \hline \end{array}$

Fill in the bubble for the correct answer choice.

18. Which is an example of the Associative Property?

MCC3.OA.5

Ⓐ $(3 \times 2) \times 3 = 3 \times (2 \times 3)$

Ⓑ $3 \times 2 = 2 \times 3$

Ⓒ $(3 \times 2) \times 3 = (2 \times 3) \times 3$

Ⓓ $(6 \times 3) = 3 \times (6 \times 2)$

19. Zach gave his cat 3 cat treats a day, for 8 days. How many cat treats did Zach give to his cat?

MCC3.OA.7

Ⓐ 3

Ⓑ 8

Ⓒ 24

Ⓓ 30

20. Elena pastes 8 stickers on a page in her album. There are 9 pages in Elena's album. Which number sentence shows how many stickers Elena has in her album? MCC3.OA.7

Ⓐ $8 \times 9 = 72$

Ⓑ $9 - 8 = 1$

Ⓒ $1 \times 8 = 8$

Ⓓ $8 + 9 = 17$

21. Olivia can make 5 bracelets in a day. How many bracelets can she make in 9 days? MCC3.OA.7

Ⓐ 4

Ⓑ 14

Ⓒ 45

Ⓓ 50

Relate Multiplication and Division

Essential Question How can you use multiplication to divide?

COMMON CORE
Georgia Performance Standard MCC3.OA.6
Understand properties of multiplication and the
relationship between multiplication and division.

 UNLOCK the Problem REAL WORLD

Pam went to the fair. She went on the same ride 6 times and used the same number of tickets each time. She used 18 tickets. How many tickets did she use each time she went on the ride?

- What do you need to find?

  _____

  _____

- Circle the numbers you need to use.

 One Way Use bar models.

You can use bar models to understand how multiplication and division are related.

Complete the bar model to show 18 tickets divided into 6 equal groups.

18 tickets

Write: 18 ÷ 6 = _____

What if the problem said Pam went on the ride 6 times and used 3 tickets each time? How many tickets did Pam use in all?

Complete the bar model to show 6 groups of 3 tickets.

3	3	3	3	3	3

_____ tickets

Write: 6 × 3 = _____

So, Pam used _____ tickets each time she went on the ride.

Multiplication and division are opposite operations, or **inverse operations**.

You can think about multiplication to solve a division problem.

To solve 18 ÷ 6 = ■, think 6 × ■ = 18.

Since 6 × 3 = 18, then 18 ÷ 6 = 3.

MATHEMATICAL PRACTICES
Math Talk What information is given in each of the bar models?

🔑 Another Way Use an array.

You can use an array to see how multiplication and division are related.

Show an array with 18 counters in 3 equal rows by completing the drawing.

There are _____ counters in each row.

Write: 18 ÷ 3 = _____

The same array can be used to find the total number if you know there are 3 rows with 6 counters in each row.

Write: 3 × 6 = _____

Share and Show 📝 MATH BOARD ·····················

1. Use the array to complete the equation.

   Think: There are 3 counters in each row.

   $6 \div 2 =$ _____

MATHEMATICAL PRACTICES

Math Talk Describe another way to find the quotient for 6 ÷ 2.

Complete.

2.

3 rows of _____ = 15

$3 \times$ _____ $= 15$

$15 \div 3 =$ _____

3.

2 rows of _____ = 12

$2 \times$ _____ $= 12$

$12 \div 2 =$ _____

✅ 4.

3 rows of _____ = 21

$3 \times$ _____ $= 21$

$21 \div 3 =$ _____

Complete the equations.

5. $5 \times$ _____ $= 40$ $40 \div 5 =$ _____

✅ 6. $6 \times$ _____ $= 18$ $18 \div 6 =$ _____

Name _____

On Your Own ....

Complete.

7.

5 rows of _____ = 30

5 × _____ = 30

30 ÷ 5 = _____

8.

4 rows of _____ = 20

4 × _____ = 20

20 ÷ 4 = _____

9.

4 rows of _____ = 28

4 × _____ = 28

28 ÷ 4 = _____

Complete the equations.

10. 7 × _____ = 21   21 ÷ 7 = _____

11. 8 × _____ = 16   16 ÷ 8 = _____

12. 4 × _____ = 32   32 ÷ 4 = _____

13. 6 × _____ = 24   24 ÷ 6 = _____

14. 9 × _____ = 18   18 ÷ 9 = _____

15. 5 × _____ = 25   25 ÷ 5 = _____

H.O.T. Algebra Complete.

16. 3 × 3 = 27 ÷ _____

17. 16 ÷ 2 = _____ × 2

18. 9 = _____ ÷ 4

19. 5 = _____ ÷ 7

20. 42 ÷ 7 = _____ × 2

21. 30 ÷ _____ = 2 × 3

Problem Solving • REAL WORLD

Model • Reason • Make Sense

Use the table for 22–23.

22. Mr. Jerome paid $24 for some students to get into the fair. How many students did Mr. Jerome pay for?

_____

23. **H.O.T.** Garrett is 8 years old. He and his family are going to the county fair. What is the price of admission for Garrett, his 2 parents, and baby sister?

_____

Cochise County Fair

Price of Admission	
Adults	$6
Students	$3
Children 5 and under free	

24. There are 20 seats on the Wildcat ride. The number of seats in each car is the same. If there are 5 cars on the ride, how many seats are there in each car? Complete the bar model to show the problem. Then answer the question.

20 seats

_____

SHOW YOUR WORK

25. **Write Math** ▶ **Pose a Problem** How many days are there in 2 weeks? Write and solve a related word problem to represent the inverse operation.

_____

_____

26. ⭐ **PARCC Test Prep** There are 35 prizes in 5 equal rows. How many prizes are in each row?

Ⓐ 6 Ⓑ 7 Ⓒ 8 Ⓓ 9

Name _____

Write Related Facts

Essential Question How can you write a set of related multiplication and division facts?

COMMON CORE
Georgia Performance Standard MCC3.0A.7
Multiply and divide within 100.

 UNLOCK the Problem

Related facts are a set of related multiplication and division equations. What related facts can you write for 2, 4, and 8?

 Activity

- What model can you use to show how multiplication and division are related?

_____

Materials ■ square tiles

STEP 1

Use 8 tiles to make an array with 2 equal rows.

Draw the rest of the tiles.

How many tiles are in each row? _____

Write a division equation for the array using the total number of tiles as the dividend and the number of rows as the divisor.

_____ ÷ _____ = _____

Write a multiplication equation for the array.

_____ × _____ = _____

STEP 2

Now, use 8 tiles to make an array with 4 equal rows.

Draw the rest of the tiles.

How many tiles are in each row? _____

Write a division equation for the array using the total number of tiles as the dividend and the number of rows as the divisor.

_____ ÷ _____ = _____

Write a multiplication equation for the array.

_____ × _____ = _____

So, $8 \div 2 =$ _____ , $2 \times 4 =$ _____ , $8 \div 4 =$ _____ ,

and $4 \times 2 =$ _____ are related facts.

Try This! Draw an array with 4 rows of 4 tiles.

Your array shows the related facts for 4, 4, and 16.

$4 \times 4 =$ _____ $16 \div 4 =$ _____

Since both factors are the same, there are only two equations in this set of related facts.

- Write another set of related facts that has only two equations.

_____

Share and Show

1. Complete the related facts for this array.

$2 \times 8 = 16$ $16 \div 2 = 8$

_____   _____

Math Talk Look at the multiplication and division equations in a set of related facts. What do you notice about the products and dividends? **Explain.**

MATHEMATICAL PRACTICES

Write the related facts for the array.

2.

_____

_____

_____

3.

_____

_____

_____

4.

_____

_____

_____

5. Why do the related facts for the array in Exercise 2 have only two equations?

_____

On Your Own ....

Write the related facts for the array.

6.

_____

_____

_____

_____

7.

_____

_____

_____

_____

8.

_____

_____

_____

_____

Write the related facts for the set of numbers.

9. 2, 5, 10

_____

_____

_____

10. 3, 8, 24

_____

_____

_____

11. 6, 6, 36

_____

_____

_____

Complete the related facts.

12. $4 \times 7 =$ _____

$7 \times$ _____ $= 28$

$28 \div$ _____ $= 4$

$28 \div 4 =$ _____

13. $5 \times$ _____ $= 30$

$6 \times$ _____ $= 30$

$30 \div 6 =$ _____

$30 \div 5 =$ _____

14. _____ $\times 9 = 27$

_____ $\times 3 = 27$

_____ $\div 9 = 3$

$27 \div$ _____ $= 9$

15. _____ $\times 5 = 20$

_____ $\times 4 = 20$

$20 \div$ _____ $= 5$

_____ $\div 5 = 4$

16. $2 \times$ _____ $= 12$

$6 \times 2 =$ _____

_____ $\div 2 = 6$

$12 \div$ _____ $= 2$

17. $5 \times 8 =$ _____

_____ $\times 5 = 40$

$40 \div 5 =$ _____

_____ $\div 8 = 5$

Problem Solving REAL WORLD

Use the table for 18–19.

18. Mr. Lee divides 1 package of clay and 1 package of glitter dough equally among 4 students. How many more glitter dough sections than clay sections does each student get?

Clay Supplies	
Item	**Number in Package**
Clay	12 sections
Clay tool set	11 tools
Glitter dough	36 sections

_____

19. **Write Math** ▶ **What's the Error?** Ty has a package of glitter dough. He says he can give 9 friends 5 equal sections. Describe his error.

SHOW YOUR WORK

_____

_____

_____

20. **H.O.T.** **Pose a Problem** Write a word problem that can be solved by using 35 ÷ 5. Solve your problem.

_____

_____

_____

_____

21. ⭐ **PARCC Test Prep** Which equation is NOT included in the same set of related facts as $9 \times 4 = 36$?

Ⓐ $4 \times 9 = 36$

Ⓑ $36 \div 6 = 6$

Ⓒ $36 \div 4 = 9$

Ⓓ $36 \div 9 = 4$

Name _____

Division Rules for 1 and 0

Essential Question What are the rules for dividing with 1 and 0?

COMMON CORE
Georgia Performance Standard MCC3.OA.5
Understand properties of multiplication and the relationship between multiplication and division.

🔑 UNLOCK the Problem   REAL WORLD

What rules for division can help you divide with 1 and 0?

If there is only 1 fishbowl, then all the fish must go in that fishbowl.

$$4 \div 1 = 4$$

↑   ↑   ↑
number   number   number in
of fish   of bowls   each bowl

Try This! There are 3 fish and 1 fishbowl. Draw a quick picture to show the fish in the fishbowl.

Write the equation your picture shows.

_____ ÷ _____ = _____

> **Rule A:** Any number divided by 1 equals that number.

MATHEMATICAL PRACTICES

Math Talk Explain how Rule A is related to the Identity Property of Multiplication.

If there is the same number of fish and fishbowls, then 1 fish goes in each fishbowl.

$$4 \div 4 = 1$$

↑   ↑   ↑
number   number   number in
of fish   of bowls   each bowl

Try This! There are 3 fish and 3 fishbowls. Draw a quick picture to show the fish divided equally among the fishbowls.

Write the equation your picture shows.

_____ ÷ _____ = _____

> **Rule B:** Any number (except 0) divided by itself equals 1.

If there are 0 fish and 4 fishbowls, there will not be any fish in the fishbowls.

$$0 \div 4 = 0$$

↑ number of fish   ↑ number of bowls   ↑ number in each bowl

Rule C: Zero divided by any number (except 0) equals 0.

If there are 0 fishbowls, then you cannot separate the fish equally into fishbowls. Dividing by 0 is not possible.

4 ÷ 0 = ▪

Rule D: You cannot divide by 0.

Try This! There are 0 fish and 3 fishbowls. Draw a quick picture to show the fishbowls.

Write the equation your picture shows.

_____ ÷ _____ = _____

Share and Show 🖊 MATH BOARD ....

1. Use the picture to find 2 ÷ 2. _____

Math Talk   MATHEMATICAL PRACTICES

Explain what happens when you divide a number (except 0) by itself.

Find the quotient.

2. 7 ÷ 1 = _____   3. 8 ÷ 8 = _____   ✓4. 0 ÷ 5 = _____   ✓5. 6 ÷ 6 = _____

Name _____

On Your Own ....

Find the quotient.

6. $0 \div 8 =$ _____   7. $5 \div 5 =$ _____   8. $2 \div 1 =$ _____   9. $0 \div 7 =$ _____

10. $5\overline{)0}$ 11. $1\overline{)9}$ 12. $7\overline{)7}$ 13. $10\overline{)10}$

Practice: Copy and Solve Find the quotient.

14. $6 \div 1$ 15. $25 \div 5$ 16. $0 \div 6$ 17. $18 \div 3$

18. $14 \div 2$ 19. $9 \div 9$ 20. $28 \div 4$ 21. $8 \div 1$

22. $3\overline{)27}$ 23. $5\overline{)10}$ 24. $3\overline{)0}$ 25. $1\overline{)0}$

Problem Solving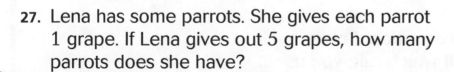

• • • • SHOW YOUR WORK • • • •

26. Claire has 7 parakeets. She puts 4 in a cage. She divides the other parakeets equally among 3 friends to hold. How many parakeets does each friend get to hold?

_____

27. Lena has some parrots. She gives each parrot 1 grape. If Lena gives out 5 grapes, how many parrots does she have?

_____

28. **H.O.T.** **Write Math** Suppose a pet store has 21 birds that are in 21 cages. Use what you know about division rules to find the number of birds in each cage. **Explain** your answer.

_____

29. ⭐ **PARCC Test Prep** Joe has 4 horses. He puts each horse in its own stall. How many stalls does Joe use?

Ⓐ 0   Ⓑ 1   Ⓒ 2   Ⓓ 4

Connect to Reading

Compare and Contrast

You have learned the rules for division with 1. Compare and contrast them to help you learn how to use the rules to solve problems.

Compare the rules. Think about how they are *alike*.
Contrast the rules. Think about how they are *different*.

Read: Rule A: Any number divided by 1 equals that number.

Rule B: Any number (except 0) divided by itself equals 1.

Compare: How are the rules alike?

• Both are division rules for 1.

Contrast: How are the rules different?

• Rule A is about dividing a number by 1.
  The quotient is that number.

• Rule B is about dividing a number (except 0) by itself.
  The quotient is always 1.

Read the problem. Write an equation. Solve.
Circle *Rule A* or *Rule B* to tell which rule you used.

30. Jamal bought 7 goldfish at the pet store. He put them in 1 fishbowl. How many goldfish did he put in the fishbowl?

_____

Rule A   Rule B

31. Ava has 6 turtles. She divides them equally among 6 aquariums. How many turtles does she put in each aquarium?

_____

Rule A   Rule B

Name _____

Divide by 10

Essential Question What strategies can you use to divide by 10?

COMMON CORE
Georgia Performance Standard MCC3.OA.7
Multiply and divide within 100.

🔑 UNLOCK the Problem REAL WORLD

There are 50 students going on a field trip to the Philadelphia Zoo. The students are separated into equal groups of 10 students each. How many groups of students are there?

- What do you need to find?

  _____

- Circle the numbers you need to use.

🔒 One Way Use repeated subtraction.

- Start with 50.
- Subtract 10 until you reach 0.
- Count the number of times you subtract 10.

$$
\begin{array}{ccccc}
50 & 40 & 30 & 20 & 10 \\
-10 & -10 & -10 & -10 & -10 \\
\hline
40 & 30 & & &
\end{array}
$$

1   2   3   4   5

You subtracted 10 five times. $50 \div 10 =$ _____

So, there are _____ groups of 10 students.

🔒 Other Ways

Ⓐ Use a number line.

- Start at 50 and count back by 10s until you reach 0.
- Count the number of times you jumped back 10.

0   5   10   15   20   25   30   35   40   45   50

You jumped back by 10 five times.

$50 \div 10 =$ _____

Math Talk MATHEMATICAL PRACTICES

How is counting on a number line to divide by 10 different from counting on a number line to multiply by 10?

B Use a multiplication table.

Divide. $50 \div 10 = $ ▪

Since division is the opposite of multiplication, you can use a multiplication table to find a quotient.

Think of a related multiplication fact.

▪ $\times 10 = 50$

STEP 1 Find the factor, 10, in the top row.

STEP 2 Look down to find the product, 50.

STEP 3 Look left to find the unknown factor, _____ .

Since _____ $\times 10 = 50$, then $50 \div 10 = $ _____ .

In Step 1, is the divisor or the dividend the given factor in the related multiplication fact?

_____

In Step 2, is the divisor or the dividend the product in the related multiplication fact?

_____

The quotient is the unknown factor.

×	0	1	2	3	4	5	6	7	8	9	10
0	0	0	0	0	0	0	0	0	0	0	0
1	0	1	2	3	4	5	6	7	8	9	10
2	0	2	4	6	8	10	12	14	16	18	20
3	0	3	6	9	12	15	18	21	24	27	30
4	0	4	8	12	16	20	24	28	32	36	40
5	0	5	10	15	20	25	30	35	40	45	50
6	0	6	12	18	24	30	36	42	48	54	60
7	0	7	14	21	28	35	42	49	56	63	70
8	0	8	16	24	32	40	48	56	64	72	80
9	0	9	18	27	36	45	54	63	72	81	90
10	0	10	20	30	40	50	60	70	80	90	100

Share and Show

1. Use repeated subtraction to find $30 \div 10$. _____

   Think: How many times do you subtract 10?

   $\begin{array}{r} 30 \\ -10 \\ \hline 20 \end{array}$ $\begin{array}{r} 20 \\ -10 \\ \hline 10 \end{array}$ $\begin{array}{r} 10 \\ -10 \\ \hline \ \end{array}$

   Math Talk MATHEMATICAL PRACTICES
   Describe two other ways to find $30 \div 10$.

Find the unknown factor and quotient.

2. $10 \times$ _____ $= 40$ _____ $= 40 \div 10$
3. $10 \times$ _____ $= 60$ $60 \div 10 = $ _____

Find the quotient.

4. _____ $= 20 \div 10$
5. $10\overline{)50}$
6. $10\overline{)70}$
7. $90 \div 10 = $ _____

224

© Houghton Mifflin Harcourt Publishing Company

Name _____

On Your Own ....

Find the unknown factor and quotient.

8. $10 \times$ _____ $= 70$ $70 \div 10 =$ _____

9. $10 \times$ _____ $= 10$ $10 \div 10 =$ _____

10. $10 \times$ _____ $= 80$ $80 \div 10 =$ _____

11. _____ $\times 2 = 12$ _____ $= 12 \div 2$

Find the quotient.

12. $50 \div 10 =$ _____

13. _____ $= 60 \div 10$

14. $16 \div 2 =$ _____

15. $90 \div 10 =$ _____

16. $10 \div 2 =$ _____

17. $30 \div 10 =$ _____

18. _____ $= 20 \div 2$

19. _____ $= 0 \div 10$

20. $10 \overline{)20}$

21. $10 \overline{)100}$

22. $10 \overline{)40}$

23. $10 \overline{)80}$

 H.O.T. **Algebra** Write $<$, $>$, or $=$.

24. $10 \div 1 \bigcirc 4 \times 10$

25. $17 - 6 \bigcirc 18 \div 2$

26. $4 \times 4 \bigcirc 8 + 8$

27. $23 + 14 \bigcirc 5 \times 8$

28. $70 \div 10 \bigcirc 23 - 16$

29. $9 \times 0 \bigcirc 9 + 0$

Problem Solving REAL WORLD

Use the picture graph for 30–32.

Animal Stickers

Elephants	☐ ☐ ☐ ☐
Giraffes	☐ ☐ ☐
Monkeys	☐ ☐ ☐ ☐

Key: Each ☐ = 10 stickers.

30. Lyle wants to add penguins to the picture graph. There are 30 stickers of penguins. How many symbols should Lyle draw for penguins?

_____

31. **Pose a Problem** Write a word problem using information from the picture graph. Then solve your problem.

_____

_____

_____

32. **H.O.T. Sense or Nonsense?** Lena wants to put the monkey stickers in an album. She says she will use more pages if she puts 5 stickers on a page instead of 10 stickers on a page. Is she correct? **Explain**.

_____

_____

_____

SHOW YOUR WORK

33. **Write Math** ▸ **Explain** how a division problem is like an unknown factor problem.

_____

_____

_____

34. ⭐ **PARCC Test Prep** Miles has 100¢ in dimes. How many dimes does Miles have?

Ⓐ 1 Ⓑ 4 Ⓒ 10 Ⓓ 100

Module 11 Assessment

▶ Vocabulary

Choose the best term from the box to complete the sentence.

Vocabulary
inverse operations
related facts
dividend

1. Multiplication and division are opposite operations,

   or _____ (p. 211)

2. _____ are a set of related multiplication and division equations. (p. 215)

▶ Concepts and Skills

Complete the equations. MCC3.OA.6

3. $3 \times$ ____ $= 24$ $24 \div 3 =$ ____

4. $5 \times$ ____ $= 15$ $15 \div 5 =$ ____

5. $7 \times$ ____ $= 49$ $49 \div 7 =$ ____

6. $9 \times$ ____ $= 18$ $18 \div 9 =$ ____

Complete the related facts. MCC3.OA.7

7. $4 \times 8 =$ ____

   $8 \times$ ____ $= 32$

   $32 \div$ ____ $= 8$

   $32 \div 8 =$ ____

8. $3 \times$ ____ $= 9$

   ____ $\div 3 = 3$

9. $6 \times$ ____ $= 42$

   $7 \times 6 =$ ____

   ____ $\div 6 = 7$

   $42 \div$ ____ $= 6$

Find the quotient. MCC3.OA.5, MCC3.OA.7

10. $8 \div 1 =$ ____

11. $60 \div 10 =$ ____

12. $0 \div 5 =$ ____

13. $9 \div 9 =$ ____

14. ____ $= 30 \div 10$

15. ____ $= 0 \div 2$

Fill in the bubble for the correct answer choice.

16. Lee plants 24 seeds in some flowerpots. If he puts 1 seed in each pot, how many flowerpots does he use? ▸MCC3.OA.5

    (A) 24   (C) 10
    (B) 12   (D) 1

17. Tan has 40 sports cards. He gives the same number of cards to each of 10 friends. Which equation can be used to find the number of sports cards each friend receives? ▸MCC3.OA.7

    (A) $40 + 10 = \blacksquare$

    (B) $40 - 10 = \blacksquare$

    (C) $40 \times 10 = \blacksquare$

    (D) $40 \div 10 = \blacksquare$

18. Which equation is NOT included in the same set of related facts as $6 \times 3 = 18$? ▸MCC3.OA.7

    (A) $3 \times 6 = 18$ (C) $18 \div 3 = 6$
    (B) $18 \div 2 = 9$ (D) $18 \div 6 = 3$

19. There are 60 people at the fair waiting in line for a ride. Each car in the ride can hold 10 people. Which equation could be used to find the number of cars needed to hold all 60 people? ▸MCC3.OA.7

    (A) $60 - 10 = \blacksquare$

    (B) $\blacksquare + 10 = 60$

    (C) $60 \div 10 = \blacksquare$

    (D) $60 \times 10 = \blacksquare$

Name _____

Divide by 3

Essential Question What strategies can you use to divide by 3?

COMMON CORE
Georgia Performance Standard MCC3.OA.7
Multiply and divide within 100.

🔑 UNLOCK the Problem REAL WORLD

For field day, 18 students have signed up for the relay race. Each relay team needs 3 students. How many teams can be made?

🔒 One Way Make equal groups.

- Look at the 18 counters below.
- Circle as many groups of 3 as you can.
- Count the number of groups.

- What do you need to find?

  _____

  _____

- Circle the numbers you need to use.

There are _____ groups of 3.

So, _____ teams can be made.

You can write $18 \div 3 =$ _____ or $3\overline{)18}$.

Math Talk MATHEMATICAL PRACTICES
Suppose the question asked how many students would be on 3 equal teams. How would you model 3 equal teams? Would the quotient be the same?

🔑 Other Ways

Ⓐ Count back on a number line.

- Start at 18.

- Count back by 3s as many times as you can.
  Complete the jumps on the number line.

- Count the number of times you jumped back 3.

> ⚠️ **ERROR Alert**
>
> Be sure to count back the same number of spaces each time you jump back on the number line.

You jumped back by 3 _____ times.

Ⓑ Use a related multiplication fact.

Since division is the opposite of multiplication, think of a related multiplication fact to find $18 \div 3$.

$$\blacksquare \times 3 = 18$$
$$6 \times 3 = 18$$

Think: What number completes the multiplication fact?

So, $18 \div 3 =$ _____ or $3\overline{)18}$.

- **What if** 24 students signed up for the relay race and there were 3 students on each team? What related multiplication fact would you use to find the number of teams?

_____

Share and Show 🖊️ MATH BOARD ....

1. Circle groups of 3 to find $12 \div 3$. _____

> **Math Talk** MATHEMATICAL PRACTICES
> **Explain** what the number of circles you made tells you.

Find the quotient.

✓ **2.** $6 \div 3 =$ ___   **3.** ___ $= 14 \div 2$ ✓ **4.** $21 \div 3 =$ ___   **5.** ___ $= 30 \div 5$

Name _____

On Your Own ....

Practice: Copy and Solve Find the quotient. Draw
a quick picture to help.

6. $9 \div 3$ 7. $10 \div 5$ 8. $18 \div 2$ 9. $24 \div 3$

Find the quotient.

10. ___ $= 12 \div 2$ 11. $40 \div 5 =$ ___   12. $60 \div 10 =$ ___   13. ___ $= 20 \div 10$

14. $27 \div 3 =$ ___   15. ___ $= 0 \div 3$ 16. $12 \div 3 =$ ___   17. ___ $= 8 \div 2$

18. $3\overline{)15}$ 19. $2\overline{)4}$ 20. $5\overline{)20}$ 21. $3\overline{)18}$

22. $2\overline{)16}$ 23. $3\overline{)12}$ 24. $3\overline{)6}$ 25. $5\overline{)35}$

26. $3\overline{)3}$ 27. $10\overline{)70}$ 28. $3\overline{)30}$ 29. $10\overline{)50}$

 Algebra Write +, −, ×, or ÷.

30. $25 \bigcirc 5 = 10 \div 2$ 31. $3 \times 3 = 6 \bigcirc 3$ 32. $16 \bigcirc 2 = 24 - 16$

33. $13 + 19 = 8 \bigcirc 4$ 34. $14 \bigcirc 2 = 6 \times 2$ 35. $21 \div 3 = 5 \bigcirc 2$

Problem Solving REAL WORLD

Use the table for 36–37.

Field Day Events	
Activity	Number of Students
Relay race	25
Beanbag toss	18
Jump-rope race	27

36. There are 5 equal teams in the relay race. How many students are on each team? Write a division equation that shows the number of students on each team.

_____

37. **H.O.T.** Students doing the jump-rope race and the beanbag toss compete in teams of 3. How many more teams participate in the jump-rope race than in the beanbag toss? **Explain** how you know.

_____

_____

_____

SHOW YOUR WORK

38. **Write Math** ➤ **What's the Question?** Michael puts 21 sports cards into stacks of 3. The answer is 7 stacks.

_____

_____

_____

39. ⭐ **PARCC Test Prep** Olivia buys 24 beanbags for field day. She buys 3 equal packs. How many beanbags are in each pack?

Ⓐ 6   Ⓒ 8

Ⓑ 7   Ⓓ 9

Divide by 4

Essential Question What strategies can you use to divide by 4?

COMMON CORE
Georgia Performance Standard MCC3.OA.7
Multiply and divide within 100.

🔑 UNLOCK the Problem REAL WORLD

A tree farmer plants 12 red maple trees in 4 equal rows. How many trees are in each row?

- What strategy could you use to solve the problem?

_____

🔒 One Way Make an array.

- Look at the array.
- Continue the array by drawing 1 tile in each of the 4 rows until all 12 tiles are drawn.
- Count the number of tiles in each row.

There are _____ tiles in each row.

So, there are _____ trees in each row.

Write: _____ ÷ _____ = _____ or $4\overline{)12}$

Read: Twelve divided by four equals three.

🔒 Other Ways

Ⓐ Make equal groups.

- Draw 1 counter in each group.
- Continue drawing 1 counter at a time until all 12 counters are drawn.

There are _____ counters in each group.

Math Talk MATHEMATICAL PRACTICES
Explain how making an array to solve the problem is like making equal groups.

B Use factors to find $12 \div 4$.

The factors of 4 are 2 and 2.

$$2 \times 2 = 4$$

factors   product

To divide by 4, use the factors.

$12 \div 4 = n$

Divide by 2. $12 \div 2 = 6$

Then divide by 2 again. $6 \div 2 = 3$

$12 \div 4 = $ _____

C Use a related multiplication fact.

$12 \div 4 = n$

$4 \times n = 12$

$4 \times 3 = 12$

Think: What number completes the multiplication fact?

$12 \div 4 = $ _____ or $4\overline{)12}$

Remember
A letter or symbol, like n, can stand for an unknown number.

Try This! Use factors of 4 to find $16 \div 4$.

The factors of 4 are 2 and 2. $16 \div 4 = $ ■

Divide by 2. $16 \div 2 = $ _____

Then divide by 2 again. $8 \div 2 = $ _____

So, $16 \div 4 = $ _____.

Think: Dividing by the factors of the divisor is the same as dividing by the divisor.

Share and Show ....

1. Use the array to find $28 \div 4$. _____

MATHEMATICAL PRACTICES

Math Talk
Explain how you used the array to find the quotient.

Find the quotient.

2. _____ $= 21 \div 3$ 3. $8 \div 4 = $ _____   4. _____ $= 40 \div 5$ ✓5. $24 \div 4 = $ _____

Find the unknown number.

6. $20 \div 4 = a$ 7. $12 \div 2 = p$ 8. $27 \div 3 = $ ▲   ✓9. $12 \div 4 = t$

   $a = $ _____ $p = $ _____   ▲ $= $ _____ $t = $ _____

234

Name _____

On Your Own ....

Practice: Copy and Solve Draw tiles to make an array.
Find the quotient.

10. $30 \div 10$ **11.** $15 \div 5$ **12.** $40 \div 4$ **13.** $16 \div 2$

Find the quotient.

14. $12 \div 3 = \underline{\quad}$ **15.** $20 \div 4 = \underline{\quad}$ **16.** $\underline{\quad} = 0 \div 4$ **17.** $\underline{\quad} = 36 \div 4$

18. $4\overline{)28}$ **19.** $2\overline{)18}$ **20.** $4\overline{)16}$ **21.** $5\overline{)25}$

Find the unknown number.

22. $45 \div 5 = b$ **23.** $20 \div 10 = e$ **24.** $8 \div 2 = \blacksquare$ **25.** $24 \div 3 = h$

     $b = \underline{\quad}$ $e = \underline{\quad}$ $\blacksquare = \underline{\quad}$ $h = \underline{\quad}$

26. $4 \div 4 = p$ **27.** $24 \div 4 = t$ **28.** $16 \div 4 = s$ **29.** $32 \div 4 = \blacksquare$

     $p = \underline{\quad}$ $t = \underline{\quad}$ $s = \underline{\quad}$ $\blacksquare = \underline{\quad}$

Algebra Complete the table.

30.

÷	9	12	15	18
3				

31.

÷	20	24	28	32
4				

H.O.T. **Algebra** Find the unknown number.

32. $14 \div \underline{\quad} = 7$ **33.** $30 \div \underline{\quad} = 6$ **34.** $8 \div \underline{\quad} = 2$ **35.** $24 \div \underline{\quad} = 8$

36. $36 \div \underline{\quad} = 9$ **37.** $40 \div \underline{\quad} = 4$ **38.** $3 \div \underline{\quad} = 1$ **39.** $35 \div \underline{\quad} = 7$

Problem Solving

Use the table for 40–41.

40. Douglas planted the birch trees in 4 equal rows. Then he added 2 more birch trees to each row. How many trees did he plant in each row?

_____

41. **H.O.T.** Mrs. Banks planted the oak trees in 4 equal rows. Mr. Webb planted the dogwood trees in 3 equal rows. Who planted more trees in each row? How many more? **Explain** how you know.

_____

_____

_____

42. **Write Math** Bryan earns $40 mowing lawns each week. He earns the same amount of money for each lawn. If he mows 4 lawns, how much does Bryan earn for each lawn? **Explain** how you found your answer.

_____

_____

_____

43. ⭐ **PARCC Test Prep** Eric planted 20 flowers in groups of 4. How many groups of flowers did he plant?

Ⓐ 4   Ⓒ 6

Ⓑ 5   Ⓓ 7

Trees Planted

Type	Number Planted
Dogwood	24
Oak	28
Birch	16

SHOW YOUR WORK

FOR MORE PRACTICE: Standards Practice Book

Divide by 6

Essential Question What strategies can you use to divide by 6?

 COMMON CORE
Georgia Performance Standard MCC3.OA.7
Multiply and divide within 100.

UNLOCK the Problem REAL WORLD

Ms. Sing needs to buy 24 juice boxes for the class picnic. Juice boxes come in packs of 6. How many packs does Ms. Sing need to buy?

- Circle the number that tells you how many juice boxes come in a pack.
- How can you use the information to solve the problem?

_____

_____

_____

🔒 One Way Make equal groups.

- Draw 24 counters.

- Circle as many groups of 6 as you can.

- Count the number of groups.

There are _____ groups of 6.

So, Ms. Sing needs to buy _____ packs of juice boxes.

You can write _____ ÷ _____ = _____ or $6\overline{)24}$.

Math Talk MATHEMATICAL PRACTICES

If you divided the 24 counters into groups of 4, how many groups would there be? **Explain** how you know.

🔑 Other Ways

A Use a related multiplication fact.

$24 \div 6 = \blacksquare$

$\blacksquare \times 6 = 24$

$4 \times 6 = 24$

Think: What number completes the multiplication fact?

$24 \div 6 = \underline{\hspace{1cm}}$ or $6\overline{)24}$

B Use factors to find $24 \div 6$.

The factors of 6 are 3 and 2.

$3 \times 2 = 6$

factors   product

To divide by 6, use the factors.

$24 \div 6 = \blacksquare$

Divide by 3. $24 \div 3 = 8$

Then divide by 2. $8 \div 2 = 4$

$24 \div 6 = \underline{\hspace{1cm}}$

• How does knowing $6 \times 9 = 54$ help you find $54 \div 6$?

_____

_____

Share and Show . . . .

1. Continue making equal groups to find $18 \div 6$. _____

MATHEMATICAL PRACTICES

Math Talk Explain how you could use factors to find $18 \div 6$.

Find the unknown factor and quotient.

2. ___ $\times 6 = 36$ $36 \div 6 =$ ___

✓3. $6 \times$ ___ $= 12$ $12 \div 6 =$ ___

Find the quotient.

4. ___ $= 0 \div 2$ 5. $6 \div 6 =$ ___   6. ___ $= 28 \div 4$ ✓7. $42 \div 6 =$ ___

© Houghton Mifflin Harcourt Publishing Company

Name _____

On Your Own ....

Find the unknown factor and quotient.

8. $6 \times$ _____ $= 30$ $30 \div 6 =$ _____

9. _____ $\times 6 = 48$ $48 \div 6 =$ _____

10. $2 \times$ _____ $= 16$ _____ $= 16 \div 2$

11. $5 \times$ _____ $= 45$ _____ $= 45 \div 5$

Find the quotient.

12. $12 \div 6 =$ _____

13. _____ $= 6 \div 1$

14. _____ $= 60 \div 6$

15. $27 \div 3 =$ _____

16. $5\overline{)35}$

17. $6\overline{)42}$

18. $6\overline{)6}$

19. $2\overline{)10}$

Find the unknown number.

20. $k = 54 \div 6$

$k =$ _____

21. $20 \div 4 = w$

$w =$ _____

22. $0 \div 6 = s$

$s =$ _____

23. $d = 36 \div 6$

$d =$ _____

24. $24 \div 6 = n$

$n =$ _____

25. $40 \div 5 = \blacktriangle$

$\blacktriangle =$ _____

26. $60 \div 10 = m$

$m =$ _____

27. $18 \div 6 = \blacksquare$

$\blacksquare =$ _____

H.O.T. **Algebra Find the unknown number.**

28. $20 \div$ _____ $= 4$

29. $24 \div$ _____ $= 8$

30. $16 \div$ _____ $= 4$

31. $3 \div$ _____ $= 3$

32. $42 \div$ _____ $= 7$

33. $30 \div$ _____ $= 10$

34. $10 \div$ _____ $= 2$

35. $32 \div$ _____ $= 4$

© Houghton Mifflin Harcourt Publishing Company

Problem Solving · REAL WORLD

36. Cody baked 12 muffins. He keeps 6 muffins. How many muffins can he give to each of his 6 friends if each friend gets the same number of muffins?

_____

37. What's the Error? Mary has 36 stickers to give to 6 friends. She says she can give each friend only 5 stickers. Use a division equation to describe Mary's error.

SHOW YOUR WORK

_____

_____

_____

38. Write Math ▸ **Pose a Problem** Write and solve a word problem for the bar model.

30

_____

_____

_____

_____

39. ⭐ **PARCC Test Prep** Each picnic table at a park can seat up to 6 people. How many tables will 48 people fill?

Ⓐ 9   Ⓒ 7

Ⓑ 8   Ⓓ 6

Name _____

Divide by 7

Essential Question What strategies can you use to divide by 7?

COMMON CORE
Georgia Performance Standard MCC3.OA.7
Multiply and divide within 100.

🔑 UNLOCK the Problem REAL WORLD

Erin used 28 large apples to make 7 apple pies. She used the same number of apples for each pie. How many apples did Erin use for each pie?

- Do you need to find the number of equal groups or the number in each group?

  _____

- What label will your answer have?

  _____

🔒 One Way Make an array.

- Draw 1 tile in each of 7 rows.

- Continue drawing 1 tile in each of the 7 rows until all 28 tiles are drawn.

- Count the number of tiles in each row.

There are _____ tiles in each row.

So, Erin used _____ for each pie.

You can write $28 \div 7 =$ _____ or $7\overline{)28}$.

MATHEMATICAL PRACTICES

Math Talk Why can you use division to solve the problem? **Explain.**

🔑 Other Ways

Ⓐ Use a related multiplication fact.

$28 ÷ 7 = a$ $7 × a = 28$ **Think:** What number $28 ÷ 7 = $ _____ or $7\overline{)28}$
                  $7 × 4 = 28$ completes the
                                   multiplication fact?

Ⓑ Make equal groups.

- Draw 7 circles to show 7 groups.

- Draw 1 counter in each group.

- Continue drawing 1 counter at a time until all 28 counters are drawn.

There are _____ counters in each group.

Share and Show ....

1. Use the related multiplication fact to find $42 ÷ 7$.
   $6 × 7 = 42$

   $42 ÷ 7 = $ _____

MATHEMATICAL PRACTICES

Math Talk **Explain** why you can use a related multiplication fact to solve a division problem.

Find the unknown factor and quotient.

2. $7 × $ _____ $= 7$ $7 ÷ 7 = $ _____   ✅ 3. $7 × $ _____ $= 35$ $35 ÷ 7 = $ _____

Find the quotient.

4. $4 ÷ 2 = $ _____   5. $56 ÷ 7 = $ _____   6. _____ $= 20 ÷ 5$ ✅ 7. _____ $= 21 ÷ 7$

Name _____

On Your Own ···

Find the unknown factor and quotient.

8. $3 \times$ _____ $= 9$ _____ $= 9 \div 3$

9. $7 \times$ _____ $= 49$ $49 \div 7 =$ _____

10. _____ $\times 7 = 63$ $63 \div 7 =$ _____

11. $4 \times$ _____ $= 32$ _____ $= 32 \div 4$

Find the quotient.

12. _____ $= 14 \div 7$

13. $15 \div 3 =$ _____

14. $0 \div 7 =$ _____

15. _____ $= 25 \div 5$

16. $48 \div 6 =$ _____

17. $7 \div 1 =$ _____

18. _____ $= 42 \div 6$

19. _____ $= 18 \div 2$

20. $7\overline{)56}$

21. $1\overline{)9}$

22. $7\overline{)21}$

23. $2\overline{)8}$

Find the unknown number.

24. $24 \div 4 = x$

$x =$ _____

25. $n = 28 \div 7$

$n =$ _____

26. $r = 54 \div 6$

$r =$ _____

27. $14 \div 7 = j$

$j =$ _____

28. $60 \div 10 = \blacksquare$

$\blacksquare =$ _____

29. $70 \div 7 = k$

$k =$ _____

30. $m = 63 \div 9$

$m =$ _____

31. $r = 12 \div 6$

$r =$ _____

 Algebra Complete the table.

32.

÷	18	30	24	36
6				

33.

÷	56	42	49	35
7				

🔑 UNLOCK the Problem REAL WORLD

34. Gavin sold 21 pies to 7 different people. Each person bought the same number of pies. How many pies did Gavin sell to each person?

Ⓐ 3 Ⓑ 4 Ⓒ 14 Ⓓ 28

a. What do you need to find? _____

_____

b. How can you use a bar model to help you decide which

operation to use to solve the problem? _____

_____

_____

c. Complete the bar model to help you find the number of pies Gavin sold to each person.

21 pies

d. What is another way you could have solved the problem?

_____

_____

e. Complete the sentences.

Gavin sold _____ pies to _____ different people.

Each person bought the same number of _____.

So, Gavin sold _____ pies to each person.

f. Fill in the bubble for the correct answer choice above.

---

35. Clare bought 35 peaches to make peach pies for a bake sale. She used 7 peaches for each pie. How many pies did Clare make?

Ⓐ 4 Ⓑ 5 Ⓒ 6 Ⓓ 7

36. There are 49 pies in all sitting on 7 shelves at a bakery. If each shelf has the same number of pies, how many pies are on each shelf?

Ⓐ 9 Ⓑ 8 Ⓒ 7 Ⓓ 6

Name _____

Divide by 9

Essential Question What strategies can you use to divide by 9?

COMMON CORE
Georgia Performance Standard MCC3.OA.7
Multiply and divide within 100.

🔑 UNLOCK the Problem · REAL · WORLD

Becket's class goes to the aquarium. The 27 students from the class are separated into 9 equal groups. How many students are in each group?

- Do you need to find the number of equal groups or the number in each group?

_____

- What label will your answer have?

_____

🔑 One Way Make equal groups.

- Draw 9 circles to show 9 groups.

- Draw 1 counter in each group.

- Continue drawing 1 counter at a time until all 27 counters are drawn.

There are _____ counters in each group.

So, there are _____ in each group.

Math Talk — MATHEMATICAL PRACTICES
What is another way you could solve the problem? **Explain.**

You can write 27 ÷ 9 = _____ or 9)27 .

🔑 Other Ways

Ⓐ Use factors to find 27 ÷ 9.

The factors of 9 are 3 and 3.

$$3 \times 3 = 9$$

factors   product

To divide by 9, use the factors.

$27 \div 9 = s$

Divide by 3. $27 \div 3 = 9$

Then divide by 3 again. $9 \div 3 = 3$

$27 \div 9 = $ _____

Ⓑ Use a related multiplication fact.

$27 \div 9 = s$

$9 \times s = 27$ **Think:** What number
                 completes the
$9 \times 3 = 27$ multiplication fact?

$27 \div 9 = $ _____ or $9\overline{)27}$

• What multiplication fact can you use to find 63 ÷ 9? _____

Share and Show

1. Draw counters in the groups to find 18 ÷ 9. _____

> **Math Talk**   MATHEMATICAL PRACTICES
> **Explain** how you would use factors to find 18 ÷ 9.

Find the quotient.

2. _____ = 45 ÷ 9   3. 36 ÷ 6 = _____   4. 9 ÷ 1 = _____   ✅5. _____ = 54 ÷ 9

6. $7\overline{)28}$ 7. $9\overline{)9}$ 8. $5\overline{)40}$ ✅9. $9\overline{)36}$

On Your Own ....

Find the quotient.

10. $8 \div 2 = $ _____

11. _____ $= 72 \div 9$

12. $56 \div 8 = $ _____

13. _____ $= 27 \div 9$

14. _____ $= 5 \div 1$

15. _____ $= 36 \div 4$

16. $81 \div 9 = $ _____

17. $30 \div 5 = $ _____

18. _____ $= 0 \div 6$

19. $21 \div 7 = $ _____

20. _____ $= 9 \div 3$

21. $42 \div 6 = $ _____

22. $9\overline{)18}$

23. $3\overline{)27}$

24. $6\overline{)48}$

25. $9\overline{)90}$

26. $4\overline{)12}$

27. $9\overline{)63}$

28. $2\overline{)16}$

29. $5\overline{)25}$

Find the unknown number.

30. $64 \div 8 = e$

$e = $ _____

31. $0 \div 9 = g$

$g = $ _____

32. ■ $= 20 \div 4$

■ $= $ _____

33. $s = 9 \div 9$

$s = $ _____

34. $35 \div 5 = $ ★

★ $= $ _____

35. $p = 4 \div 1$

$p = $ _____

36. $54 \div 9 = w$

$w = $ _____

37. $a = 14 \div 2$

$a = $ _____

H.O.T. Algebra Complete the table.

38.

$\div$	24	40	32	48
8				

39.

$\div$	54	45	72	63
9				

🔑 UNLOCK the Problem ▸ REAL WORLD

40. Carlos has 28 blue tang fish and 17 yellow tang fish in one large fish tank. He wants to separate the fish so that there are the same number of fish in each of 9 smaller tanks. How many tang fish will Carlos put in each smaller tank?

a. What do you need to find? _____

_____

b. Why do you need to use two operations to solve the problem? _____

_____

c. Write the steps to find how many tang fish Carlos will put in each smaller tank.

d. Complete the sentences.

Carlos has _____ blue tang fish

and _____ yellow tang fish in one large fish tank.

He wants to separate the fish so that there are the same number

of fish in each of _____ smaller tanks.

So, Carlos will put _____ fish in each smaller tank.

41. Sophie has a new fish. She feeds it 9 fish pellets each day. If Sophie has fed her fish 72 pellets, for how many days has she had her fish?

_____

42. ⭐ **PARCC Test Prep** At the aquarium, Ms. Brady separates 36 students into 9 equal groups. How many students are in each group?

(A) 2   (C) 4

(B) 3   (D) 5

Name _____

 Module 12 Assessment

▶ **Concepts and Skills**

1. Explain how to find 20 ÷ 4 by making an array.
   🔖 MCC3.OA.7

   _____

   _____

   _____

2. Explain how to find 30 ÷ 6 by making equal groups.
   🔖 MCC3.OA.7

   _____

   _____

   _____

Find the unknown factor and quotient. 🔖 MCC3.OA.7

3. $6 \times$ ____ $= 18$ ____ $= 18 \div 6$ | **4.** $7 \times$ ____ $= 28$ ____ $= 28 \div 7$

5. $6 \times$ ____ $= 48$ ____ $= 48 \div 6$ | **6.** $5 \times$ ____ $= 20$ ____ $= 20 \div 5$

Find the quotient. 🔖 MCC3.OA.7

7. ____ $= 6 \div 3$ **8.** $21 \div 3 =$ ____   **9.** ____ $= 14 \div 7$ **10.** $36 \div 9 =$ ____

11. $7\overline{)35}$ **12.** $4\overline{)24}$ **13.** $6\overline{)54}$ **14.** $6\overline{)42}$

© Houghton Mifflin Harcourt Publishing Company

Fill in the bubble for the correct answer choice.

15. Jose has 24 new books. He plans to read 3 of them each week. How many weeks will it take Jose to read all of his new books? MCC3.OA.7

    Ⓐ 3 weeks

    Ⓑ 8 weeks

    Ⓒ 15 weeks

    Ⓓ 21 weeks

16. Alyssa made 4 pancakes for breakfast. She has 36 berries to put on top of the pancakes. She will put an equal number of berries on each pancake. How many berries will Alyssa put on each pancake?

    MCC3.OA.7

    Ⓐ 4

    Ⓑ 6

    Ⓒ 9

    Ⓓ 10

17. Lavinia buys 30 cups for her party. She buys 6 equal packs. How many cups are in each pack? MCC3.OA.7

    Ⓐ 9

    Ⓑ 6

    Ⓒ 5

    Ⓓ 2

18. A baker placed 63 muffins on 7 shelves at the bakery. If each shelf has the same number of muffins, how many muffins are on each shelf? MCC3.OA.7

    Ⓐ 4

    Ⓑ 6

    Ⓒ 7

    Ⓓ 9

Name _____

✓ Unit 3 Assessment

▶ **Vocabulary**

Choose the best term from the box.

Vocabulary
Commutative
Property of
Multiplication
inverse operations

1. The property that states that you can multiply two factors in any order and get the same product.

_____. (p. 180)

▶ **Concepts and Skills**

Find the quotient. ▮MCC3.OA.5, MCC3.OA.7

2. $12 \div 4 =$ _____   3. $35 \div 7 =$ _____   4. _____ $= 54 \div 9$ 5. _____ $= 27 \div 3$

6. $7\overline{)49}$ 7. $3\overline{)9}$ 8. $10\overline{)70}$ 9. $9\overline{)72}$

10. $\begin{array}{r} 6 \\ \times\ 8 \\ \hline \end{array}$ 11. $\begin{array}{r} 10 \\ \times\ 4 \\ \hline \end{array}$ 12. $\begin{array}{r} 5 \\ \times\ 9 \\ \hline \end{array}$ 13. $\begin{array}{r} 6 \\ \times\ 3 \\ \hline \end{array}$ 14. $\begin{array}{r} 5 \\ \times\ 8 \\ \hline \end{array}$ 15. $\begin{array}{r} 8 \\ \times\ 8 \\ \hline \end{array}$

16. $9 \times 0 =$ _____   17. $7 \times 8 =$ _____   18. $4 \times 8 =$ _____   19. $7 \times 3 =$ _____

Find the unknown factor and quotient. ▮MCC3.OA.6, MCC3.OA.7

20. $6 \times$ _____ $= 42$ $42 \div 6 =$ _____ | 21. $7 \times$ _____ $= 28$ _____ $= 28 \div 7$

22. _____ $\times 4 = 16$ $16 \div 4 =$ _____ | 23. $6 \times$ _____ $= 60$ _____ $= 60 \div 6$

GO
Online
Assessment Options
Unit Test

Fill in the bubble for the correct answer choice.

24. Maria has 54 flower seeds and 9 pots. If she wants to put an equal number of seeds in each pot, how many seeds will Maria put in each pot? ▶ MCC3.OA.7

 (A) 6

 (B) 7

 (C) 8

 (D) 9

25. Kim went to the store and bought 3 shirts. They cost $9 each. How much did she spend? ▶ MCC3.OA.7

 (A) $27

 (B) $24

 (C) $9

 (D) $3

26. Bao bought 24 tickets to go on his favorite ride at the fair. The ride costs 3 tickets. How many times can Bao go on his favorite ride? ▶ MCC3.OA.7

 (A) 24

 (B) 18

 (C) 9

 (D) 8

27. Which of the following multiplication equations can be used to find $42 \div 7$? ▶ MCC3.OA.6

 (A) $6 \times 6 = 36$

 (B) $5 \times 8 = 40$

 (C) $8 \times 6 = 48$

 (D) $7 \times 6 = 42$

Fill in the bubble for the correct answer choice.

28. There are 42 students going on a field trip. They are riding in 7 vans. Each van has the same number of students. How many students are riding in each van?

MCC3.OA.7

(A) 8

(B) 7

(C) 6

(D) 5

29. The girl scout group is going on a camping trip. There are 7 tents and 4 girls in each tent. How many girls are going on the camping trip? MCC3.OA.7

(A) 4

(B) 7

(C) 21

(D) 28

30. Kendall baked 30 muffins. Each of her baking trays holds 6 muffins. How many trays of muffins did Kendall bake? MCC3.OA.7

(A) 4

(B) 5

(C) 24

(D) 36

31. There are 54 students in the marching band. They form equal rows, and there are no fewer than 5 rows and no more than 10 students in each row.

★ How many rows can they form and how many students will be in each row? **Explain** how you got your answer.

_____

_____

_____

★★ Two new students join the marching band. How many rows can all of the students form and how many students will be in each row? **Explain** how you got your answer.

_____

_____

_____

_____

★★★ One day, only 47 students came to practice. There were 5 students marching in the first row. What is the greatest number of rows that could be used to arrange the rest of the students in equal rows? **Explain** your answer.

_____

_____

_____

_____

_____

_____

Show What You Know

Check your understanding of important skills.

Name _____

▶ **Think Addition to Subtract**
Write the missing numbers.

1. $11 - 5 = $ ■

Think 5 + ■ = 11

5 + _____ = 11

So, 11 − 5 = _____.

2. $13 - 4 = $ ■

Think 4 + ■ = 13

4 + _____ = 13

So, 13 − 4 = _____.

▶ **Add 3 Numbers** **Write the sum.**

3. $2 + 7 + 3 = $ _____

4. $3 + 5 + 2 = $ _____

5. $6 + 1 + 9 = $ _____

▶ **Model with Arrays** **Use the array. Complete.**

6. 3 rows of 4

_____ × _____ = _____

7. 4 rows of 2

_____ × _____ = _____

MATH DETECTIVE
WITH
CARMEN SANDIEGO™

The butterfly exhibit at the museum will display 60 different butterfly species arranged in an array. Each row has 6 butterflies. Be a Math Detective to find the number of rows in the butterfly exhibit.

The butterfly exhibit will open soon.

Vocabulary Builder

▶ **Visualize It** ••••••••••••••••••••••••••••••••••••

Complete the tree map by using the words with a ✓.

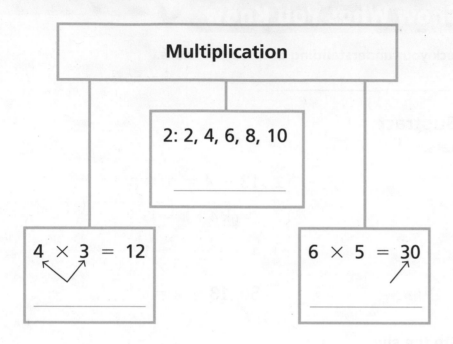

Multiplication

2: 2, 4, 6, 8, 10

_____

4 × 3 = 12

_____

6 × 5 = 30

_____

Review Words

addition

✓ products

Distributive Property

inverse operations

✓ factors

multiplication

pattern

rectangle

repeated addition

✓ multiples

Preview Words

area

order of operations

✓ square unit (sq un)

✓ unit square

▶ **Understand Vocabulary** ••••••••••••••••••••••••

Complete the sentences by using the review and preview words.

1. The _____ is the measure of the number of unit squares needed to cover a surface.

2. You can count, use _____, or multiply to find the area of a rectangle.

3. A _____ is a square with a side length of 1 unit and is used to measure area.

4. The _____ shows that you can break apart a rectangle into smaller rectangles and add the area of each smaller rectangle to find the total area.

© Houghton Mifflin Harcourt Publishing Company

GO Online • eStudent Edition • Multimedia eGlossary

Name _____

Number Patterns

Essential Question How can you use properties to explain patterns on the addition table?

 COMMON CORE
Georgia Performance Standard MCC3.OA.9
Solve problems involving the four operations, and identify and explain patterns in arithmetic.

🔑 UNLOCK the Problem

A **pattern** is an ordered set of numbers or objects. The order helps you predict what will come next.

You can use the addition table to explore patterns.

🔓 Activity 1

Materials orange and green crayons

- Look across each row and down each column. What pattern do you see?

_____

_____

- Shade the row and column orange for the addend 0. Compare the shaded squares to the yellow row and the blue column. What pattern do you see?

_____

What happens when you add 0 to a number?

_____

- Shade the row and column green for the addend 1. What pattern do you see?

_____

What happens when you add 1 to a number?

_____

_____

+	0	1	2	3	4	5	6	7	8	9	10
0	0	1	2	3	4	5	6	7	8	9	10
1	1	2	3	4	5	6	7	8	9	10	11
2	2	3	4	5	6	7	8	9	10	11	12
3	3	4	5	6	7	8	9	10	11	12	13
4	4	5	6	7	8	9	10	11	12	13	14
5	5	6	7	8	9	10	11	12	13	14	15
6	6	7	8	9	10	11	12	13	14	15	16
7	7	8	9	10	11	12	13	14	15	16	17
8	8	9	10	11	12	13	14	15	16	17	18
9	9	10	11	12	13	14	15	16	17	18	19
10	10	11	12	13	14	15	16	17	18	19	20

The **Identity Property of Addition** states that the sum of any number and zero is that number.
$$7 + 0 = 7$$

MATHEMATICAL PRACTICES

Math Talk What other patterns can you find in the addition table?

Activity 2

Materials ■ orange crayon

- Shade all the sums of 5 orange. What pattern do you see?

_____

_____

- Write two addition sentences for each sum of 5. The first two are started for you.

  $5 + 0 =$ _____ and $0 + 5 =$ _____

  _____ + _____ = _____ and _____ + _____ = _____

  _____ + _____ = _____ and _____ + _____ = _____

- What pattern do you see?

_____

_____

+	0	1	2	3	4	5	6	7	8	9	10
0	0	1	2	3	4	5	6	7	8	9	10
1	1	2	3	4	5	6	7	8	9	10	11
2	2	3	4	5	6	7	8	9	10	11	12
3	3	4	5	6	7	8	9	10	11	12	13
4	4	5	6	7	8	9	10	11	12	13	14
5	5	6	7	8	9	10	11	12	13	14	15
6	6	7	8	9	10	11	12	13	14	15	16
7	7	8	9	10	11	12	13	14	15	16	17
8	8	9	10	11	12	13	14	15	16	17	18
9	9	10	11	12	13	14	15	16	17	18	19
10	10	11	12	13	14	15	16	17	18	19	20

> The **Commutative Property of Addition** states that you can add two or more numbers in any order and get the same sum.
>
> $$3 + 4 = 4 + 3$$
> $$7 = 7$$

Activity 3

Materials ■ orange and green crayons

- Shade a diagonal from left to right orange. Start with a square for 1. What pattern do you see?

_____

- Shade a diagonal from left to right green. Start with a square for 2. What pattern do you see?

_____

> **Remember**
> Even numbers end in 0, 2, 4, 6, or 8. Odd numbers end in 1, 3, 5, 7, or 9.

- Write addition sentences for the shaded boxes. Write *even* or *odd* under each addend.

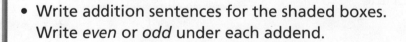

_____ + _____ = 6   _____ + _____ = 7   _____ + _____ = 8

↑   ↑   ↑   ↑   ↑   ↑   ↑   ↑   ↑

_____ + _____ = even   _____ + _____ = odd   _____ + _____ = even

MATHEMATICAL PRACTICES

Math Talk **Explain** how you know when the sum of two numbers will be odd.

Name _____

Share and Show

Use the addition table on page 6 for 1–15.

Use the addition table on page 6 for 1–15.

1. Complete the addition sentences to show the Commutative Property of Addition.

$$3 + \underline{\hspace{1cm}} = \underline{\hspace{1cm}} \qquad 4 + \underline{\hspace{1cm}} = \underline{\hspace{1cm}}$$

Math Talk MATHEMATICAL PRACTICES
Explain why you can use the Commutative Property of Addition to write a related addition sentence.

Find the sum. Then use the Commutative Property of Addition to write the related addition sentence.

2. $8 + 5 = \underline{\hspace{1cm}}$
$\underline{\hspace{1cm}} + \underline{\hspace{1cm}} = \underline{\hspace{1cm}}$

3. $7 + 9 = \underline{\hspace{1cm}}$
$\underline{\hspace{1cm}} + \underline{\hspace{1cm}} = \underline{\hspace{1cm}}$

4. $10 + 4 = \underline{\hspace{1cm}}$
$\underline{\hspace{1cm}} + \underline{\hspace{1cm}} = \underline{\hspace{1cm}}$

Is the sum even or odd? Write _even_ or _odd_.

5. $8 + 1$ _____

6. $3 + 9$ _____

7. $4 + 8$ _____

On Your Own

Find the sum. Then use the Commutative Property of Addition to write the related addition sentence.

8. $0 + 8 = \underline{\hspace{1cm}}$
$\underline{\hspace{1cm}} + \underline{\hspace{1cm}} = \underline{\hspace{1cm}}$

9. $7 + 3 = \underline{\hspace{1cm}}$
$\underline{\hspace{1cm}} + \underline{\hspace{1cm}} = \underline{\hspace{1cm}}$

10. $8 + 7 = \underline{\hspace{1cm}}$
$\underline{\hspace{1cm}} + \underline{\hspace{1cm}} = \underline{\hspace{1cm}}$

Is the sum even or odd? Write _even_ or _odd_.

11. $6 + 4$ _____

12. $5 + 9$ _____

13. $2 + 3$ _____

Problem Solving

14. **H.O.T.** **Write Math** Look back at the shaded diagonals in Activity 2. Why does the orange diagonal show only odd numbers? **Explain.**

_____

_____

_____

_____

15. ⭐ **PARCC Test Prep** Which describes the number sentence?

$$5 + 0 = 5$$

(A) Commutative Property of Addition

(B) Identity Property of Addition

(C) even + even = even

(D) odd + odd = odd

H.O.T. Sense or Nonsense?

16. Whose statement makes sense? Whose statement is nonsense? **Explain** your reasoning.

The sum of an odd number and an odd number is odd.

The sum of an even number and an even number is even.

Joey's Work

odd + odd = odd
5 + 7

I can circle pairs of tiles in each addend and there is 1 left over in each addend. So, the sum will be odd.

_____

_____

_____

Kayley's Work

even + even = even
4 + 6

I can circle pairs of tiles with no tiles left over. So, the sum is even.

_____

_____

_____

- For the statement that is nonsense, correct the statement.

_____

Problem Solving •
Model Addition and Subtraction

Essential Question How can you use the strategy *draw a diagram* to solve one- and two-step addition and subtraction problems?

COMMON CORE
Georgia Performance Standard MCC3.OA.8
Solve problems involving the four operations, and identify and explain patterns in arithmetic.

 UNLOCK the Problem REAL WORLD

Sami scored 84 points in the first round of a new computer game. He scored 21 more points in the second round than in the first round. What was Sami's total score?

You can use a bar model to solve the problem.

Read the Problem

What do I need to find?	**What information do I need to use?**	**How will I use the information?**
I need to find _____.	Sami scored _____ points in the first round. He scored _____ more points than that in the second round.	I will draw a bar model to show the number of points Sami scored in each round. Then I will use the bar model to decide which operation to use.

Solve the Problem

- Complete the bar model to show the number of points Sami scored in the second round.

_____ points	_____ points

■ points

_____ + _____ = ■

_____ = ■

- Complete another bar model to show Sami's total score.

_____ points	_____ points

▲ points

_____ + _____ = ▲

_____ = ▲

1. How many points did Sami score in the second round? _____

2. What was Sami's total score? _____

🔓 Try Another Problem

Anna scored 265 points in a computer game. Greg scored 142 points. How many more points did Anna score than Greg?

You can use a bar model to solve the problem.

GAME OVER
ANNA 265 GREG 142

1000

Read the Problem

What do I need to find?	What information do I need to use?	How will I use the information?

Solve the Problem

Record the steps you used to solve the problem.

Anna _____ points

Greg _____ points

■ points

---

3. How many more points did Anna score than Greg?

_____

4. How do you know your answer is reasonable?

_____

_____

_____

5. How did your drawing help you solve the problem?

_____

_____

Name _____

Share and Show

? UNLOCK the Problem
√ Use the problem solving MathBoard.
√ Choose a strategy you know.

1. Sara received 73 votes in the school election. Ben received 25 fewer votes than Sara. How many students voted?

   First, find how many students voted for Ben.

   Think: $73 - 25 = \blacksquare$

   Write the numbers in the bars.

   So, Ben received _____ votes.

   Next, find the total number of votes.

   Think: $73 + 48 = \blacktriangle$

   Write the numbers in the bars.

   So, _____ students voted.

Sara _____ votes

Ben _____ votes

$\blacksquare$ votes

$\blacksquare = $ _____ votes

_____ votes _____ votes

$\blacktriangle$ votes

$\blacktriangle = $ _____ votes

2. **H.O.T.** **What if** there were 3 students in another election and the total number of votes was the same? What would the bar model for the total number of votes look like? How many votes might each student get?

   _____

   _____

3. **Pose a Problem** Use the bar model at the right. Write a problem to match it.

   _____

   _____

   _____

89 $\blacksquare$

157

4. Solve your problem. Will you add or subtract?

   _____

On Your Own . . . .

Choose a
STRATEGY

Act It Out

Draw a Diagram

Find a Pattern

Make a Table

5. Tony's Tech Store is having a sale. The store had 142 computers in stock. During the sale, 91 computers were sold. How many computers were not sold?

_____

6. The number of computer games sold during the sale was 257. This is 162 more than the number sold the week before the sale. How many computer games were sold the week before the sale?

_____

SHOW YOUR WORK

7. In one week, 128 cell phones were sold. The following week, 37 more cell phones were sold than the week before. How many cell phones were sold in those two weeks?

_____

8. **H.O.T.** **Write Math** ▶ On Monday, the number of customers in the store, rounded to the nearest hundred, was 400. What is the greatest number of customers that could have been in the store? **Explain.**

_____

_____

_____

_____

9. ★ **PARCC Test Prep** The number of laptop computers sold in one day was 42. That is 18 fewer than the number of desktop computers sold. How many desktop computers were sold?

  Ⓐ 24   Ⓒ 60

  Ⓑ 50   Ⓓ 61

Name _____

Problem Solving • Model Multiplication

Essential Question How can you use the strategy *draw a diagram* to solve one- and two-step problems?

COMMON CORE
Georgia Performance Standard MCC3.OA.8
Solve problems involving the four operations, and identify and explain patterns in arithmetic.

🔑 UNLOCK the Problem REAL WORLD

Three groups of students are taking drum lessons. There are 8 students in each group. How many students are taking lessons in all?

Read the Problem

What do I need to find?

I need to find how many _____

are taking drum lessons.

What information do I need to use?

There are _____ groups of

students taking drum lessons. There are

_____ students in each group.

How will I use the information?

I will draw a bar model to help me see

_____

_____.

Solve the Problem

Complete the bar model to show the drummers.

Write 8 in each box to show the 8 students in each of the 3 groups.

8	_____	_____

■ students

Since there are equal groups, I can multiply to find the number of students taking lessons.

_____ × _____ = ■

_____ = ■

So, there are _____ students in all.

MATHEMATICAL PRACTICES

Math Talk How would the bar model change if there were 6 groups of 4 students? Solve.

🔒 Try Another Problem

Twelve students in Mrs. Taylor's class want to start a band. Seven students each made a drum. The rest made 2 maracas each. How many maracas in all were made?

Read the Problem	Solve the Problem
What do I need to find?	**Record the steps you used to solve the problem.**
What information do I need to use?	
How will I use the information?	

Solve the Problem table:

7	_____

12 students

1. How many maracas in all did the students make? _____

2. How do you know your answer is reasonable? _____

MATHEMATICAL PRACTICES

Math Talk Why wouldn't you draw 2 boxes and write 5 in each box?

Name _____

Share and Show . . . .

Choose a STRATEGY

Act It Out
Draw a Diagram
Find a Pattern
Make a Table

1. There are 6 groups of 4 students who play the trumpet in the marching band. How many students play the trumpet in the band?

    First, draw a bar model to show each group of students.

    Draw _____ boxes and write _____ in each box.

    ▮ students

    Then, multiply to find the total number of trumpet players.

    _____ × _____ = ▮

    _____ = ▮

    So, _____ students play the trumpet in the marching band.

2. **H.O.T.** **What if** there are 4 groups of 7 students who play the saxophone? How many students play the saxophone or trumpet?

    _____

3. Suppose there are 5 groups of 4 trumpet players. In front of the trumpet players are 18 saxophone players. How many students play the trumpet or saxophone?

    _____

4. There are 3 rows of flute players in the marching band. There are 7 students in each row. How many flute players are in the marching band?

    _____

SHOW YOUR WORK

© Houghton Mifflin Harcourt Publishing Company

On Your Own . . . .

Use the picture graph for 5–7.

5. The picture graph shows how students in Jillian's class voted for their favorite instrument. How many students voted for the guitar?

_____

6. **Write Math** ➤ On the day of the survey, two students were absent. The picture graph shows the votes of all the other students in the class, including Jillian. How many students are in the class? **Explain** your answer.

_____

_____

_____

Favorite Instrument Survey

Instrument	Number of Votes
Flute	
Trumpet	
Guitar	
Drum	

Key: Each 🛢 = 2 votes.

 SHOW YOUR WORK

7. **H.O.T.** Jillian added the number of votes for two instruments and got a total of 12 votes. For which two instruments did she add the votes?

_____ and _____

8. The flute was invented 26 years after the harmonica. The electric guitar was invented 84 years after the flute. How many years was the electric guitar invented after the harmonica?

_____

9. ⭐ **PARCC Test Prep** After music class, the students filled 4 cabinets with their instruments. Each cabinet has space for 8 instruments. How many instruments did the students put away?

Ⓐ 32

Ⓑ 24

Ⓒ 16

Ⓓ 12

© Houghton Mifflin Harcourt Publishing Company

Patterns on the Multiplication Table

Essential Question How can you use properties to explain patterns on the multiplication table?

COMMON CORE
Georgia Performance Standard MCC3.OA.9
Solve problems involving the four operations, and identify and explain patterns in arithmetic.

🔑 UNLOCK the Problem REAL WORLD

You can use a multiplication table to explore number patterns.

🔑 Activity 1

Materials ■ MathBoard

- Write the products for the green squares. What do you notice about the products?

_____

_____

Write the multiplication sentences for the products on your MathBoard. What do you notice about the factors?

_____

_____

×	0	1	2	3	4	5	6	7	8	9	10
0											
1											
2											
3											
4											
5											
6											
7											
8											
9											
10											

- Will this be true in the yellow squares? **Explain** using a property you know.

_____

Write the products for the yellow squares.

- Complete the columns for 1, 5, and 6. Look across each row and compare the products. What do you notice?

_____

What property does this show?

_____

Math Talk MATHEMATICAL PRACTICES
Explain how you can use these patterns to find other products.

🔑 Activity 2

Materials ■ yellow and blue crayons

- Shade the rows for 0, 2, 4, 6, 8, and 10 yellow.

- What pattern do you notice about each

  shaded row? _____

  _____

- Compare the rows for 2 and 4. What do you

  notice about the products? _____

  _____

×	0	1	2	3	4	5	6	7	8	9	10
0	0	0	0	0	0	0	0	0	0	0	0
1	0	1	2	3	4	5	6	7	8	9	10
2	0	2	4	6	8	10	12	14	16	18	20
3	0	3	6	9	12	15	18	21	24	27	30
4	0	4	8	12	16	20	24	28	32	36	40
5	0	5	10	15	20	25	30	35	40	45	50
6	0	6	12	18	24	30	36	42	48	54	60
7	0	7	14	21	28	35	42	49	56	63	70
8	0	8	16	24	32	40	48	56	64	72	80
9	0	9	18	27	36	45	54	63	72	81	90
10	0	10	20	30	40	50	60	70	80	90	100

- Shade the columns for 1, 3, 5, 7, and 9 blue.

- What do you notice about the products for each shaded column?

  _____

- Compare the products for the green squares. What do you
  notice? What do you notice about the factors?

  _____

- What other patterns do you see?

  _____

  _____

Share and Show ....

1. Use the table to write the products for the row for 2.

   _____, _____, _____, _____, _____,

   _____, _____, _____, _____, _____, _____

   Describe a pattern you see.

   _____

> **MATHEMATICAL PRACTICES**
> **Math Talk** What do you notice about the product of any number and 2?

Is the product even or odd? Write *even* or *odd*.

2. 5×8 _____   3. 6×3 _____   4. 3×5 _____   ✓ 5. 4×4 _____

Name _____

Use the multiplication table. Describe a pattern you see.

6. in the column for 10

_____
_____

7. in the column for 8

_____
_____

On Your Own ·

Is the product even or odd? Write _even_ or _odd_.

8. 4×8 _____

9. 5×5 _____

10. 7×4 _____

11. 2×9 _____

Use the multiplication table. Describe a pattern you see.

12. in the row for 3

_____
_____

13. in the columns for 4 and 8

_____
_____

14. H.O.T. Correct the pattern. Rewrite your pattern.

6, 12, 18, 22, 30, 36 _____

Problem Solving ·

Complete the table. Then describe a pattern you see in the products.

15.

×	2	4	6	8	10
5					

_____
_____

16.

×	1	3	5	7	9
5					

_____
_____

17. Write Math ▶ **Explain** how patterns of the ones digits in the products relate to the factors in Exercises 15 and 16.

_____
_____

18. ★ **PARCC Test Prep** Which of the following describes this pattern?

12, 16, 20, 24, 28

Ⓐ Multiply by 4.　　Ⓑ Add 4.　　Ⓒ Multiply by 5.　　Ⓓ Subtract 4.

H.O.T.   **Sense or Nonsense?**

19. Whose statement makes sense? Whose statement is nonsense? **Explain** your reasoning.

The product of an odd number and an even number is even.

The product of two even numbers is even.

Gunter's Work

odd   even   even
↓   ↓   ↓
3   ×   4   =   12

I can circle 2 equal groups of 6 with no tiles left over. So, the product is even.

Giselle's Work

even   even   even
↓   ↓   ↓
2   ×   6   =   12

I can circle 6 pairs with no tiles left over. So, the product is even.

_____

_____

• **Write** a statement about the product of two odd numbers. Give an example to show why your statement is true.

_____

_____

_____

Problem Solving • Multiplication

Essential Question How can you use the strategy *make a table* to solve multiplication problems?

COMMON CORE
Georgia Performance Standard MCC3.OA.8
Solve problems involving the four operations, and identify and explain patterns in arithmetic.

🔑 UNLOCK the Problem REAL WORLD

Scott has a stamp album. Some pages have 1 stamp on them, and other pages have 2 stamps on them. If Scott has 18 stamps, show how many different ways he could put them in the album. Use the graphic organizer below to solve the problem.

Read the Problem

What do I need to find?

_____

_____

_____

What information do I need to use?

Scott has _____ stamps. Some of the

pages have _____ stamp on them, and

the other pages have _____ stamps.

How will I use the information?

I will make a _____ showing all the different ways of arranging the stamps in the album.

Solve the Problem

Make a table to show the number of pages with 1 stamp and with 2 stamps. Each row must equal

_____, the total number of stamps.

Pages with 2 Stamps	Pages with 1 Stamp	Total Stamps
8	2	18
7	4	18
6	6	18
5		18
	10	18
3	12	
2		

So, there are _____ different ways.

1. What number patterns do you see in the table?

_____

_____

🔒 Try Another Problem

What if Scott bought 3 more stamps and now has 21 stamps? Some album pages have 1 stamp and some pages have 2 stamps. Show how many different ways he could put the odd number of stamps in the album.

Read the Problem	Solve the Problem
What do I need to find?	_____
	_____
	_____
What information do I need to use?	_____
	_____
	_____
	_____
	_____
How will I use the information?	_____
	_____
	So, there are _____ different ways.

2. What patterns do you see in this table? _____

_____

3. How are these patterns different from the patterns in

the table on page 171? _____

_____

Name _____

Share and Show

1. Aaron's mother is making lemonade. For each pitcher, she uses 1 cup of lemon juice, 1 cup of sugar, and 6 cups of water. What is the total number of cups of ingredients she will use to make 5 pitchers of lemonade?

   First, make a table to show the number of cups of lemon juice, sugar, and water that are in 1 pitcher of lemonade.

   Next, multiply to find the number of cups of water needed for each pitcher of lemonade.

   Think: For every pitcher, the number of cups of water increases by 6.

   Last, use the table to solve the problem.

Number of Pitchers	1	2	3		5
Cups of Lemon Juice	1		3		
Cups of Sugar	1	2			
Cups of Water	6	12		24	
Total Number of Cups of Ingredients	8				

So, in 5 pitchers of lemonade, there are _____ cups of

lemon juice, _____ cups of sugar, and _____ cups of water.

This makes a total of _____ cups of ingredients.

2. **What if** it takes 4 lemons to make 1 cup of lemon juice? How many lemons would it take to make 5 pitchers? **Explain** how you can use the table to help you find the answer.

   _____

   _____

3. What pattern do you see in the total number of cups of ingredients?

   _____

   _____

On Your Own . . . .

Choose a
STRATEGY
Act It Out
Draw a Diagram
Find a Pattern
Make a Table

4. Julie saw 3 eagles each day she went bird-watching. How many eagles did Julie see in 6 days?

_____

5. **H.O.T.** Greg has a dollar bill, quarters, and dimes. How many ways can he make $1.75?

Name the ways. _____

_____

_____

SHOW YOUR WORK

6. **Write Math** ▶ Cammi needs 36 postcards. She buys 4 packages of 10 postcards. How many postcards will Cammi have left over? **Explain**.

_____

_____

_____

7. Phillip has 8 books on 3 bookshelves. How many books does Phillip have? Complete the bar model.

books

_____

8. ⭐ **PARCC Test Prep** Each year for 8 years, the Williams family visited 6 different states on vacation. How many more states do they need to visit before they have seen all 50 states?

Ⓐ 48   Ⓒ 24

Ⓑ 36   Ⓓ 2

Module 13 Assessment

▶ **Vocabulary**

Choose the best term from the box to complete the sentence.

Vocabulary
Commutative
Property of Addition
Identity Property of
Addition
pattern

1. The _____ states that the sum of any number and zero is that number. (p. 257)

2. The _____ states that you can add two or more numbers in any order and get the same sum. (p. 258)

▶ **Concepts and Skills**

Is the sum even or odd? Write *even* or *odd*. MCC3.OA.9

3. $8 + 5$ _____

4. $9 + 7$ _____

5. $4 + 6$ _____

Is the product even or odd? Write *even* or *odd*. MCC3.OA.9

6. 5×6 _____

7. 7×5 _____

8. 8×4 _____

9. On Monday, 85 books were taken out from the library. On Tuesday, 22 more books were taken out than on Monday. How many books were taken out during those two days combined? MCC3.OA.8

_____

10. There are 4 rows of student desks in Mr. Fraioli's classroom. There are 6 desks in each row. Including Mr. Fraioli's desk, how many desks are in the classroom? MCC3.OA.8

_____

Fill in the bubble for the correct answer choice.

11. Just Bread sold 385 loaves of bread on Monday, 147 on Tuesday, and 126 on Wednesday. How many more loaves were sold on Monday than on Tuesday and Wednesday? MCC3.OA.8

Ⓐ 112

Ⓑ 122

Ⓒ 273

Ⓓ 658

12. Josh has 4 dogs. Each dog gets 2 dog biscuits every day. How many biscuits will Josh need for all of his dogs for Saturday and Sunday? MCC3.OA.8

Ⓐ 4

Ⓑ 8

Ⓒ 12

Ⓓ 16

13. When Chloe finds the multiplication facts for 2, which digit will NOT be in the ones place of the products?
MCC3.OA.9

Ⓐ 8   Ⓒ 4

Ⓑ 6   Ⓓ 3

14. Each month for 6 months, Earl read 3 books. His goal was to read 25 books this year. How many more books does Earl need to read to achieve his goal?
MCC3.OA.8

Ⓐ 7

Ⓑ 16

Ⓒ 18

Ⓓ 34

Name _____

Describe Patterns

Essential Question . What are some ways you can describe a pattern in a table?

COMMON CORE
Georgia Performance Standard MCC3.OA.9
Solve problems involving the four operations, and identify and explain patterns in arithmetic.

🔑 UNLOCK the Problem REAL WORLD

The outdoor club is planning a camping trip. Each camper will need a flashlight. One flashlight uses 4 batteries. How many batteries are needed for 8 flashlights?

You can describe a pattern in a table.

Flashlights	1	2	3	4	5	6	7	8
Batteries	4	8	12	16	20	24	28	■

Think: Count by 1s.

Think: Count by 4s.

🔒 One Way Describe a pattern across the rows.

STEP 1 Look for a pattern to complete the table. As you look across the rows, you can see that the number of batteries increases by 4 for each flashlight.

So, for every flashlight add _____ batteries.

STEP 2 Use the pattern to find the number of batteries in 8 flashlights.

Add _____ to 28 batteries. $28 + 4 =$ _____

So, _____ batteries are needed for 8 flashlights.

> ⚠️ **ERROR Alert**
> Check that your pattern will work for all the numbers in the table.

🔒 Another Way Describe a pattern in the columns.

STEP 1 Look for a pattern by comparing the columns in the table. You can multiply the number of flashlights by 4 to find the number of batteries that are needed.

STEP 2 Use the pattern to find how many batteries are needed for 8 flashlights.

$8 \times 4 =$ _____

> MATHEMATICAL PRACTICES
> **Math Talk** Why is it important to know how many batteries are needed for 1 flashlight?

© Houghton Mifflin Harcourt Publishing Company

Try This! Describe a pattern. Then complete the table.

The campers need 5 packs of batteries. If there are 8 batteries in each pack, how many batteries will be in 5 packs?

Packs of Batteries	Number of Batteries
1	8
2	16
3	
4	32
5	

Use addition.

Describe a pattern.

Add _____ batteries for each pack.

Use multiplication.

Describe a pattern.

Multiply the number of packs of batteries by _____.

So, there will be _____ batteries in 5 packs.

Share and Show

1. How can you describe a pattern to find the cost of 4 packs of batteries?

_____

_____

Packs of Batteries	1	2	3	4
Cost	$3	$6	$9	

Describe a pattern for the table. Then complete the table.

2.

Tents	Lanterns
2	4
3	6
4	8
5	10
6	
7	

_____

3.

Adults	1	2	3	4	5
Campers	6	12	18		

_____

MATHEMATICAL PRACTICES

Math Talk Explain how you use your description for a pattern to complete a table.

Name _____

On Your Own . . . .

Describe a pattern for the table. Then complete the table.

4.

Hours	1	2	3	4	5
Miles Hiked	2	4	6		

5.

Cabins	3	4	5	6	7
Campers	27	36	45		

6.

Cabins	Beds
1	5
2	10
3	
4	20
5	
6	

7.

Adults	Students
2	12
3	18
4	
5	30
6	
7	

8.

Canoes	4	5	6	7	8
Campers	12	15	18		

9.

Canoes	2	3	4	5	6
Paddles	4	6	8		

10. 🔺H.O.T. Students made a craft project at camp. They used 2 small pine cone patterns and 1 large pine cone pattern. Complete the table to find how many patterns were used for the different numbers of projects.

Projects	1	2	3	4	5	6	7	8	9	10
Small Pattern	2									
Large Pattern	1									

© Houghton Mifflin Harcourt Publishing Company

Problem Solving REAL WORLD

Use the picture graph for 11–13.

11. Jena bought 3 fishing poles. How much did she spend?

_____

12. Noah bought 1 fishing pole, 2 corks, and 1 carton of worms. What was the total cost?

_____

13. **Write Math** ▸ Ryan bought 8 corks. **Explain** how you can use the Commutative Property to find the cost.

_____

_____

14. **H.O.T.** The cost to rent a raft is $7 per person. A raft can hold up to 6 people. There is a $3 launch fee per raft. What is the total cost for a group of 6? **Explain**.

_____

15. Taylor bought 4 boxes of granola bars. There are 6 bars in each box. How many granola bars did Taylor buy?

_____

16. ★ **PARCC Test Prep** Which of the following describes a pattern in the table?

Lifeguards	1	2	3	4	5
Swimmers	10	20	30	40	50

Ⓐ Add 9.   Ⓒ Subtract 9.

Ⓑ Multiply by 2.   Ⓓ Multiply by 10.

Cost of Fishing Supplies

Corks	
Poles	
Worms	

Key: Each 🐟 = $2.

SHOW YOUR WORK

Name _____

Problem Solving • Two-Step Problems

Essential Question How can you use the strategy *act it out* to solve two-step problems?

COMMON CORE
Georgia Performance Standard MCC3.OA.8
Solve problems involving the four operations, and identify and explain patterns in arithmetic.

🔑 UNLOCK the Problem REAL WORLD

Madilyn bought 2 packs of pens and a notebook for $11. The notebook cost $3. Each pack of pens cost the same amount. What is the price of 1 pack of pens?

Read the Problem	Solve the Problem
What do I need to find?	**Describe how to act out the problem.**
I need to find the price of 1 pack of _____.	Start with 11 counters. Take away 3 counters.
	total cost ↓ cost of notebook ↓ p, cost of 2 packs of pens ↓
	_____ − _____ = p
What information do I need to use?	_____ = p
Madilyn spent _____ in all.	Now I know that 2 packs of pens cost _____.
She bought _____ packs of pens and _____ notebook.	Next, make _____ equal groups with the 8 remaining counters.
The notebook cost _____.	p, cost of 2 packs of pens ↓ number of packs ↓ c, cost of 1 pack of pens ↓
	$8 ÷ _____ = c
How will I use the information?	_____ = c
I will use the information to _____ out the problem.	So, the price of 1 pack of pens is _____.

Math Talk MATHEMATICAL PRACTICES
Why do you need to use two operations to solve the problem? **Explain.**

© Houghton Mifflin Harcourt Publishing Company

Module 14   283

🔓 Try Another Problem

Chad bought 4 packs of T-shirts. He gave 5 T-shirts to his brother. Now Chad has 19 shirts. How many T-shirts were in each pack?

Read the Problem	Solve the Problem
What do I need to find?	**Describe how to act out the problem.**
What information do I need to use?	
How will I use the information?	

• How can you use multiplication and subtraction to check your answer?

_____

_____

_____

Math Talk MATHEMATICAL PRACTICES
Explain another strategy you could use to solve this problem.

Name _____

Share and Show

Tips

♦ UNLOCK the Problem

✓ Circle the question.
✓ Underline the important facts.
✓ Choose a strategy you know.

1. Mac bought 4 packs of toy cars. Then his friend gave him 9 cars. Now Mac has 21 cars. How many cars were in each pack?

Act out the problem by using counters or the picture and by writing equations.

First, subtract the cars Mac's friend gave him.

total cars		cars given to Mac		c, cars in 4 packs
↓		↓		↓
21	−	_____	=	c
		_____	=	c

Then, divide to find the number of cars in each pack.

c, cars in 4 packs		number of packs		p, number in each pack
↓		↓		↓
12	÷	_____	=	p
		_____	=	p

So, there were _____ cars in each pack.

2. **H.O.T. What if** Mac bought 8 packs of cars and then he gave his friend 3 cars? If Mac has 13 cars now, how many cars were in each pack?

_____

✓ 3. Ryan gave 7 of his model cars to a friend. Then he bought 6 more cars. Now Ryan has 13 cars. How many cars did Ryan start with?

_____

✓ 4. Chloe bought 5 sets of books. She donated 9 of her books to her school. Now she has 26 books. How many books were in each set?

_____

SHOW YOUR WORK

On Your Own. . . . .

Choose a
STRATEGY

Act It Out
Draw a Diagram
Find a Pattern
Make a Table

5. Raul bought 2 packs of erasers. He found 2 erasers in his backpack. Now Raul has 8 erasers. How many erasers were in each pack?

_____

6. Blair cuts a ribbon into 2 equal pieces. Then she cuts 4 inches off one piece. That piece is now 5 inches long. What was the length of the original ribbon?

_____

SHOW YOUR WORK

7. ⚡H.O.T. ▸Write Math▸ Rose saw a movie, shopped, and ate at a restaurant. She did not see the movie first. She shopped right after she ate. In what order did Rose do these activities? **Explain** how you know.

_____

_____

_____

_____

_____

_____

8. ★ **PARCC Test Prep** Mr. Acosta bought 3 packs of markers. Each pack had the same number of markers. He gave 4 markers to his daughter. Now he has 14 markers. How many markers were in each pack?

Ⓐ 6

Ⓑ 11

Ⓒ 14

Ⓓ 26

Order of Operations

Essential Question Why are there rules such as the order of operations?

COMMON CORE
Georgia Performance Standard MCC3.OA.8
Solve problems involving the four operations, and identify and explain patterns in arithmetic.

Investigate

CONNECT You can use what you know about acting out a two-step problem to write one equation to describe and solve a two-step problem.

- If you solved a two-step problem in a different order, what do you think might happen?

_____

Use different orders to find $4 + 16 \div 2$.

A. Make a list of all the possible orders you can use to find the answer to $4 + 16 \div 2$.

_____

B. Use each order in your list to find the answer. Show the steps you used.

_____

_____

Draw Conclusions ....

1. Did following different orders change the answer? _____

2. If a problem has more than one type of operation, how does the order in which you perform the operations affect the answer?

_____

3. **H.O.T.** **Explain** the need for setting an order of operations that everyone follows.

_____

_____

Make Connections

When solving problems with more than one type of operation, you need to know which operation to do first. A special set of rules, called the **order of operations**, gives the order in which calculations are done in a problem.

First, multiply and divide from left to right.

Then, add and subtract from left to right.

Meghan buys 2 books for $4 each. She pays with a $10 bill. How much money does she have left?

You can write $10 - 2 × $4 = c to describe and solve the problem.

Use the order of operations to solve $10 - 2 × $4 = c.

STEP 1

Multiply from left to right. $10 - 2 × $4 = c
                                $10 - $8   = c

STEP 2

Subtract from left to right. $10 - $8 = c
                                         $2 = c

So, Meghan has _____ left.

- Does your answer make sense? **Explain.**

  _____

  _____

  _____

Math Talk What operation should you do first to find: $12 - 6 ÷ 2$ and $12 ÷ 6 - 2$? What is the answer to each problem?

Share and Show

Write *correct* if the operations are listed in the correct order. If not correct, write the correct order of operations.

1. $4 + 5 × 2$ multiply, add

   _____

☑ 2. $8 ÷ 4 × 2$ multiply, divide

   _____

3. $12 + 16 ÷ 4$ add, divide

   _____

4. $9 + 2 × 3$ add, multiply

   _____

5. $4 + 6 ÷ 3$ divide, add

   _____

6. $36 - 7 × 3$ multiply, subtract

   _____

**Follow the order of operations to find the unknown number.
Use your MathBoard.**

7. $63 \div 9 - 2 = f$

$f = $ _____

8. $7 - 5 + 8 = y$

$y = $ _____

9. $3 \times 6 - 2 = h$

$h = $ _____

10. $80 - 64 \div 8 = n$

$n = $ _____

11. $3 \times 4 + 6 = a$

$a = $ _____

12. $2 \times 7 \div 7 = c$

$c = $ _____

13. $20 \div 5 + 5 = g$

$g = $ _____

14. $42 \div 6 - 4 = b$

$b = $ _____

15. $20 + 12 - 5 = t$

$t = $ _____

H.O.T. Algebra Use the numbers listed to make the equation true.

16. 2, 6, and 5

_____ + _____ × _____ = 16

17. 4, 12, and 18

_____ − _____ ÷ _____ = 15

18. 8, 9, and 7

_____ × _____ − _____ = 47

19. 2, 4, and 9

_____ ÷ _____ + _____ = 11

20. **H.O.T. Pose a Problem** Write a word problem that can
be solved by using $2 \times 5 \div 5$. Solve your problem.

_____

_____

_____

_____

21. **Write Math** Is $4 + 8 \times 3$ equal to $4 + 3 \times 8$? **Explain**
how you know without finding the answers.

_____

_____

_____

Picture Book Art

The Eric Carle Museum of Picture Book Art in Amherst, Massachusetts, is the first museum in the United States that is devoted to picture book art. Picture books introduce literature to young readers.

The museum has 3 galleries, a reading library, a café, an art studio, an auditorium, and a museum shop. The exhibits change every 3 to 6 months, depending on the length of time the picture art is on loan and how fragile it is.

The table shows prices for some souvenirs in the bookstore in the museum.

Souvenir Prices	
Souvenir	**Price**
Firefly Picture Frame	$25
Exhibition Posters	$10
Caterpillar Note Cards	$8
Caterpillar Pens	$4
Sun Note Pads	$3

22. Kallon bought 3 Caterpillar note cards and 1 Caterpillar pen. How much did he spend on souvenirs?

_____

23. Raya and 4 friends bought their teacher 1 Firefly picture frame. They shared the cost equally. Then Raya bought an Exhibition poster. How much money did Raya spend in all? **Explain.**

_____

_____

_____

24. In Jaylene's class, 7 people bought Caterpillar pens and 1 person bought a poster. What was the total amount spent?

_____

Name _____

▶ **Vocabulary**

Choose the best term from the box to complete the sentence.

Vocabulary
order of operations
pattern
repeated addition

1. The _____ gives the order in which calculations are done in a problem. (p. 288)

2. A _____ is an ordered set of numbers or objects. (p. 258)

Describe a pattern for the table. Then complete the table. MCC3.OA.9

3.

Weeks	1	2	3	4	5
Days	7	14	21		

_____

4.

Tickets	2	3	4	5	6
Cost	$8	$12	$16		

_____

5.

Project Teams	Members
3	9
4	12
5	
6	18
7	

_____

6.

Tables	Chairs
1	8
2	16
3	
4	32
5	

_____

Follow the order of operations to find the unknown number. MCC3.OA.8

7. $42 \div 6 + 3 = g$

$g =$ _____

8. $6 - 3 \times 2 = b$

$b =$ _____

9. $5 \times 3 - 4 = k$

$k =$ _____

Fill in the bubble for the correct answer choice.

10. Emma bought 3 packs of pencils. She found 6 pencils in her desk. Now Emma has 24 pencils. How many pencils were in each pack? ◣ MCC3.OA.8

Ⓐ 6

Ⓑ 8

Ⓒ 10

Ⓓ 15

11. Which of the following describes a pattern in the table? ◣ MCC3.OA.9

Bags	1	2	3	4	5
Lemons	4	8	12	16	20

Ⓐ Add 3.   Ⓒ Multiply by 2.

Ⓑ Subtract 3.   Ⓓ Multiply by 4.

12. What is the unknown number? ◣ MCC3.OA.8

$$30 \div 5 = n$$

Ⓐ 3

Ⓑ 6

Ⓒ 10

Ⓓ 12

13. The camping club rents 4 rafts. How many people can 4 rafts hold? ◣ MCC3.OA.9

Rafts	1	2	3	4
People	8	16	24	■

Ⓐ 20

Ⓑ 26

Ⓒ 32

Ⓓ 40

Name _____

Understand Area

Essential Question How is finding the area of a shape different from finding the perimeter of a shape?

COMMON CORE Georgia Performance Standards
MCC3.MD.5, MCC3.MD.5a
Geometric measurement: understand concepts of area and relate area to multiplication and to addition.

🔑 UNLOCK the Problem   REAL WORLD

CONNECT You learned that perimeter is the measure around a shape. It is measured in linear units, or units that are used to measure the distance between two points.

Area is the measure of the number of unit squares needed to cover a flat surface. A **unit square** is a square with a side length of 1 unit. It has an area of 1 **square unit (sq un)**.

Unit Square

Perimeter

1 unit + 1 unit + 1 unit + 1 unit = 4 units

Area

1 square unit

Math Idea
You can count the number of units on each side of a shape to find its perimeter. You can count the number of unit squares inside a shape to find its area in square units.

🔑 Activity Materials ■ geoboard ■ rubber bands

Ⓐ Use your geoboard to form a shape made from 2 unit squares. Record the shape on this dot paper.

What is the area of this shape?

Area = _____ square units

Ⓑ Change the rubber band so that the shape is made from 3 unit squares. Record the shape on this dot paper.

What is the area of this shape?

Area = _____ square units

Math Talk   MATHEMATICAL PRACTICES
For B, did your shape look like your classmate's shape? **Explain.**

Try This! Draw three different shapes that are each made from 4 unit squares. Find the area of the shape.

Shape 1   Shape 2   Shape 3

Area = _____ square units   Area = _____ square units   Area = _____ square units

- How are the shapes the same? How are the shapes different?

_____

Share and Show

1. Shade each unit square in the shape shown. Count the unit squares to find the area.

   Area = _____ square units

Count to find the area of the shape.

2.

3.

✓4.

Area = _____ square units   Area = _____ square units   Area = _____ square units

Write *area* or *perimeter* for the situation.

5. buying a rug for a room

_____

✓6. putting a fence around a garden

_____

MATHEMATICAL PRACTICES

Math Talk What are other situations where you need to find area?

Name _____

On Your Own ....

Count to find the area of the shape.

7.

Area = _____ square units

8.

Area = _____ square units

9.

Area = _____ square units

10.

Area = _____ square units

11.

Area = _____ square units

12.

Area = _____ square units

13.

Area = _____ square units

14.

Area = _____ square units

15.

Area = _____ square units

Write *area* or *perimeter* for the situation.

16. painting a wall

_____

17. covering a patio with tiles

_____

18. putting a wallpaper border
around a room

_____

19. gluing a ribbon around a
picture frame

_____

Problem Solving REAL WORLD

Billy is building an enclosure for his small dog, Eli. Use the diagram for 20–22.

Eli's Enclosure

20. Billy will put fencing around the outside of the enclosure. How much fencing does he need for the enclosure?

_____

21. Billy will use sod to cover the ground in the enclosure. How much sod does Billy need?

_____

22. **Write Math** ➤ **Explain** how the perimeter and the area of the enclosure are different.

_____

_____

23. **H.O.T.** Draw two different shapes, each with an area of 10 square units.

24. **★PARCC Test Prep** What is the area of the shape at the right?

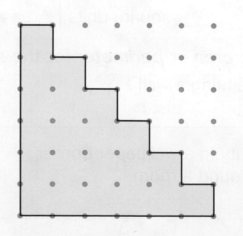

Ⓐ 6 square units

Ⓑ 21 square units

Ⓒ 24 square units

Ⓓ 36 square units

Measure Area

Essential Question How can you find the area of a plane shape?

COMMON CORE Georgia Performance Standards
MCC3.MD.5b, MCC3.MD.6
Geometric measurement: understand concepts of area and
relate area to multiplication and to addition.

🔑 UNLOCK the Problem

Jaime is measuring the area of the rectangles with
1-inch square tiles.

Activity 1 Materials ■ 1-inch grid paper ■ scissors

Cut out eight 1-inch squares. Use the dashed lines as
guides to place tiles for A–C.

A Place 4 tiles on Rectangle A.

• Are there any gaps? _____

• Are there any overlaps? _____

• Jaime says that the area is 4 square
inches. Is Jaime's measurement correct? _____

So, when you measure area, there can be
no space between the tiles, or no gaps.

B Place 8 tiles on Rectangle B.

• Are there any gaps? _____

• Are there any overlaps? _____

• Jaime says that the area is 8 square
inches. Is Jaime's measurement correct? _____

So, when you measure the area, the tiles
cannot overlap.

C Place 6 tiles on Rectangle C.

• Are there any gaps? _____

• Are there any overlaps? _____

• Jaime says that the area is 6 square
inches. Is Jaime's measurement correct? _____

So, the area of the rectangles is

_____ square inches.

1 square inch

Rectangle A

Rectangle B

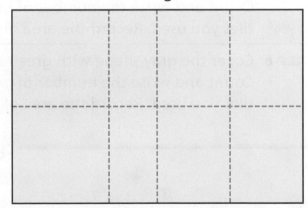

Rectangle C

🔓 Activity 2 Materials ■ green and blue paper ■ scissors

STEP 1 Estimate the number of blue square tiles it will take to cover the gray shape.

_____ blue square tiles

STEP 2 Estimate the number of green tiles it will take to cover the gray shape.

_____ green square tiles

STEP 3 Trace the blue square pattern ten times and cut out the squares.

STEP 4 Trace the green square pattern thirty-six times and cut out the squares.

STEP 5 Cover the gray shape with blue square tiles. Count and write the number of blue square tiles you used. Record the area of the shape.

_____ blue square tiles

Area = _____ blue square units

STEP 6 Cover the gray shape with green square tiles. Count and write the number of green square tiles you used. Record the area of the shape.

_____ green square tiles

Area = _____ green square units

MATHEMATICAL PRACTICES

Math Talk Explain why the number of green square tiles needed to cover the shape is different than the number of blue square tiles needed.

Try This! Count to find the area of the shape.

☐ is 1 square centimeter.

There are _____ unit squares in the shape.

1					
2					

So, the area is _____ square centimeters.

Name _____

Share and Show

1. Count to find the area of the shape. Each unit square is 1 square centimeter.

   Think: Are there any gaps? Are there any overlaps?

   There are _____ unit squares in the shape.

   So, the area is _____ square centimeters.

Math Talk MATHEMATICAL PRACTICES
Explain how you can use square centimeters to find the area of the shapes in Exercises 2 and 3.

**Count to find the area of the shape.
Each unit square is 1 square centimeter.**

2.

   Area = _____ square centimeters

3.

   Area = _____ square centimeters

On Your Own

**Count to find the area of the shape.
Each unit square is 1 square inch.**

4.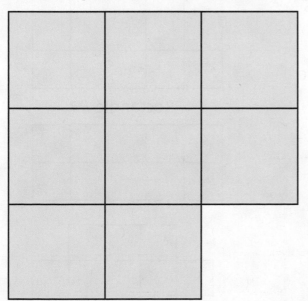

   Area = _____ square inches

5.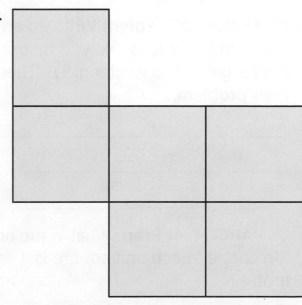

   Area = _____ square inches

Problem Solving REAL WORLD

6. Danny is placing tiles on the floor of an office lobby. Each tile is 1 square meter. The diagram shows the lobby. What is the area of the lobby?

_____

7. Angie is painting a space shuttle mural on a wall. She divides the area into sections that are each one square foot. The diagram shows the mural. What is the area of the mural?

_____

8. **Write Math** ▷ **Sense or Nonsense?** Tom places green square tiles on the shape shown. He says that the shape has an area of 12 square units. Does this make sense? **Explain.**

_____

_____

Rectangle A

9. **H.O.T.** **Pose a Problem** Write an area problem that can be solved by using Rectangle A and Rectangle B. Then solve your problem.

_____

_____

Rectangle B

_____

10. ⭐ **PARCC Test Prep** What is the area of the shape? Each unit square is 1 square foot.

   (A) 3 square feet   (C) 13 square feet

   (B) 10 square feet   (D) 15 square feet

Name _____

Problem Solving • Area of Rectangles

Essential Question How can you use the strategy *find a pattern* to solve area problems?

COMMON CORE
Georgia Performance Standard MCC3.MD.7b
Geometric measurement: understand concepts of area and relate area to multiplication and to addition.

🔑 UNLOCK the Problem REAL WORLD

Mr. Koi wants to build storage buildings, so he drew plans for the buildings. He wants to know how the areas of the buildings are related. How will the areas of Buildings A and B change? How will the areas of Buildings C and D change?

Use the graphic organizer to help you solve the problem.

Read the Problem

What do I need to find?	**What information do I need to use?**	**How will I use the information?**
I need to find how the areas will change from A to B and from _____ to _____.	I need to use the _____ and _____ of each building to find its area.	I will record the areas in a table. Then I will look for a pattern to see how the _____ will change.

Solve the Problem

I will complete the table to find patterns to solve the problem.

	Length	Width	Area		Length	Width	Area
Building A	3 ft			Building C		4 ft	
Building B	3 ft			Building D		8 ft	

I see that the lengths will be the same and the widths will be doubled.

The areas will change from _____ to _____ and from _____ to _____.

So, when the lengths are the same and the widths are doubled,

the areas will be _____.

🔑 Try Another Problem

Mr. Koi is building more storage buildings. He wants to know how the areas of the buildings are related. How will the areas of Buildings E and F change? How will the areas of Buildings G and H change?

Use the graphic organizer to help you solve the problem.

Read the Problem

What do I need to find?	What information do I need to use?	How will I use the information?

Solve the Problem

I will complete the table to find patterns to solve the problem.

	Length	Width	Area		Length	Width	Area
Building E				Building G			
Building F				Building H			

• How did your table help you find a pattern?

_____

_____

© Houghton Mifflin Harcourt Publishing Company

MATHEMATICAL PRACTICES

Math Talk What if the length of both sides is doubled? How would the areas change?

Name _____

Share and Show

Use the table for 1–2.

1. Many pools come in rectangular shapes. How do the areas of the swimming pools change when the widths change?

   First, complete the table by finding the area of each pool.

   Think: I can find the area by multiplying the length and the width.

   Then, find a pattern of how the lengths change and how the widths change.

   The _____ stays the same.

   The widths _____.

   Last, describe a pattern of how the area changes.

   The areas _____ by ____ square feet.

Swimming Pool Sizes			
Pool	Length (in feet)	Width (in feet)	Area (in square feet)
A	8	20	
B	8	30	
C	8	40	
D	8	50	

2. 🗹 **H.O.T.** **What if** the length of each pool was 16 feet? **Explain** how the areas would change.

   _____

   _____

3. 🗹 Elizabeth built a sandbox that is 4 feet long and 4 feet wide. She also built a flower garden that is 4 feet long and 6 feet wide. She built a vegetable garden that is 4 feet long and 8 feet wide. How do the areas change?

   _____

   _____

   _____

SHOW YOUR WORK

On Your Own . . . .

Choose a
STRATEGY

Act It Out

Draw a Diagram

Find a Pattern

Make a Table

4. Danielle is baking cookies. She makes 30 cookies and sets them in 6 equal rows on the baking tray. How many cookies are in each row? Draw a bar model to find your answer.

5. ⚡H.O.T.⚡ A diagram of Paula's bedroom is at the right. Her bedroom is in the shape of a rectangle. Write the measures for the other sides. What is the perimeter of the room? (Hint: The two pairs of opposite sides are equal lengths.)

17 ft

12 ft

6. ⚡H.O.T.⚡ Jacob has a rectangular garden with an area of 56 square feet. The length of the garden is 8 feet. What is the width of the garden?

7. ⭐ **PARCC Test Prep** Heather owns a carpet cleaning company. Her prices are based on the area of the carpet. What is the price of cleaning a room with an area of 200 square feet?

Total Area (in square feet)	50	100	150	200
Price (in dollars)	15	30	45	■

Ⓐ $30

Ⓒ $60

Ⓑ $45

Ⓓ $245

Name _____

Area of Combined Rectangles

Essential Question How can you break apart a shape to find the area?

COMMON CORE Georgia Performance Standards
MCC3.MD.7c, MCC3.MD.7d
Geometric measurement: understand concepts of area and relate area to multiplication and to addition.

🔑 UNLOCK the Problem REAL WORLD

Anna's rug has side lengths of 4 feet and 9 feet. What is the area of Anna's rug?

Remember

You can use the Distributive Property to break apart an array.

$3 \times 3 = 3 \times (2 + 1)$

🔒 Activity Materials ■ square tiles

STEP 1 Use square tiles to model 4×9.

STEP 2 Draw a rectangle on the grid paper to show your model.

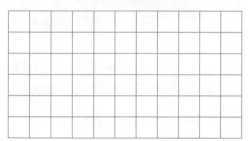

STEP 3 Draw a vertical line to break apart the model to make two smaller rectangles.

The side length 9 is broken into _____ plus _____.

STEP 4 Find the area of each of the two smaller rectangles.

Rectangle 1: _____ × _____ = _____

Rectangle 2: _____ × _____ = _____

STEP 5 Add the products to find the total area.

_____ + _____ = _____ square feet

STEP 6 Check your answer by counting the number of square feet.

_____ square feet

So, the area of Anna's rug is _____ square feet.

Math Talk MATHEMATICAL PRACTICES
Did you draw a line in the same place as your classmates? **Explain** why you found the same total area.

CONNECT Using the Distributive Property, you found that you could break apart a rectangle into smaller rectangles, and add the area of each smaller rectangle to find the total area.

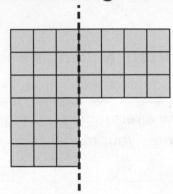

How can you break apart this shape into rectangles to find its area?

🔑 One Way Use a horizontal line. | **🔑 Another Way** Use a vertical line.

STEP 1 Write a multiplication equation for each rectangle.

Rectangle 1: ____ × ____ = ____

Rectangle 2: ____ × ____ = ____

STEP 2 Add the products to find the total area.

____ + ____ = ____ square units

So, the area is _____ square units.

STEP 1 Write a multiplication equation for each rectangle.

Rectangle 1: ____ × ____ = ____

Rectangle 2: ____ × ____ = ____

STEP 2 Add the products to find the total area.

____ + ____ = ____ square units

MATHEMATICAL PRACTICES

Math Talk **Explain** how you can check your answer.

Share and Show

1. Draw a line to break apart the shape into rectangles. Find the total area of the shape.

   Think: I can draw vertical or horizontal lines to break apart the shape to make rectangles.

   Rectangle 1: ____ × ____ = ____

   Rectangle 2: ____ × ____ = ____

   ____ + ____ = ____ square units

310

© Houghton Mifflin Harcourt Publishing Company

Name _____

Use the Distributive Property to find the area. Show your multiplication and addition equations.

 2.

_____

_____ square units

 3.

_____

_____ square units

On Your Own ....

Use the Distributive Property to find the area. Show your multiplication and addition equations.

4.

_____

_____ square units

5.

_____

_____ square units

Draw a line to break apart the shape into rectangles. Find the area of the shape.

6.

Rectangle 1: ___ ✕ ___ = ___

Rectangle 2: ___ ✕ ___ = ___

___ + ___ = ___ square units

7. H.O.T.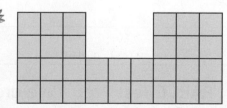

Rectangle 1: ___ ✕ ___ = ___

Rectangle 2: ___ ✕ ___ = ___

Rectangle 3: ___ ✕ ___ = ___

___ + ___ + ___ = ___ square units

© Houghton Mifflin Harcourt Publishing Company

Problem Solving REAL WORLD

8. Ms. Lee's classroom is shown at the right. Each unit square is 1 square foot. Draw a line to break apart the shape into rectangles. What is the total area of Ms. Lee's classroom?

_____

9. Jared has a rectangular bedroom with a rectangular closet. Each unit square is 1 square foot. Draw a line to break apart the shape into rectangles. What is the total area of Jared's bedroom?

_____

10. **Write Math** ➤ **Explain** how to break apart the shape to find the area of the shape.

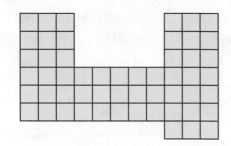

1 unit square = 1 square meter

_____

_____

_____

_____

_____

11. **H.O.T.** Use the Distributive Property to find the area of the shape at the right. Write your multiplication and addition equations.

1 unit square = 1 square centimeter

_____

_____

12. ⭐ **PARCC Test Prep** Pete drew a diagram of his backyard on grid paper. Each unit square is 1 square meter. The area surrounding the patio is grass. How many square meters of grass are in his backyard?

Ⓐ 4 square meters   Ⓒ 26 square meters

Ⓑ 18 square meters   Ⓓ 30 square meters

Module 15 Assessment

▶ **Vocabulary**

Choose the best term from the box to complete the sentence.

Vocabulary
area
square unit
unit squares
perimeter

1. The measure of the number of unit squares needed to cover a shape with no gaps or overlaps is the _____. **(p. 293)**

2. A square with sides of 1 unit is a _____. **(p. 293)**

3. You can count _____ to find the area of a shape. **(p. 293)**

▶ **Concepts and Skills**

Find the area of the shape.

Each unit square is 1 square yard. MCC3.MD.7, MCC3.MD.7a

4.

_____

5.

_____

Draw a line to break apart the shape into rectangles.
Find the area of the shape. MCC3.MD.7c, MCC3.MD.7d

6.

Rectangle 1: ____ × ____ = ____

Rectangle 2: ____ × ____ = ____

____ + ____ = ____ square units

7.

Rectangle 1: ____ × ____ = ____

Rectangle 2: ____ × ____ = ____

____ + ____ = ____ square units

8. Peter drew this rectangle. Which multiplication equation can be used to find the area? ◗MCC3.MD.7a

Ⓐ 4 × 4 = 16   Ⓒ 4 + 7 + 4 + 7 = 22

Ⓑ 7 + 7 + 7 + 7 = 28   Ⓓ 4 × 7 = 28

9. What is the area of the shape shown? Each square is 1 square foot. ◗MCC3.MD.5b, MCC3.MD.6

Ⓐ 20 square feet   Ⓒ 27 square feet

Ⓑ 23 square feet   Ⓓ 28 square feet

10. Which statement is true about the two rectangles?

◗MCC3.MD.7b

Ⓐ The area of Rectangle *B* is double the area of Rectangle *A*.

Ⓑ The area of Rectangle *A* is double the area of Rectangle *B*.

Ⓒ The area of Rectangle *B* is half of the area of Rectangle *A*.

Ⓓ The area of Rectangle *A* is the same as the area of Rectangle *B*.

Rectangle *A*   Rectangle *B*

Name _____

Unit 4 Assessment

▶ **Vocabulary**

Choose the best term from the box to complete the sentence.

Vocabulary
area
Commutative Property of Addition
Identity Property of Addition
order of operations

1. The measure of the number of unit squares needed to cover a shape with no gaps or overlaps is the _____. (p. 293)

2. The _____ gives the order in which calculations are done in a problem. (p. 288)

3. The _____ states that you can add two or more numbers in any order and get the same sum. (p. 258)

▶ **Concepts and Skills**

Is the sum even or odd? Write *even* or *odd*. ◣MCC3.OA.9

4. 6 + 4 _____   5. 3 + 8 _____   6. 9 + 7 _____

Describe a pattern in the table. Then complete the table. ◣MCC3.OA.9

7.

Tens	1	2	3	4	5
Ones	10	20	30		

8.

Jars	2	3	4	5	6
Pickles	16	24		40	

_____   _____

Find the area of the shape. Each unit square is 1 square meter.

◣MCC3.MD.5, MCC3.MD.5a, MCC3.MD.5b, MCC3.MD.6, MCC3.MD.7, MCC3.MD.7a

9.

_____ square meters

10.

_____ square meters

GO Online Assessment Options Unit Test

Fill in the bubble for the correct answer choice.

11. Which describes the number sentence? ◣MCC3.OA.9

$$7 + 6 = 6 + 7$$

- Ⓐ Commutative Property of Addition
- Ⓑ Identity Property of Addition
- Ⓒ even + even = even
- Ⓓ odd + odd = odd

12. Sasha has 64 books in her collection. That is 38 more books than Caroline has. How many books do they have together? ◣MCC3.OA.8

- Ⓐ 26
- Ⓑ 90
- Ⓒ 92
- Ⓓ 102

13. Which of the following describes this pattern?
◣MCC3.OA.9

$$1, 2, 4, 8, 16$$

- Ⓐ Add 1.
- Ⓑ Add 2.
- Ⓒ Multiply by 2.
- Ⓓ Multiply by 4.

14. Lisa has quarters, nickels, and dimes. How many ways can she make $0.50? ◣MCC3.OA.8

- Ⓐ 6
- Ⓑ 8
- Ⓒ 9
- Ⓓ 10

Fill in the bubble for the correct answer choice.

15. What is the area of the shape? MCC3.MD.5, MCC3.MD.5a

Ⓐ 8 square units

Ⓑ 8 units

Ⓒ 12 square units

Ⓓ 12 units

16. Alfredo used the Distributive Property to find the area of this rectangle. Which set of multiplication and addition equations could he have used?

MCC3.MD.7c, MCC3.MD.7d

Ⓐ 4 + 5 = 9; 4 + 5 = 9; 9 + 9 = 18

Ⓑ 4 + 5 = 9; 4 + 5 = 9; 9 × 9 = 81

Ⓒ 4 × 5 = 20; 4 × 5 = 20; 20 + 20 = 40

Ⓓ 4 × 10 = 40; 4 × 10 = 40; 40 + 40 = 80

17. Margo will sweep a room. A diagram of the floor that she needs to sweep is shown at the right. What is the area of the floor? MCC3.MD.5b, MCC3.MD.6

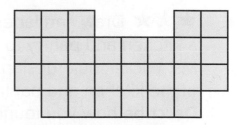

Ⓐ 8 square units Ⓒ 27 square units

Ⓑ 21 square units Ⓓ 32 square units

► Performance Assessment Task

MCC3.MD.5b, MCC3.MD.6, MCC3.MD.7, MCC3.MD.7a, MCC3.MD.7b, MCC3.MD.7c, MCC3.MD.7d

18. Ms. Wicks is designing a house. The kitchen will have an area between 70 square feet and 85 square feet. The pantry next to the kitchen will have an area between 8 square feet and 15 square feet.

★ Will a kitchen that is 10 feet long and 8 feet wide have the correct area? **Explain** how you know.

_____

_____

_____

★★ Make a list of 3 possible measurements for kitchens and for pantries that Ms. Wicks could include in her design. **Explain** how you decided which measurements to list.

_____

_____

_____

★★★ Draw and label a design for a kitchen and pantry to show what Ms. Wicks could design. Find the area of the kitchen and pantry combined. **Describe** how you found your answer.

_____

_____

_____

_____

Show What You Know

Check your understanding of important skills.

Name _____

▶ **Plane Shapes**

1. Color the triangles blue.

2. Color the rectangles red.

▶ **Number of Sides** Write the number of sides.

3. _____ sides

4. _____ sides

5. Circle the shapes that have 4 or more sides.

MATH DETECTIVE
WITH
CARMEN SANDIEGO™

Whitney found this drawing that shows 9 small squares.
Be a Math Detective to find larger squares in the drawing.
How many squares are there in all? Explain.

GO
Online Assessment Options: Soar to Success Math

▶ **Visualize It** ••

Complete the tree map by using the words with a ✓.

polygon

▶ **Understand Vocabulary** •••••••••••••••••••••••••

Draw a line to match the word with its definition.

1. closed shape •

• A part of a line that includes two endpoints and all the points between them

2. line segment •

• A shape formed by two rays that share an endpoint

3. right angle •

• A shape that starts and ends at the same point

4. hexagon •

• An angle that forms a square corner

5. angle •

• A closed plane shape made up of line segments

6. polygon •

• A polygon with 6 sides and 6 angles

Preview Words
angle
closed shape
hexagon
intersecting lines
line
line segment
open shape
parallel lines
perpendicular lines
point
polygon
✓ quadrilateral
ray
✓ rectangle
✓ rhombus
right angle
✓ square
✓ trapezoid
✓ triangle
Venn diagram
vertex

Name _____

Identify Polygons

Essential Question How can you use line segments and angles to make polygons?

COMMON CORE
Georgia Performance Standard MCC3.G.1
Reason with shapes and their attributes.

CONNECT In earlier lessons, you learned about line segments and angles. In this lesson, you will see how line segments and angles make polygons.

A **polygon** is a closed plane shape that is made up of line segments that meet only at their endpoints. Each line segment in a polygon is a **side**.

Math Idea
All polygons are closed shapes. Not all closed shapes are polygons.

🔑 UNLOCK the Problem REAL WORLD

Circle all the words that describe the shape.

A

B

C

D

A	B	C	D
plane shape	plane shape	plane shape	plane shape
open shape	open shape	open shape	open shape
closed shape	closed shape	closed shape	closed shape
curved paths	curved paths	curved paths	curved paths
line segments	line segments	line segments	line segments
polygon	polygon	polygon	polygon

Try This!

Fill in the blanks with *sometimes*, *always*, or *never*.

Polygons are _____ plane shapes.

Polygons are _____ closed shapes.

Polygons are _____ open shapes.

Plane shapes are _____ polygons.

Math Talk MATHEMATICAL PRACTICES
Explain why not all closed shapes are polygons.

Name Polygons Polygons are named by the number of sides and angles they have.

Some traffic signs are in the shape of polygons. A stop sign is in the shape of which polygon?

angle

side → **STOP**

🔑 **Count the number of sides and angles.**

triangle	**quadrilateral**	**pentagon**
3 sides	4 sides	_____ sides
3 angles	_____ angles	5 angles

hexagon	**octagon**	**decagon**
_____ sides	8 sides	_____ sides
6 angles	_____ angles	10 angles

How many sides does the stop sign have? _____

How many angles? _____

So, a stop sign is in the shape of an _____.

Math Talk

MATHEMATICAL PRACTICES

Compare the number of sides and angles. What is a true statement about all polygons?

Share and Show   ●

1. The shape at the right is a polygon. Circle all the words that describe the shape.

   plane shape   open shape   closed shape   pentagon

   curved paths   line segments   hexagon   quadrilateral

Name _____

Is the shape a polygon? Write *yes* or *no*.

2.

_____

3.

_____

☑ 4.

_____

Math Talk MATHEMATICAL PRACTICES
Explain how you can change the shape in Exercise 4 to make it a polygon.

Write the number of sides and the number of angles. Then name the polygon.

5.
YIELD

_____ sides

_____ angles

_____

6.

_____ sides

_____ angles

_____

☑ 7.

_____ sides

_____ angles

_____

On Your Own ....

Is the shape a polygon? Write *yes* or *no*.

8.

_____

9.

_____

10.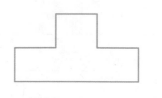

_____

Write the number of sides and the number of angles. Then name the polygon.

11.

_____ sides

_____ angles

_____

12.

_____ sides

_____ angles

_____

13.

_____ sides

_____ angles

_____

Problem Solving...

14. **Write Math** ► **Sense or Nonsense?** Jake said Shapes *A—E* are all polygons. Does this statement make sense? **Explain** your answer.

_____

_____

_____

15. **What if** Kim wants to draw a polygon? How can she check her drawing?

_____

_____

16. I am a closed shape made of 6 line segments. I have 2 angles less than a right angle and no right angles. What shape am I? Draw an example in the workspace.

_____

17. **H.O.T.** Is every closed shape a polygon? Use a drawing to help **explain** your answer.

_____

_____

_____

18. **What's the Error?** Eric says that the shape at the right is an octagon. Do you agree or disagree?

Explain. _____

_____

19. ★ **PARCC Test Prep** Alicia drew the polygon at the right. What is the name of the polygon she drew?

Ⓐ octagon   Ⓒ pentagon

Ⓑ hexagon   Ⓓ quadrilateral

Module 16 Assessment

▶ Vocabulary

Choose the best term from the box to complete the sentence.

1. An _____ is formed by two rays that share an endpoint. (p. 325)

2. A _____ is a closed shape made up of line segments. (p. 329)

3. A _____ forms a square corner. (p. 325)

▶ Concepts and Skills

Use the corner of a sheet of paper to tell whether the angle is a right angle, less than a right angle, or greater than a right angle.
MCC3.G.1

4.

_____

5.

_____

6.

_____

Write the number of sides and the number of angles. Then name the polygon. MCC3.G.1

7.

_____ sides

_____ angles

_____

8.

_____ sides

_____ angles

_____

9.

_____ sides

_____ angles

_____

Fill in the bubble for the correct answer choice.

10. Anne drew a closed shape. Which of these could be the shape Anne drew? MCC3.G.1

 Ⓐ Ⓒ

 Ⓑ Ⓓ

11. This sign tells drivers there is a steep hill ahead. Look at the shape of the sign. How many sides and angles are there? MCC3.G.1

Ⓐ 4 sides and 4 angles

Ⓑ 5 sides and 5 angles

Ⓒ 6 sides and 6 angles

Ⓓ 7 sides and 7 angles

12. Which shape is NOT a polygon? MCC3.G.1

Ⓐ Ⓒ

Ⓑ Ⓓ

13. Sean drew a shape with 2 fewer sides than an octagon. Which shape did he draw? MCC3.G.1

Ⓐ triangle   Ⓒ hexagon

Ⓑ pentagon   Ⓓ quadrilateral

14. John drew a polygon with two line segments that meet to form a right angle. Which words describe the line segments? MCC3.G.1

Ⓐ parallel and perpendicular

Ⓑ parallel and intersecting

Ⓒ intersecting and perpendicular

Ⓓ intersecting and curved

Classify Quadrilaterals

Essential Question How can you use sides and angles to help you describe quadrilaterals?

COMMON CORE
Georgia Performance Standard MCC3.G.1
Reason with shapes and their attributes.

 UNLOCK the Problem

Quadrilaterals are named by their sides and their angles.

 Describe quadrilaterals.

quadrilateral

_____ sides

_____ angles

 ERROR Alert

Some quadrilaterals cannot be classified as a trapezoid, rectangle, square, or rhombus.

---

trapezoid

exactly _____ pair of opposite sides that are parallel

lengths of sides could be the same

---

rectangle

_____ pairs of opposite sides that are parallel

_____ pairs of sides that are of equal length

_____ right angles

square

_____ pairs of opposite sides that are parallel

_____ sides that are of equal length

_____ right angles

rhombus

_____ pairs of opposite sides that are parallel

_____ sides that are of equal length

Math Talk Explain why a square can also be named a rectangle or a rhombus.

MATHEMATICAL PRACTICES

Share and Show

Look at the quadrilateral at the right.

1. Outline each pair of opposite sides that are parallel with a different color. How many pairs of opposite

   sides appear to be parallel? _____

2. Look at the parallel sides you colored.

   The sides in each pair are of _____ length.

Think: All the angles are right angles.

✓3. Name the quadrilateral. _____

Circle all the words that describe the quadrilateral.

4.

   rectangle

   rhombus

   square

   trapezoid

5.

   rhombus

   quadrilateral

   square

   rectangle

✓6.

   rectangle

   rhombus

   trapezoid

   quadrilateral

MATHEMATICAL PRACTICES

Math Talk **Explain** how you can have a rhombus that is not a square.

On Your Own

Circle all the words that describe the quadrilateral.

7.

   rectangle

   trapezoid

   quadrilateral

   rhombus

8.

   rectangle

   rhombus

   trapezoid

   square

9.

   quadrilateral

   square

   rectangle

   rhombus

Name _____

Problem Solving. . . . .

Use the quadrilaterals at the right for 10–12.

10. Which quadrilaterals appear to have
    4 right angles?

    _____

11. Which quadrilaterals appear to have
    2 pairs of opposite sides that are parallel?

    _____

12. Which quadrilaterals appear to have no
    right angles?

    _____

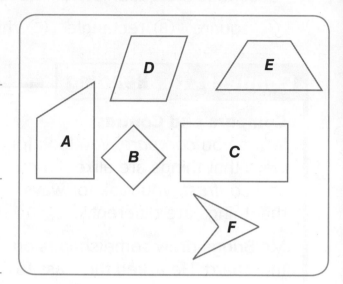

Write *all* or *some* to complete the sentence for 13–18.

13. The opposite sides of _____
    rectangles are parallel.

14. _____ sides of a rhombus are the
    same length.

15. _____ squares are rectangles.

16. _____ rhombuses are squares.

17. _____ quadrilaterals are polygons.

18. _____ polygons are quadrilaterals.

19. **Write Math** ► Circle the shape at the
    right that is not a quadrilateral. **Explain**
    your choice.

    _____

    _____

    _____

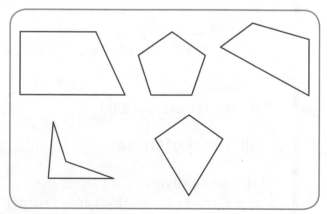

20. **H.O.T.** I am a polygon that has 4 sides and 4 angles. At
    least one of my angles is less than a right angle. Circle all
    the shapes that I could be.

    quadrilateral   rectangle   square   rhombus   trapezoid

21. ⭐ **PARCC Test Prep** Rita glued craft sticks together to make this shape. Which best describes the quadrilateral Rita made?

Ⓐ square Ⓑ rectangle Ⓒ rhombus Ⓓ trapezoid

Connect to Reading

Compare and Contrast

When you *compare,* you look for ways that things are alike. When you *contrast,* you look for ways that things are different.

Mr. Briggs drew some shapes on the board. He asked the class to tell how the shapes are alike and how they are different.

Complete the sentences.

- Shapes _____, _____, _____, _____, _____, _____, and _____ are polygons.

- Shapes _____, _____, and _____ are not polygons.

- Shapes _____, _____, _____, and _____ are quadrilaterals.

- Shapes _____, _____, and _____ appear to have only 1 pair of opposite sides that are parallel.

- Shapes _____, _____, and _____ appear to have 2 pairs of opposite sides that are parallel.

- All 4 sides of shapes _____ and _____ appear to be the same length.

- In these polygons, all sides do not appear to be the same length. _____

- These shapes can be called rhombuses. _____

- Shapes _____ and _____ are quadrilaterals, but cannot be called rhombuses.

- Shape _____ is a rhombus and can be called a square.

Name _____

Draw Quadrilaterals

Essential Question How can you draw quadrilaterals?

COMMON CORE
Georgia Performance Standard MCC3.G.1
Reason with shapes and their attributes.

🔑 UNLOCK the Problem REAL WORLD

CONNECT You have learned to classify quadrilaterals by the number of pairs of opposite sides that are parallel, by the number of pairs of sides of equal length, and by the number of right angles.

How can you draw quadrilaterals?

🔓 Activity 1 Use grid paper to draw quadrilaterals.

Materials ■ ruler

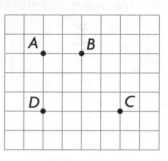

• Use a ruler to draw line segments from points A to B, from B to C, from C to D, and from D to A.

• Write the name of your quadrilateral.

_____

🔓 Activity 2 Draw a shape that does not belong.

Materials ■ ruler

🅐 Here are three examples of a quadrilateral. Draw an example of a polygon that is not a quadrilateral.

• **Explain** why your polygon is not a quadrilateral.

_____

_____

B Here are three examples of a square.
Draw a quadrilateral that is not a square.

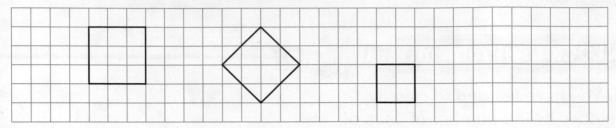

- **Explain** why your quadrilateral is not a square.

_____

_____

C Here are three examples of a rectangle.
Draw a quadrilateral that is not a rectangle.

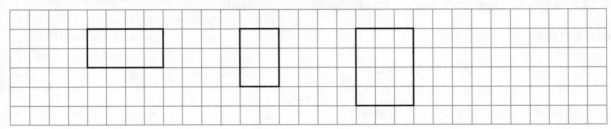

- **Explain** why your quadrilateral is not a rectangle.

_____

_____

D Here are three examples of a rhombus.
Draw a quadrilateral that is not a rhombus.

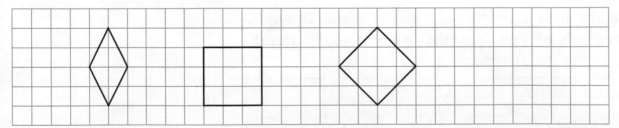

- **Explain** why your quadrilateral is not a rhombus.

_____

_____

© Houghton Mifflin Harcourt Publishing Company

MATHEMATICAL PRACTICES

Math Talk Compare your drawings with your classmates. **Explain** how your drawings are alike and how they are different.

Name _____

Share and Show

1. Choose four endpoints that connect to make a rectangle.

   Think: A rectangle has 2 pairs of opposite sides that are parallel, 2 pairs of sides of equal length, and 4 right angles.

Draw a quadrilateral that is described.
Name the quadrilateral you drew.

✓ 2. 2 pairs of equal sides

Name _____

✓ 3. 4 sides of equal length

Name _____

Math Talk

MATHEMATICAL PRACTICES

Explain one way the quadrilaterals you drew are alike and one way they are different.

On Your Own

Practice: Copy and Solve Use grid paper to draw a quadrilateral that is described. Name the quadrilateral you drew.

4. exactly 1 pair of opposite sides that are parallel

5. 4 right angles

6. 2 pairs of sides of equal length

Draw a quadrilateral that does not belong. Then explain why.

7.

8.

Problem Solving REAL WORLD

9. **Write Math** → **What's the Error?** Jacki drew the shape at the right. She said it is a rectangle because it has 2 pairs of opposite sides that are parallel. **Describe** her error.

_____

_____

10. Adam drew three quadrilaterals. One quadrilateral had no pairs of parallel sides, one quadrilateral had 1 pair of opposite sides that are parallel, and the last quadrilateral had 2 pairs of opposite sides that are parallel. Draw the three quadrilaterals that Adam could have drawn. Name the quadrilaterals.

_____   _____   _____

11. **H.O.T.** Amy has 4 straws of equal length. Name the quadrilaterals

that can be made using these 4 straws. _____
Amy cuts one of the straws in half. She uses the two halves and two of the other straws to make a quadrilateral. Name a

quadrilateral that can be made using these 4 straws. _____

12. ⭐ **PARCC Test Prep** Jordan drew a quadrilateral with 2 pairs of opposite sides that are parallel. Which shape could NOT be the quadrilateral Jordan drew?

Ⓐ   Ⓑ   Ⓒ   Ⓓ

Name _____

Describe Triangles

Essential Question How can you use sides and angles to help you describe triangles?

COMMON CORE
Georgia Performance Standard MCC3.G.1
Reason with shapes and their attributes.

🔑 UNLOCK the Problem

How can you use straws of different lengths to make triangles?

🔓 Activity Materials ■ straws ■ scissors ■ MathBoard

STEP 1 Cut straws into different lengths.

STEP 2 Find straw pieces that you can put together to make a triangle. Draw your triangle on the MathBoard.

STEP 3 Find straw pieces that you cannot put together to make a triangle.

1. Compare the lengths of the sides. **Describe** when you can make a triangle.

_____

_____

MATHEMATICAL PRACTICES

Math Talk What if you had three straws of equal length? Can you make a triangle? **Explain.**

2. **Describe** when you cannot make a triangle.

_____

_____

_____

3. **Explain** how you can change the straw pieces in

Step 3 to make a triangle. _____

_____

Ways to Describe Triangles

What are two ways triangles can be described?

🔒 One Way

Triangles can be described by the number of sides that are of equal length.

Draw a line to match the description of the triangle(s).

•   •   •

•   •   •

No sides are equal in length.

Two sides are equal in length.

Three sides are equal in length.

🔒 Another Way

Triangles can be described by the types of angles they have.

Draw a line to match the description of the triangle(s).

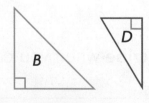

•   •   •

•   •   •

One angle is a right angle.

One angle is greater than a right angle.

Three angles are less than a right angle.

Math Talk MATHEMATICAL PRACTICES
Can a triangle have two right angles? **Explain.**

Name _____

Share and Show

1. Write the number of sides of equal length the triangle appears to have.

_____

Use the triangles for 2–4. Write F, G, or H.

Math Talk Explain another way you can describe triangle H.

2. Triangle _____ has 1 right angle.

✓3. Triangle _____ has 1 angle greater than a right angle.

✓4. Triangle _____ has 3 angles less than a right angle.

On Your Own

Use the triangles for 5–7. Write K, L, or M.
Then complete the sentences.

5. Triangle _____ has 1 right angle and appears to have

_____ sides of equal length.

6. Triangle _____ has 3 angles less than a right angle and

appears to have _____ sides of equal length.

7. Triangle _____ has 1 angle greater than a right angle

and appears to have _____ sides of equal length.

Problem Solving REAL WORLD

MATHEMATICAL PRACTICES

Model • Reason • Make Sense

8. **Sense or Nonsense?** Martin said a triangle can have two sides that are parallel. Does his statement make sense? **Explain.**

_____

_____

9. **Write Math** Compare Triangles *R* and *S*. How are they alike? How are they different?

_____

_____

_____

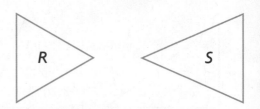

10. **Describe** the shape of the front of the building by its sides and by its angles.

_____

_____

11. **H.O.T.** Use a ruler to draw a straight line from one corner of this rectangle to the opposite corner. What shapes did you make? What do you notice about the shapes?

_____

_____

12. **PARCC Test Prep** Savannah made a group with Triangles *L, N, P,* and *R*. How are these triangles alike?

Ⓐ All of their sides are of equal length.

Ⓑ They all have 1 right angle.

Ⓒ They all have 1 angle greater than a right angle.

Ⓓ They all have 3 angles less than a right angle.

© Houghton Mifflin Harcourt Publishing Company

350 **FOR MORE PRACTICE:**
Standards Practice Book

Name _____

Problem Solving • Classify Plane Shapes

Essential Question How can you use the strategy *draw a diagram* to classify plane shapes?

COMMON CORE
Georgia Performance Standard MCC3.G.1
Reason with shapes and their attributes.

🔑 UNLOCK the Problem · REAL WORLD

A **Venn diagram** shows how sets of things are related. In the Venn diagram at the right, one circle has shapes that are rectangles. Shapes that are rhombuses are in the other circle. The shapes in the section where the circles overlap are both rectangles and rhombuses.

What type of quadrilateral is in both circles?

Rectangles   Rhombuses

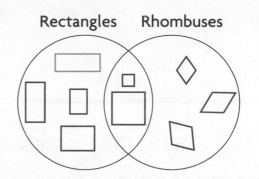

Read the Problem	Solve the Problem
What do I need to find? _____ _____	**What is true about all quadrilaterals?** _____ **Which quadrilaterals have 2 pairs of opposite sides that are parallel?** _____
What information do I need to use? the circles labeled _____ and _____	**Which quadrilaterals have 4 sides of equal length?** _____ **Which quadrilaterals have 4 right angles?** _____
How will I use the information? _____ _____ _____	The quadrilaterals in the section where the circles overlap have _____ pairs of opposite sides that are parallel, _____ sides of equal length, and _____ right angles. So, _____ are in both circles.

MATHEMATICAL PRACTICES

Math Talk Does a ▱ fit in the Venn diagram? **Explain.**

🔒 Try Another Problem

The Venn diagram shows the shapes Abbie used to make a picture. Where would the shape shown below be placed in the Venn diagram?

Read the Problem	**Solve the Problem**
What do I need to find?	**Record the steps you used to solve the problem.**
What information do I need to use?	
How will I use the information?	

1. How many shapes do not have right angles?

   _____

2. How many red shapes have right angles but are

   not quadrilaterals? _____

3. What is a different way to sort the shapes?

   _____

   _____

MATHEMATICAL PRACTICES

Math Talk What name can be used to describe all the shapes in the Venn diagram? **Explain** how you know.

Name _____

Share and Show

Use the Venn diagram for 1–3.

1. Jordan is sorting the shapes at the right in a Venn diagram. Where does the ◇ go?

   First, look at the sides and angles of the polygons.

   Next, draw the polygons in the Venn diagram.

   The shape has _____ sides of equal length

   and _____ right angles.

   So, the shape goes in the

   _____ .

2. **H.O.T. What if** Jordan sorted the shapes by Polygons with Right Angles and Polygons with Angles Less Than a Right Angle? Would the circles still overlap? **Explain.**

   _____

   _____

   Polygons with Right Angles   Polygons with All Sides Equal in Length

3. Where would you place a ⌂?

   _____

4. **H.O.T.** Eva drew the Venn diagram below. What labels could she have used for the diagram?

   _____   _____

   _____   _____

On Your Own.........................

5. Ben and Marta are both reading the same book. Ben has read $\frac{1}{3}$ of the book. Marta has read $\frac{1}{4}$ of the book. Who has read more? _____

6. There are 42 students from 6 different classes in the school spelling bee. Each class has the same number of students in the spelling bee. Use the bar model to find how many students are from each class.

42 students

_____ students ÷ _____ classes = _____ students

7. **H.O.T.** **Write Math** ▶ Cara baked 16 cupcakes. She took half of them to school. She gave Frank one fourth of what was left. How many cupcakes does Cara have now? **Explain** how you know.

_____

_____

_____

8. Ashley is making a quilt with squares of fabric. There are 9 rows with 8 squares in each row. How many squares of fabric are there?

_____

9. ⭐ **PARCC Test Prep** What label could describe Circle *A*?

Ⓐ Polygons with Perpendicular Sides

Ⓑ Polygons with 2 Pairs of Opposite Sides That Are Parallel

Ⓒ Polygons with 2 Pairs of Sides of Equal Length

Ⓓ Polygons with All Sides of Equal Length

A   Quadrilaterals with Right Angles

FOR MORE PRACTICE:
Standards Practice Book

Name _____

Relate Shapes, Fractions, and Area

Essential Question How can you divide shapes into parts with equal areas and write the area as a unit fraction of the whole?

COMMON CORE
Georgia Performance Standard MCC3.G.2
Reason with shapes and their attributes.

Investigate

Materials ■ pattern blocks ■ color pencils ■ ruler

CONNECT You can use what you know about combining and separating plane shapes to explore the relationship between fractions and area.

A. Trace a hexagon pattern block.

B. Divide your hexagon into two parts with equal area.

C. Write the names of the new shapes. _____

D. Write the fraction that names each part of the

whole you divided. _____
Each part is $\frac{1}{2}$ of the whole shape's area.

E. Write the fraction that names the whole area. _____

Math Idea
Equal parts of a whole have equal area.

Draw Conclusions . . . .

1. **Explain** how you know the two shapes have the same area.

_____

_____

2. **Predict** what would happen if you divide the hexagon into three shapes with equal area. What fraction names the area of each part of the divided hexagon? What fraction names the whole area?

_____

3. 🌟**H.O.T.** **Apply** Show how you can divide the hexagon into four shapes with equal area.

Each part is _____ of the whole shape's area.

Make Connections

The rectangle at the right is divided into four parts with equal area.

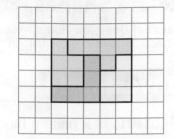

- Write the unit fraction that names each part of the divided whole. _____

- What is the area of each part? _____

- How many $\frac{1}{4}$ parts does it take to make one whole? _____

- Is the shape of each of the $\frac{1}{4}$ parts the same? _____

- Is the area of each of the $\frac{1}{4}$ parts the same? **Explain** how you know.

_____

_____

Divide the shape into equal parts.

Draw lines to divide the rectangle below into six parts with equal area.

MATHEMATICAL PRACTICES

Math Talk **Explain** how you know the areas of all the parts are equal.

- Write the fraction that names each part of the divided whole. _____

- Write the area of each part. _____

- Each part is _____ of the whole shape's area.

Share and Show

1. Divide the trapezoid into 3 parts with equal area. Write the names of the new shapes. Then write the fraction that names the area of each part of the whole.

_____

Name _____

Draw lines to divide the shape into equal parts that show the fraction given.

2.

$\frac{1}{6}$

3.

$\frac{1}{2}$

✓4.

$\frac{1}{8}$

Draw lines to divide the shape into parts with equal area. Write the area of each part as a unit fraction.

5.
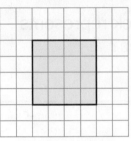
8 equal parts

_____

✓6.

6 equal parts

_____

7.
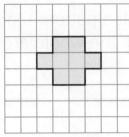
4 equal parts

_____

8.
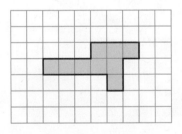
3 equal parts

_____

9.
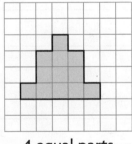
4 equal parts

_____

10.
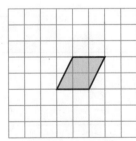
2 equal parts

_____

11. **H.O.T.** **Write Math** ▶ If the area of three ◇ is equal to the area of one ⬡, the area of how many ◇ equals four ⬡? **Explain** your answer.

_____

Problem Solving REAL WORLD

12. **H.O.T.** Sense or Nonsense?

Divide the hexagon into six equal parts.

Which pattern block represents $\frac{1}{6}$ of the whole area?

_____

Divide the trapezoid into three equal parts.

Which pattern block represents $\frac{1}{3}$ of the whole area?

_____

Alexis said the area of $\frac{1}{3}$ of the trapezoid is greater than the area of $\frac{1}{6}$ of the hexagon because $\frac{1}{3} > \frac{1}{6}$. Does her statement make sense? **Explain** your answer.

_____

_____

_____

_____

- Write a statement that makes sense.

_____

_____

- **What if** you divide the hexagon into 3 equal parts? Write a sentence that compares the area of each equal part of the hexagon to each equal part of the trapezoid.

_____

_____

Name _____

▶ **Vocabulary**

Choose the best term from the box to complete the sentence.

Vocabulary
rectangle
rhombus
square
trapezoid

1. A _____ has 4 right angles and 4 equal sides. (p. 339)

2. A _____ has exactly 1 pair of opposite sides that are parallel. (p. 339)

▶ **Concepts and Skills**

Circle all the words that describe the quadrilateral. MCC3.G.1

3.

rectangle

rhombus

square

trapezoid

4.

rectangle

rhombus

square

trapezoid

5.

rectangle

rhombus

square

trapezoid

Draw lines to divide the shape into equal parts that show the fraction given. MCC3.G.2

6.

$\frac{1}{6}$

7.

$\frac{1}{2}$

8.

$\frac{1}{4}$

Fill in the bubble for the correct answer choice.

9. Which quadrilateral has exactly 2 right angles? MCC3.G.1

Ⓐ

Ⓒ

Ⓑ

Ⓓ

10. Reggie divided the shape into parts with equal area. Which fraction names the area of each part of the divided shape? MCC3.G.2

Ⓐ $\frac{1}{2}$

Ⓒ $\frac{1}{4}$

Ⓑ $\frac{1}{3}$

Ⓓ $\frac{1}{8}$

11. Which label could describe Circle *E*? MCC3.G.1

Polygons with at Least 2 Pairs of Opposite Sides that are Parallel

E

Ⓐ Polygons with at Least 2 Perpendicular Sides

Ⓑ Polygons with All Sides of Equal Length

Ⓒ Polygons with Less than 5 Sides

Ⓓ Polygons with No Right Angles

Name _____

Unit 5 Assessment

▶ Vocabulary

Choose the best term from the box to complete the sentence.

Vocabulary
hexagon
parallel lines
perpendicular lines
plane shape

1. A _____ has 6 sides and 6 angles.
   (p. 330)

2. A _____ is formed by points that make curved paths, line segments, or both. (p. 321)

3. _____ appear to never cross or meet and are always the same distance apart. (p. 333)

▶ Concepts and Skills

Look at the green sides of the polygon. Tell if they appear to be *intersecting, perpendicular,* or *parallel*. Write all the words that describe the sides. ▌MCC3.G.1

4.

_____

_____

5.

_____

_____

6.

_____

_____

Circle all the words that describe the quadrilateral. ▌MCC3.G.1

7.

rectangle

rhombus

trapezoid

square

8.

quadrilateral

rhombus

trapezoid

rectangle

9.

rhombus

rectangle

square

trapezoid

GO Online | Assessment Options **Unit Test**

Fill in the bubble for the correct answer choice.

10. Which is NOT an example of a closed shape?

MCC3.G.1

Ⓐ

Ⓒ

Ⓑ

Ⓓ

11. Anne drew a line segment. Which of these could be the shape Anne drew? MCC3.G.1

Ⓐ

Ⓒ

Ⓑ

Ⓓ

12. Which shape is NOT a polygon? MCC3.G.1

Ⓐ

Ⓒ

Ⓑ

Ⓓ

13. Sam divided the shape into parts with equal area. Which fraction names the area of each part of the divided shape? MCC3.G.2

Ⓐ $\frac{1}{2}$ Ⓒ $\frac{1}{4}$

Ⓑ $\frac{1}{3}$ Ⓓ $\frac{1}{6}$

Name _____

Fill in the bubble for the correct answer choice.

14. Philip drew a shape with 2 fewer sides than a hexagon. Which shape did he draw? MCC3.G.1

Ⓐ triangle　Ⓑ pentagon　Ⓒ octagon　Ⓓ quadrilateral

15. Jennifer drew these polygons. Which shape is NOT a rhombus? MCC3.G.1

Ⓐ 　　Ⓒ

Ⓑ 　　Ⓓ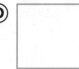

16. Which quadrilateral appears to have only 1 pair of parallel sides? MCC3.G.1

Ⓐ 　　Ⓒ

Ⓑ 　　Ⓓ

17. Which polygon does NOT have a right angle? MCC3.G.1

Ⓐ 　　Ⓒ

Ⓑ 　　Ⓓ

18. Jack drew a picture of his house for the art fair. His teacher copied the picture and used it for math class.

★ **Describe** four of the shapes you see in Jack's house.

_____

_____

_____

_____

_____

★★ **Describe** all of the quadrilaterals you see in Jack's house.

_____

_____

_____

_____

★★★ Draw a house like Jack's house. Use different shapes, including triangles and pentagons. **Identify** and list the shapes that you used.

_____

_____

_____

_____

Unit 6 Representing and Comparing Fractions

Show What You Know

Check your understanding of important skills.

Name _____

▶ Halves and Fourths

1. Find the shape that is divided into 2 equal parts. Color $\frac{1}{2}$.

2. Find the shape that is divided into 4 equal parts. Color $\frac{1}{4}$.

▶ Count Equal Groups Complete.

3.

_____ groups

_____ in each group

4.

_____ groups

_____ in each group

▶ Fractions of a Whole

Write the fraction that names the shaded part of each shape.

5. _____

6. _____

7. _____

MATH DETECTIVE WITH CARMEN SANDIEGO™

Casey shared a pizza with some friends. They each ate $\frac{1}{3}$ of the pizza. Be a Math Detective to find how many people shared the pizza.

Vocabulary Builder

▶ **Visualize It** ⋅⋅⋅

Complete the bubble map by using the
words with a ✓.

Preview Words
denominator
✓ eighths
equal parts
✓ fourths
fraction
fraction greater than 1
✓ halves
numerator
✓ sixths
✓ thirds
unit fraction
✓ whole

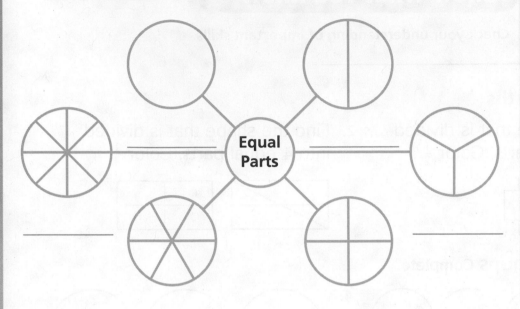

▶ **Understand Vocabulary** ⋅⋅

Read the description. Write the preview word.

1. It is a number that names part of a whole or part

    of a group. _____

2. It is the part of a fraction above the line, which tells
   how many parts are being counted.

    _____

3. It is the part of a fraction below the line, which tells
   how many equal parts there are in the whole or in

    the group. _____

4. It is a number that names 1 equal part of a whole

    and has 1 as its numerator. _____

GO Online • eStudent Edition • Multimedia eGlossary

Name _____

Equal Parts of a Whole

Essential Question What are equal parts of a whole?

COMMON CORE
Georgia Performance Standard MCC3.NF.1
Develop understanding of fractions as numbers.

🔑 UNLOCK the Problem REAL WORLD

Lauren shares a sandwich with her brother. They each get an equal part. How many equal parts are there?

🔒 Each whole shape below is divided into equal parts. A **whole** is all of the parts of one shape or group. **Equal parts** are exactly the same size.

• What do you need to find?

_____

_____

• How many people share the

sandwich? _____

2 halves

3 thirds

4 fourths

_____ **sixths**

_____ **eighths**

Lauren's sandwich is divided into halves.

So, there are _____ equal parts.

• Draw a picture to show a different way Lauren's sandwich could have been divided into halves.

MATHEMATICAL PRACTICES

Math Talk Are your halves the same shape as your classmates' halves? **Explain** why both halves represent the same size.

Try This! Write whether the shape is divided into *equal* parts or *unequal* parts.

A

4 _____ parts
    fourths

B

6 _____ parts
    sixths

C

2 _____ parts
These are not halves.

 ERROR Alert
Be sure the parts are
equal in size.

equal   unequal

Share and Show

1. This shape is divided into 3 equal parts. What is the name for the parts?

MATHEMATICAL PRACTICES
Math Talk **Explain** how you know if parts are equal.

_____

Write the number of equal parts. Then write the name for the parts.

2.

_____ equal parts

_____

3.

_____ equal parts

_____

☑ 4.

_____ equal parts

_____

Write whether the shape is divided into *equal* parts or *unequal* parts.

5.

_____ parts

6.

_____ parts

☑ 7.

_____ parts

Name _____

On Your Own ....

Write the number of equal parts. Then write the name
for the parts.

8.

_____ equal parts

_____

9.

_____ equal parts

_____

10.

_____ equal parts

_____

11.

_____ equal parts

_____

12.

_____ equal parts

_____

13.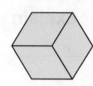

_____ equal parts

_____

Write whether the shape is divided into *equal* parts
or *unequal* parts.

14.

_____ parts

15.

_____ parts

16.

_____ parts

Draw lines to divide the circles into equal parts.

17. 2 halves

18. 4 fourths

19. 8 eighths

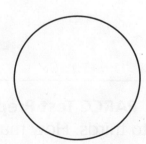

Problem Solving REAL WORLD

Use the pictures for 20–21.

Pan A   **Pan B**

20. Mrs. Rivera made 2 pans of brownies for Alex's party. She cut each pan into parts. What is the name of the parts for Pan A?

_____

21. **H.O.T.** **Sense or Nonsense?** Alex said his mom divided Pan B into eighths. Does his statement make sense? **Explain.**

_____

_____

22. **H.O.T.** **Write Math** **Explain** why the rectangle is divided into 4 equal parts.

_____

_____

23. Shelby cut a triangle out of paper. She wants to divide the triangle into 2 equal parts. Draw a quick picture to show what her triangle could look like.

24. Andrew wants to divide a square piece of paper into 4 equal parts. Draw two different quick pictures to show what his paper could look like.

25. ★ **PARCC Test Prep** Parker divides a fruit bar into thirds. How many equal parts are there?

(A) 2   (C) 4

(B) 3   (D) 8

Name _____

Equal Shares

Essential Question Why do you need to know how to make equal shares?

COMMON CORE
Georgia Performance Standard MCC3.NF.1
Develop understanding of fractions as numbers.

 UNLOCK the Problem REAL WORLD

Four friends share 2 small pizzas equally. What are two ways the pizza could be divided equally? How much pizza will each friend get?

🔑 **Draw to model the problem.**

Draw 2 circles to show the pizzas.

• How might the two ways be different?

_____

_____

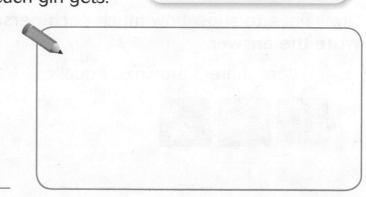

🔑 One Way

There are _____ friends.

So, cut each pizza into 4 slices.

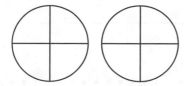

There are _____ equal parts.

Each friend can have 2 equal parts. Each friend will get 2 eighths of all the pizza.

🔑 Another Way

There are _____ friends.

So, cut all the pizza into 4 slices.

There are _____ equal parts.

Each friend can have 1 equal part. Each friend will get 1 half of a pizza.

MATHEMATICAL PRACTICES

Math Talk **Explain** why both ways let the friends have an equal share.

Try This! Four girls share 3 oranges equally. Draw a quick picture to find out how much each girl gets.

• Draw 3 circles to show the oranges.

• Draw lines to divide the circles equally.

• Shade the part 1 girl gets.

• Describe what part of an orange each girl gets.

_____

🔒 Example

Melissa and Kyle are planning to share one pan of lasagna with 6 friends. They do not agree on the way to cut the pan into equal parts. Will each friend get an equal share using Melissa's way? Using Kyle's way?

Melissa's Way   **Kyle's Way**

• Will Melissa's shares and Kyle's shares have the same shape? _____

• Will their shares using either way be the same size? _____

So, each friend will get an _____ share using either way.

• H.O.T. **Explain** why both ways let the friends have the same amount.

_____

_____

Share and Show MATH BOARD . . . .

1. Two friends share 4 cookies equally. Use the picture to find how much each friend gets.

Think: There are more cookies than friends.

MATHEMATICAL PRACTICES

Math Talk **Explain** another way the cookies could have been divided. Tell how much each friend will get.

_____

Draw lines to show how much each person gets. Write the answer.

☑ 2. 8 sisters share 3 brownies equally.

_____

☑ 3. 6 neighbors share 4 pies equally.

© Houghton Mifflin Harcourt Publishing Company

Name _____

On Your Own . . . .

Draw lines to show how much each person gets. Write the answer.

4. 3 classmates share 2 granola bars equally.

_____

5. 4 brothers share 2 sandwiches equally.

_____

Draw to show how much each person gets. Shade the amount that one person gets. Write the answer.

6. 8 friends share 4 sheets of construction paper equally.

_____

7. 4 sisters share 3 muffins equally.

_____

8. 6 students share 5 small pizzas equally.

_____

UNLOCK the Problem   REAL WORLD

9. Julia has 4 adults and 3 children coming over for dessert. She is going to serve 2 small blueberry pies. If she plans to give each person, including herself, an equal share of pie, how much pie will each person get?

a. What do you need to find? _____

_____

b. How will you use what you know about drawing equal

shares to solve the problem? _____

_____

c. Draw a quick picture to find the share of pie each person will get.

d. Complete the sentences.

Julia has _____ adults and

_____ children coming over.

In all, there will be _____ people having pie.

She is going to serve _____ blueberry pies.

So, each person will get

_____ of a blueberry pie.

---

10. Abby baked 5 cherry pies. She wants to share them equally among 8 of her neighbors. How much of a pie will each neighbor get?

_____

11. ⭐ **PARCC Test Prep** Six friends share 2 pizzas equally. How much of a pizza does each friend get?

Ⓐ 2 sixths   Ⓒ 6 halves

Ⓑ 3 sixths   Ⓓ 6 thirds

Name _____

Unit Fractions of a Whole

Essential Question What do the top and bottom numbers of a fraction tell?

COMMON CORE
Georgia Performance Standard MCC3.NF.1
Develop understanding of fractions as numbers.

A **fraction** is a number that names part of a whole or part of a group.

In a fraction, the top number tells how many equal parts are being counted.

The bottom number tells how many equal parts are in the whole or in the group.

$\longrightarrow \dfrac{1}{6}$

A **unit fraction** names 1 equal part of a whole. It has 1 as its top number. $\frac{1}{6}$ is a unit fraction.

🔑 UNLOCK the Problem REAL WORLD

Luke's family picked strawberries. They used them to make a strawberry pie. They cut it into 6 equal pieces. Luke ate 1 piece. What fraction of the strawberry pie did he eat?

🔒 Find part of a whole.

Shade 1 of the 6 equal parts.

Read: one sixth   **Write:** $\frac{1}{6}$

So, Luke ate _____ of the strawberry pie.

🔒 Use a fraction to find a whole.

This shape [ ] is $\frac{1}{4}$ of the whole. Here are examples of what the whole could look like.

MATHEMATICAL PRACTICES

Math Talk Explain how you can make a whole if you know what one equal part looks like.

Ⓐ   Ⓑ   Ⓒ

© Houghton Mifflin Harcourt Publishing Company

Try This! Look again at the examples at the bottom of page 315.
Draw two other pictures of how the whole might look.

Share and Show

1. What fraction names the shaded part? _____

   Think: 1 out of 3 equal parts is shaded.

**Write the number of equal parts in the whole.
Then write the fraction that names the shaded part.**

2.

   _____ equal parts

   _____

3.

   _____ equal parts

   _____

✓ 4.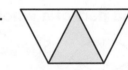

   _____ equal parts

   _____

5.

   _____ equal parts

   _____

6.

   _____ equal parts

   _____

✓ 7.

   _____ equal parts

   _____

On Your Own ....

Write the number of equal parts in the whole.
Then write the fraction that names the shaded part.

8.

_____ equal parts

_____

9.

_____ equal parts

_____

10.

_____ equal parts

_____

11.

_____ equal parts

_____

12.

_____ equal parts

_____

13. **H.O.T.**

_____ equal parts

_____

Draw a picture of the whole.

14. $\frac{1}{2}$ is

15. $\frac{1}{3}$ is

16. $\frac{1}{6}$ is

17. $\frac{1}{4}$ is

Problem Solving REAL WORLD

Use the pictures for 18–20.

Kylie's Lunch	Dylan's Lunch
sandwich	pizza
cookie	fruit bar

18. The missing parts of the pictures show what Kylie and Dylan ate for lunch. What fraction of the pizza did Dylan eat?

_____

19. What fraction of the cookie did Kylie eat? Write the fraction in numbers and in words.

_____ _____

20. **Write Math** ▶ **What's the Question?**
The answer is $\frac{1}{4}$.

_____

_____

21. Diego drew lines to divide the square into 6 pieces as shown. Then he shaded part of the square. Diego says he shaded $\frac{1}{6}$ of the square. Is he correct? **Explain** how you know.

_____

_____

22. **H.O.T.** Riley's granola bar is broken into equal pieces. She ate one piece, which was $\frac{1}{4}$ of the bar. How many more pieces does Riley need to eat to finish the granola bar? Draw a picture.

_____

23. ⭐ **PARCC Test Prep** Mary shaded part of a rectangle. What fraction names the part she shaded?

Ⓐ $\frac{1}{2}$ Ⓒ $\frac{1}{4}$

Ⓑ $\frac{1}{3}$ Ⓓ $\frac{3}{1}$

FOR MORE PRACTICE:
Standards Practice Book

Name _____

Fractions of a Whole

Essential Question How does a fraction name part of a whole?

COMMON CORE
Georgia Performance Standard MCC3.NF.1
Develop understanding of fractions as numbers.

🔑 UNLOCK the Problem REAL WORLD

The first pizzeria in America opened in New York in 1905. The pizza recipe came from Italy. Look at Italy's flag. What fraction of the flag is not red?

🔒 **Name equal parts of a whole.**

A fraction can name more than 1 equal part of a whole.

The flag is divided into 3 equal parts, and 2 parts are not red.

2 parts not red → $\dfrac{2}{3}$ ← numerator
3 equal parts in all → ← denominator

Read: two thirds or two parts out of three equal parts

Write: $\dfrac{2}{3}$

So, _____ of the flag is not red.

▲ Italy's flag has three equal parts.

Math Idea

When all the parts are shaded, one whole shape is equal to all of its parts. It represents the whole number 1.

$$\dfrac{3}{3} = 1$$

The **numerator** tells how many parts are being counted.

The **denominator** tells how many equal parts are in the whole or in the group.

You can count equal parts, such as sixths, to make a whole.

One $\frac{1}{6}$ part	Two $\frac{1}{6}$ parts	Three $\frac{1}{6}$ parts	Four $\frac{1}{6}$ parts	Five $\frac{1}{6}$ parts	Six $\frac{1}{6}$ parts
$\dfrac{1}{6}$	$\dfrac{2}{6}$	$\dfrac{3}{6}$	$\dfrac{}{6}$	$\dfrac{}{6}$	$\dfrac{}{6}$

For example, $\dfrac{6}{6}$ = one whole, or 1.

Try This! Write the missing word or number to name the shaded part.

A

$\frac{2}{6}$

_____ sixths

B

$\frac{5}{8}$

_____ eighths

C

$\frac{}{3}$

two thirds

D

$\frac{}{6}$, or 1

six sixths, or one whole

Share and Show ·

1. Shade two parts out of eight equal parts. Write a fraction in words and in numbers to name the shaded part.

   Think: Each part is $\frac{1}{8}$.

   Read: _____ eighths   **Write:** _____

Math Talk **Explain** what the numerator and denominator of a fraction tell you.

Write the fraction that names each part. Write a fraction in words and in numbers to name the shaded part.

2.

   Each part is _____.

   _____ fourths

   _____

3.

   Each part is _____.

   _____ sixths

   _____

4.

   Each part is _____.

   _____ fourths

   _____

Name _____

On Your Own ....

Write the fraction that names each part. Write a fraction
in words and in numbers to name the shaded part.

5.

Each part is _____.

_____ eighths

_____

6.

Each part is _____.

_____ thirds

_____

7.

Each part is _____.

_____ sixths

_____

8.

Each part is _____.

_____ fourths

_____

9.

Each part is _____.

_____ halves

_____

10.

Each part is _____.

_____ eighths

_____

Shade the fraction circle to model the fraction.
Then write the fraction in numbers.

11. six out of eight

_____

12. three fourths

_____

13. three out of three

_____

14. one out of two

_____

15. five sixths

_____

16. one out of four

_____

Problem Solving REAL WORLD

Use the pictures for 17–19.

17. Mrs. Ormond ordered pizza. Each pizza had 8 equal slices. What fraction of the pepperoni pizza was eaten?

Pepperoni   Cheese   Veggie

_____

18. What fraction of the cheese pizza is left?

_____

19. **Pose a Problem** Use the picture of the veggie pizza to write a problem that has a fraction as the answer. Solve your problem.

_____

_____

_____

20. **What's the Error?** Kate says that $\frac{2}{4}$ of the rectangle is shaded. Describe her error. Write the correct fraction for the shaded part.

_____

_____

_____

21. ⭐ **PARCC Test Prep** What fraction names the shaded part of the shape?

Ⓐ $\frac{2}{8}$

Ⓑ $\frac{2}{6}$

Ⓒ $\frac{6}{8}$

Ⓓ $\frac{8}{6}$

FOR MORE PRACTICE:
Standards Practice Book

Fractions on a Number Line

Essential Question How can you represent and locate fractions on a number line?

 COMMON CORE Georgia Performance Standards
MCC3.NF.2a, MCC3.NF.2b
Develop understanding of fractions as numbers.

🔑 UNLOCK the Problem REAL WORLD

Billy's family is traveling from his house to his grandma's house. They stop at gas stations when they are $\frac{1}{4}$ and $\frac{3}{4}$ of the way there. How can he represent those distances on a number line?

You can use a number line to show fractions. The length from one whole number to the next whole number represents one whole. The line can be divided into any number of equal parts, or lengths.

Math Idea
A point on a number line shows the endpoint of a length, or distance, from zero. A number or fraction can name the distance.

🔑 Activity Locate fractions on a number line.

Materials ■ fraction strips

Billy's House   Grandma's House

   0   1

$\frac{1}{4}$

$\frac{0}{4}$ $\frac{4}{4}$

STEP 1 Divide the line into four equal lengths, or fourths. Place four $\frac{1}{4}$-fraction strips end-to-end above the line to help.

STEP 2 At the end of each strip, draw a mark on the line.

STEP 3 Count the fourths from zero to 1 to label the distances from zero.

STEP 4 Think: $\frac{1}{4}$ is 1 out of 4 equal lengths.
Draw a point at $\frac{1}{4}$ to represent the distance from 0 to $\frac{1}{4}$.
Label the point *G1*.

STEP 5 Think: $\frac{3}{4}$ is 3 out of 4 equal lengths.
Draw a point at $\frac{3}{4}$ to represent the distance from 0 to $\frac{3}{4}$.
Label the point *G2*.

🔑 Example Complete the number line to name the point.

Materials ■ color pencils

Write the fraction that names the point on the number line.

Think: This number line is divided into six equal lengths, or sixths.

The length of one equal part is _____.

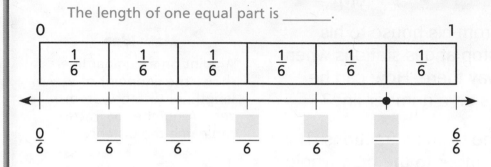

Shade the fraction strips to show the location of the point.

There are _____ out of _____ equal lengths shaded.

The shaded length shows $\frac{5}{6}$.

So, _____ names the point.

Share and Show 📝

1. Complete the number line. Draw a point to show $\frac{2}{3}$.

MATHEMATICAL PRACTICES

Math Talk **Explain** what the length between each mark on this number line represents.

Write the fraction that names the point.

2. point A _____

✔ 3. point B _____

✔ 4. point C _____

Name _____

On Your Own ·

Use fraction strips to help you complete the number line. Then locate and draw a point for the fraction.

5. $\frac{2}{6}$

6. $\frac{1}{2}$

7. $\frac{2}{3}$

Write the fraction that names the point.

8. point C _____   9. point D _____   10. point E _____

UNLOCK the Problem REAL WORLD

11. Javia ran 8 laps around a track to run a total of 1 mile on Monday. How many laps will she need to run on Tuesday to run $\frac{3}{8}$ of a mile?

Ⓐ 1   Ⓑ 3   Ⓒ 6   Ⓓ 8

a. What do you need to find?

_____

b. How will you use what you know about number lines to help you solve the problem?

_____

_____

c. H.O.T. Make a model to solve the problem.

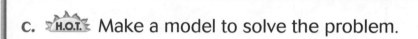

d. Complete the sentences.

There are _____ laps in 1 mile.

Each lap represents _____ of a mile.

_____ laps represent the distance of three eighths of a mile.

So, Javia will need to run _____ laps to run $\frac{3}{8}$ of a mile.

e. Fill in the bubble for the correct answer choice above.

12. Which fraction names point *F* on the number line?

Ⓐ $\frac{1}{6}$ Ⓑ $\frac{2}{6}$ Ⓒ $\frac{6}{2}$ Ⓓ $\frac{6}{6}$

Module 18 Assessment

► **Vocabulary**

Choose the best term from the box to complete the sentence.

Vocabulary
denominator
fraction
numerator

1. A _____ is a number that names part of a whole or part of a group. (p. 375)

2. The _____ tells how many parts are being counted. (p. 379)

► **Concepts and Skills**

Write the number of equal parts. Then write the name for the parts. MCC3.NF.1

3.

_____ equal parts

_____

4.

_____ equal parts

_____

5.

_____ equal parts

_____

Write the number of equal parts in the whole. Then write the fraction in numbers that names the shaded part. MCC3.NF.1

6.

_____ equal parts

_____

7.

_____ equal parts

_____

8.

_____ equal parts

_____

Write the fraction that names the point. MCC3.NF.2a, MCC3.NF.2b

9. point A _____

10. point B _____

11. point C _____

Fill in the bubble for the correct answer choice.

12. Jessica ordered a pizza. What fraction of the pizza has mushrooms? MCC3.NF.1

(A) $\frac{2}{6}$ (C) $\frac{6}{8}$

(B) $\frac{2}{8}$ (D) $\frac{8}{6}$

13. Which fraction names the shaded part?

MCC3.NF.1

(A) $\frac{8}{8}$ (C) $\frac{3}{8}$

(B) $\frac{5}{8}$ (D) $\frac{1}{8}$

14. Six friends share 3 oatmeal squares equally. How much of an oatmeal square does each friend get?

MCC3.NF.1

(A) 1 half

(B) 1 third

(C) 1 fourth

(D) 1 sixth

Name _____

Relate Fractions and Whole Numbers

Essential Question When might you use a fraction greater than 1 or a whole number?

COMMON CORE
Georgia Performance Standard MCC3.NF.3c
Develop understanding of fractions as numbers.

🔑 UNLOCK the Problem · REAL WORLD

Steve ran 1 mile and Jenna ran $\frac{4}{4}$ of a mile. Did Steve and Jenna run the same distance?

🔑 **Locate 1 and $\frac{4}{4}$ on a number line.**

- Shade 4 lengths of $\frac{1}{4}$ and label the number line.
- Draw a point at 1 and $\frac{4}{4}$.

> **Math Idea**
> If two numbers are located at the same point on a number line, then they are equal and represent the same distance.

Since the distance _____ and _____ end at the same point, they are equal.

So, Steve and Jenna ran the _____ distance.

Try This! Complete the number line. Locate and draw points at $\frac{3}{6}$, $\frac{6}{6}$, and 1.

A Are $\frac{3}{6}$ and 1 equal? **Explain.**

Think: Do the distances end at the same point?

_____

So, $\frac{3}{6}$ and 1 are _____.

B Are $\frac{6}{6}$ and 1 equal? **Explain.**

Think: Do the distances end at the same point?

_____

So, $\frac{6}{6}$ and 1 are _____.

CONNECT The number of equal parts the whole is divided into is the denominator of a fraction. The number of parts being counted is the numerator. A **fraction greater than 1** has a numerator greater than its denominator.

Examples

Each shape is 1 whole. Write a whole number and a fraction greater than 1 for the parts that are shaded.

Remember

$\frac{4}{1}$ ← numerator
← denominator

A

There are 2 wholes.

Each whole is divided into 4 equal parts, or fourths. $2 = \frac{8}{4}$

There are _____ equal parts shaded.

B

There are 3 wholes.

Each whole is divided into 1 equal part. $3 = \frac{3}{1}$

There are _____ equal parts shaded.

1. **Explain** what *each whole is divided into 1 equal part* means in Example B.

_____

_____

Read Math

Read $\frac{3}{1}$ as *three ones*.

2. How do you divide a whole into 1 equal part?

_____

_____

Try This!

Each shape is 1 whole. Write a whole number and a fraction greater than 1 for the parts that are shaded.

☐ = ☐/☐

Name _____

Share and Show...

1. Each shape is 1 whole. Write a whole number and a fraction greater than 1 for the parts that are shaded.

There are _____ wholes.

Each whole is divided into _____ equal parts.

There are _____ equal parts shaded.

$\square = \dfrac{\ \ }{\ \ }$

Use the number line to find whether the two numbers are equal. Write *equal* or *not equal*.

2. $\dfrac{1}{8}$ and $\dfrac{8}{8}$ _____

☑ 3. $\dfrac{8}{8}$ and 1 _____

☑ 4. 1 and $\dfrac{4}{8}$ _____

On Your Own..

Use the number line to find whether the two numbers are equal. Write *equal* or *not equal*.

> **Math Talk** MATHEMATICAL PRACTICES
> Explain how you know whether the two fractions are equal or not equal in Exercise 4.

5. $\dfrac{0}{3}$ and 1 _____

6. 1 and $\dfrac{2}{3}$ _____

7. $\dfrac{3}{3}$ and 1 _____

Each shape is 1 whole. Write a fraction greater than 1 for the parts that are shaded.

8.

$2 = \underline{\quad\quad}$

9.

$1 = \underline{\quad\quad}$

10.

$3 = \underline{\quad\quad}$

11.

$2 = \underline{\quad\quad}$

☀ **H.O.T.** **Draw a model of the fraction or fraction greater than 1. Then write it as a whole number.**

12. $\frac{8}{4} =$ _____

13. $\frac{6}{6} =$ _____

14. $\frac{5}{1} =$ _____

Problem Solving

15. Jeff rode his bike around a bike trail that was $\frac{1}{3}$ of a mile long. He rode around the trail 9 times. Write a fraction greater than 1 for the distance. How many miles did Jeff ride?

_____

16. ☀ **H.O.T.** **Write Math** ▶ **What's the Error?** Andrea drew the number line below. She said that $\frac{9}{8}$ and 1 were equal. **Explain** her error.

0   1

$\frac{1}{8}$ $\frac{2}{8}$ $\frac{3}{8}$ $\frac{4}{8}$ $\frac{5}{8}$ $\frac{6}{8}$ $\frac{7}{8}$ $\frac{8}{8}$ $\frac{9}{8}$

_____

17. ⭐ **PARCC Test Prep** Each shape is 1 whole. Which fraction greater than 1 names the parts that are shaded?

  Ⓐ $\frac{4}{6}$ Ⓒ $\frac{24}{4}$

  Ⓑ $\frac{24}{6}$ Ⓓ $\frac{4}{24}$

FOR MORE PRACTICE:
Standards Practice Book

© Houghton Mifflin Harcourt Publishing Company

Fractions of a Group

Essential Question How can a fraction name part of a group?

COMMON CORE
Georgia Performance Standard MCC3.NF.1
Develop understanding of fractions as numbers.

 UNLOCK the Problem REAL WORLD

Jake and Emma each have a collection of marbles.
What fraction of each collection is blue?

🔑 You can use a fraction to name part of a group.

Jake's Marbles	Emma's Marbles

number of blue marbles → ☐ ← numerator total number → $\overline{8}$ ← denominator of marbles	bags of blue marbles → ☐ ← numerator total number → $\overline{4}$ ← denominator of bags
Read: three eighths, or three out of eight	**Read:** one fourth, or one out of four
Write: $\frac{3}{8}$	**Write:** $\frac{1}{4}$
So, _____ of Jake's marbles are blue.	So, _____ of Emma's marbles are blue.

Try This! **Name part of a group.**

Draw 2 red counters and 6 yellow counters.

Write the fraction of counters that are red.

☐ ← number of red counters
___
☐ ← total number of counters

Write the fraction of counters that are not red.

☐ ← number of yellow counters
___
☐ ← total number of counters

So, _____ of the counters are red and _____ are not red.

Fractions Greater Than 1

Sometimes a fraction can name more than a whole group.

Daniel collects baseballs. He has collected 8 so far. He puts them in cases that hold 4 baseballs each. What part of the baseball cases has Daniel filled?

Think: 1 case = 1

Daniel has two full cases of 4 baseballs each.

So, 2, or $\frac{8}{4}$, baseball cases are filled.

Try This! Complete the whole number and the fraction greater than 1 to name the part filled.

A

Think: 1 pan = 1

_____, or $\frac{}{6}$

B

Think: 1 box = 1

_____, or $\frac{}{8}$

Share and Show

1. What fraction of the counters are red? _____

Think: How many red counters are there? How many counters are there in all?

Math Talk

MATHEMATICAL PRACTICES

Explain another way to name the fraction for Exercise 3.

Write a fraction to name the red part of each group.

2. _____

3. _____

Name _____

Write a whole number and a fraction greater than 1 to name the part filled.

4.

Think: 1 carton = 1

_____

☑ 5.

Think: 1 container = 1

_____

On Your Own...

Write a fraction to name the blue part of each group.

6.

_____

7.

_____

8.

_____

9.

_____

Write a whole number and a fraction greater than 1 to name the part filled.

10.

Think: 1 container = 1

_____

11.

Think: 1 carton = 1

_____

Draw a quick picture on your MathBoard. Then write a fraction to name the shaded part of the group.

12. Draw 8 circles.
    Shade 8 circles.

_____

13. Draw 8 triangles.
    Make 4 groups.
    Shade 1 group.

_____

14. Draw 4 rectangles.
    Shade 2 rectangles.

_____

Problem Solving REAL WORLD

Use the graph for 15–16.

15. The bar graph shows the winners of the Smith Elementary School Marble Tournament. How many games were played? What fraction of the games did Scott win?

_____ _____

16. What fraction of the games did Robyn NOT win?

_____

 SHOW YOUR WORK

17. **H.O.T.** Liam has 6 marbles. Of them, $\frac{1}{3}$ are blue. The rest are red. Draw a picture to show Liam's marbles.

18. **Write Math** **What's the Question?** A bag has 2 yellow cubes, 3 blue cubes, and 1 white cube. The answer is $\frac{1}{6}$.

_____

_____

19. ★**PARCC Test Prep** Makayla picked some flowers. What fraction of her flowers are yellow?

(A) $\frac{1}{8}$ (B) $\frac{2}{8}$ (C) $\frac{3}{8}$ (D) $\frac{4}{8}$

Name _____

Find Part of a Group Using Unit Fractions

Essential Question How can a fraction tell how many are in part of a group?

COMMON CORE
Georgia Performance Standard MCC3.NF.1
Develop understanding of fractions as numbers.

🔑 UNLOCK the Problem REAL WORLD

Audrey buys a bouquet of 12 flowers. One third of them are red. How many of the flowers are red?

- How many flowers does Audrey buy in all? _____
- What fraction of the flowers are red? _____

🔓 Activity

Materials ■ two-color counters ■ MathBoard

- Put 12 counters on your MathBoard.
- Since you want to find $\frac{1}{3}$ of the group, there should be _____ equal groups. Draw the counters below.

- Circle one of the groups to show _____.

  Then count the number of counters in that group.

There are _____ counters in 1 group. $\frac{1}{3}$ of 12 = _____

So, _____ of the flowers are red.

- **What if** Audrey buys a bouquet of 9 flowers and one third of them are yellow? Use your MathBoard and counters to find how many of the flowers are yellow.

  _____

Math Talk MATHEMATICAL PRACTICES
Explain how you can use the numerator and denominator in a fraction to find part of a group.

Try This! Find part of a group.

Joseph picks 20 flowers from his mother's garden. One fourth of them are purple. How many of the flowers are purple?

STEP 1 Draw a row of 4 counters.

Think: To find $\frac{1}{4}$, make 4 equal groups.

_____

STEP 2 Continue to draw as many rows of 4 counters as you can until you have 20 counters.

_____

STEP 3 Then circle _____ equal groups.

Think: Each group represents $\frac{1}{4}$ of the flowers.

There are _____ counters in 1 group.

$\frac{1}{4}$ of 20 = _____

$\frac{1}{4}$ $\frac{1}{4}$ $\frac{1}{4}$ $\frac{1}{4}$

So, _____ of the flowers are purple.

Share and Show MATH BOARD ....

1. Use the model to find $\frac{1}{2}$ of 8. _____

   Think: How many counters are in 1 of the 2 equal groups?

> MATHEMATICAL PRACTICES
>
> **Math Talk** **Explain** why you count the number of counters in just one of the groups in Exercise 1.

Circle equal groups to solve. Count the number of flowers in 1 group.

2. $\frac{1}{4}$ of 8 = _____

3. $\frac{1}{3}$ of 6 = _____

4. $\frac{1}{6}$ of 12 = _____

398

On Your Own

Circle equal groups to solve. Count the number
of flowers in 1 group.

5. $\frac{1}{4}$ of 12 = _____

6. $\frac{1}{3}$ of 15 = _____

7. $\frac{1}{4}$ of 16 = _____

8. $\frac{1}{3}$ of 9 = _____

9. $\frac{1}{6}$ of 18 = _____

10. $\frac{1}{8}$ of 8 = _____

11. $\frac{1}{6}$ of 30 = _____

12. $\frac{1}{3}$ of 12 = _____

13. H.O.T. $\frac{1}{2}$ of 6 = _____

H.O.T. **Draw counters. Then circle equal groups to solve.**

14. $\frac{1}{8}$ of 16 = _____

15. $\frac{1}{6}$ of 24 = _____

Problem Solving REAL WORLD

Use the table for 16–17.

Flower Seeds Bought	
Name	**Number of Packs**
Ryan	8
Brooke	12
Cole	20

16. One fourth of the seed packs Ryan bought are violet seeds. How many packs of violet seeds did Ryan buy? Draw counters to solve.

_____

17. **H.O.T.** **Write Math** One third of Brooke's seed packs and one fourth of Cole's seed packs are daisy seeds. How many packs of daisy seeds did they buy altogether? **Explain** how you know.

_____

_____

_____

SHOW YOUR WORK

18. **Sense or Nonsense?** Sophia bought 12 pots. One sixth of them are green. Sophia said she bought 2 green pots. Does her answer make sense? **Explain** how you know.

_____

_____

_____

_____

19. ★**PARCC Test Prep** Bailey picked 15 flowers. One third of them are yellow. How many yellow flowers did Bailey pick?

(A) 3   (C) 10

(B) 5   (D) 15

Problem Solving • Find the Whole Group Using Unit Fractions

Essential Question How can you use the strategy *draw a diagram* to solve fraction problems?

COMMON CORE
Georgia Performance Standard MCC3.NF.1
Develop understanding of fractions as numbers.

🔑 UNLOCK the Problem REAL WORLD

Cameron has 4 clown fish in his fish tank. One third of the fish in the tank are clown fish. How many fish does Cameron have in his tank?

Use the graphic organizer to help you solve the problem.

Read the Problem	Solve the Problem
What do I need to find? I need to find _____ are in Cameron's fish tank.	**Describe how to draw a diagram to solve.** The denominator in $\frac{1}{3}$ tells you that there are _____ equal parts in the whole group. Draw 3 circles to show _____ equal parts. Since 4 fish are $\frac{1}{3}$ of the whole group,
What information do I need to use? Cameron has _____ clown fish. _____ of the fish in the tank are clown fish.	draw _____ counters in the first circle. Since there are _____ counters in the first circle, draw _____ counters in each of the remaining circles. Then find the total number of counters.
How will I use the information? I will use the information in the problem to draw a _____ .	So, Cameron has _____ fish in his tank.

🔒 Try Another Problem

A pet store has 2 gray rabbits. One eighth of the rabbits at the pet store are gray. How many rabbits does the pet store have?

Read the Problem	**Solve the Problem**
What do I need to find?	
What information do I need to use?	
How will I use the information?	

1. How do you know that your answer is reasonable?

_____

_____

2. How did your diagram help you solve the problem? _____

_____

Math Talk
MATHEMATICAL PRACTICES

Suppose $\frac{1}{2}$ of the rabbits are gray. **Explain** how you can find the number of rabbits at the pet store.

Name _____

Share and Show   . . . .

🔑 UNLOCK the Problem **Tips**

✓ Circle the question.
✓ Underline important facts.
✓ Put the problem in your own words.
✓ Choose a strategy you know.

1. Lily has 3 dog toys that are red. One fourth of all her dog toys are red. How many dog toys does Lily have?

   First, draw _____ circles to show _____ equal parts.

   SHOW YOUR WORK

   Next, draw _____ toys in _____ circle since

   _____ circle represents the number of red toys.

   Last, draw _____ toys in each of the remaining circles. Find the total number of toys.

   So, Lily has _____ dog toys.

2. **H.O.T.** **What if** Lily had 4 toys that are red? How many dog toys would she have?

   _____

3. The pet store sells bags of pet food. There are 4 bags of cat food. One sixth of the bags of food are bags of cat food. How many bags of pet food does the pet store have?

   _____

4. Rachel owns 2 parakeets. One fourth of all her birds are parakeets. How many birds does Rachel own?

   _____

On Your Own. . . . .

Choose a
STRATEGY

Act It Out
Draw a Diagram
Find a Pattern
Make a Table

Draw a quick picture to solve for 5–6.

5. There are 18 bottlenose dolphins at an aquarium. One sixth of them are not adults. How many of the bottlenose dolphins are not adults?

_____

SHOW YOUR WORK

6. **H.O.T.** Six friends share 5 small pizzas. Each friend first eats half of a pizza. How much more pizza does each friend need to eat to finish all the pizzas and share them equally?

_____

7. **Write Math** Braden bought 4 packs of dog treats. He gave 4 treats to his neighbor's dog. Now Braden has 24 treats left for his dog. How many dog treats were in each pack? **Explain** how you know.

_____

_____

_____

_____

8. ★ **PARCC Test Prep** Two hats are $\frac{1}{3}$ of the group. How many hats are in the whole group?

Ⓐ 4   Ⓒ 6

Ⓑ 5   Ⓓ 8

Module 19 Assessment

▶ **Vocabulary**

Choose the best term from the box to complete the sentence.

1. A _____ has a numerator greater than its denominator. (p. 390)

2. The number that names the number of equal parts in a fraction is the _____. (p. 379)

▶ **Concepts and Skills**

Each shape is 1 whole. Write a fraction greater than 1 for the parts that are shaded. ▌MCC3.NF.3c

3.

2 = _____

4.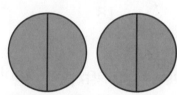

2 = _____

Write a fraction to name the red part of each group. ▌MCC3.NF.1

5.

_____

6.

_____

Circle equal groups to solve. Count the number of objects in 1 group. ▌MCC4.NF.1

7. $\frac{1}{2}$ of 12 = _____

8. $\frac{1}{4}$ of 16 = _____

9. $\frac{1}{3}$ of 12 = _____

Fill in the bubble for the correct answer choice.

10 What is $\frac{1}{4}$ of 12 ? MCC3.NF.1

Ⓐ 2   Ⓒ 4

Ⓑ 3   Ⓓ 6

11. Mrs. Cooper bought 2 pizzas that are shown below.

Which fraction can be used to represent the number
of pizzas? MCC3.NF.3c

Ⓐ $\frac{2}{8}$ Ⓒ $\frac{16}{8}$

Ⓑ $\frac{8}{8}$ Ⓓ $\frac{18}{8}$

12. Marva has these shapes on a table.

What fraction of the shapes are triangles? MCC3.NF.1

Ⓐ $\frac{1}{6}$ Ⓒ $\frac{1}{3}$

Ⓑ $\frac{1}{4}$ Ⓓ $\frac{1}{2}$

13. Jimmy has 3 red marbles. One fourth of Jimmy's marbles
are red. How many marbles does Jimmy have? MCC3.NF.1

Ⓐ 4   Ⓒ 9

Ⓑ 7   Ⓓ 12

Name _____

Problem Solving • Compare Fractions

Essential Question How can you use the strategy *act it out* to solve comparison problems?

COMMON CORE
Georgia Performance Standard MCC3.NF.3d
Develop understanding of fractions as numbers.

🔑 UNLOCK the Problem · REAL WORLD

Mary and Vincent climbed up a rock wall at the park. Mary climbed $\frac{3}{4}$ of the way up the wall. Vincent climbed $\frac{3}{8}$ of the way up the wall. Who climbed higher?

You can act out the problem by using manipulatives to help you compare fractions.

Remember
$<$ is less than
$>$ is greater than
$=$ is equal to

Read the Problem	**Solve the Problem**
What do I need to find? _____	**Record the steps you used to solve the problem.** \[1 \] \[$\frac{1}{4}$ \] \[$\frac{1}{4}$ \] \[$\frac{1}{4}$ \] \[$\frac{1}{8}$ \] \[$\frac{1}{8}$ \] \[$\frac{1}{8}$ \]
What information do I need to use? Mary climbed _____ of the way. Vincent climbed _____ of the way.	Compare the lengths. _____ ◯ _____ The length of the $\frac{3}{4}$ model is _____ than the length of the $\frac{3}{8}$ model.
How will I use the information? I will use _____ and _____ the lengths of the models to find who climbed _____.	So, _____ climbed higher on the rock wall.

Math Talk | MATHEMATICAL PRACTICES
 How do you know who climbed higher?

© Houghton Mifflin Harcourt Publishing Company

🔑 Try Another Problem

The camp leader is making waffles for breakfast. Tracy ate $\frac{3}{6}$ of her waffle. Kim ate $\frac{5}{6}$ of her waffle. Who ate more of her waffle?

Read the Problem	Solve the Problem
What do I need to find?	**Record the steps you used to solve the problem.**
What information do I need to use?	
How will I use the information?	

Math Talk **Explain** how you know that $\frac{5}{6}$ is greater than $\frac{3}{6}$ without using models.

1. How did your model help you solve the problem?_____

_____

2. Tracy and Kim each had a carton of milk with lunch. Tracy drank $\frac{5}{8}$ of her milk. Kim drank $\frac{7}{8}$ of her milk. Who drank more of her milk? **Explain**.

_____

_____

Name _____

Share and Show

UNLOCK the Problem Tips
✓ Circle the question.
✓ Underline important facts.
✓ Act out the problem using manipulatives.

1. At the park, people can climb a rope ladder to its top. Rosa climbed $\frac{2}{8}$ of the way up the ladder. Justin climbed $\frac{2}{6}$ of the way up the ladder. Who climbed higher on the rope ladder?

   First, what are you asked to find?

   _____

   Then, model and compare the fractions.

   Think: Compare $\frac{2}{8}$ and $\frac{2}{6}$.

   Last, find the greater fraction.

   _____ ◯ _____

   So, _____ climbed higher on the rope ladder.

☑ 2. **H.O.T.** **What if** Cara also tried the rope ladder and climbed $\frac{2}{4}$ of the way up? Who climbed highest on the rope ladder: Rosa, Justin, or Cara? **Explain** how you know.

   _____

   _____

   _____

   _____

☑ 3. Ted walked $\frac{2}{3}$ mile to his soccer game. Then he walked $\frac{1}{3}$ mile to his friend's house. Which distance is shorter? **Explain** how you know.

   _____

   _____

SHOW YOUR WORK

On Your Own

Choose a
STRATEGY

Act It Out
Draw a Diagram
Find a Pattern
Make a Table

Use the table for 4–5.

4. Suri is frosting 8 cupcakes for her party. The table shows the fraction of cupcakes frosted with each frosting flavor. Which flavor did Suri use on the most cupcakes?

   Hint: Use 8 counters to model the cupcakes.

   _____

5. **Write Math** ▶ **What's the Question?** The answer is strawberry.

   _____

   _____

Suri's Cupcakes

Frosting Flavor	Fraction of Cupcakes
Vanilla	$\frac{3}{8}$
Chocolate	$\frac{4}{8}$
Strawberry	$\frac{1}{8}$

6. **H.O.T.** Suppose Suri had also used peanut butter frosting on the cupcakes. She frosted $\frac{1}{2}$ of the cupcakes with vanilla, $\frac{1}{4}$ with chocolate, $\frac{1}{8}$ with strawberry, and $\frac{1}{8}$ with peanut butter. Which flavor of frosting did Suri use on the most cupcakes?

   _____

7. Ms. Gordon has many cookie recipes. One recipe uses $\frac{1}{3}$ cup oatmeal and $\frac{1}{2}$ cup flour. Will Ms. Gordon use more oatmeal or more flour? **Explain**.

   _____

8. ★ **PARCC Test Prep** Rick lives $\frac{4}{6}$ mile from school. Noah lives $\frac{3}{6}$ mile from school. Which of the following correctly compares the fractions?

   Ⓐ $\frac{4}{6} = \frac{3}{6}$ Ⓒ $\frac{4}{6} > \frac{3}{6}$

   Ⓑ $\frac{4}{6} < \frac{3}{6}$ Ⓓ $\frac{3}{6} > \frac{4}{6}$

SHOW YOUR WORK

Compare Fractions with the Same Denominator

COMMON CORE
Georgia Performance Standard MCC3.NF.3d
Develop understanding of fractions as numbers.

Essential Question How can you compare fractions with the same denominator?

🔑 UNLOCK the Problem REAL WORLD

Jeremy and Christina are each making quilt blocks. Both blocks are the same size and both are made of 4 equal-size squares. $\frac{2}{4}$ of Jeremy's squares are green. $\frac{1}{4}$ of Christina's squares are green. Whose quilt block has more green squares?

- Circle the two fractions you need to compare.
- How are the two fractions alike?

_____

Jeremy's Quilt Block   **Christina's Quilt Block**

🔒 Compare fractions of a whole.

- Shade $\frac{2}{4}$ of Jeremy's quilt block.
- Shade $\frac{1}{4}$ of Christina's quilt block.
- Compare $\frac{2}{4}$ and $\frac{1}{4}$.

The greater fraction will have the larger amount of the whole shaded.

$$\frac{2}{4} \bigcirc \frac{1}{4}$$

Math Idea
You can compare two fractions when they refer to the same whole or to groups that are the same size.

So, _____ quilt block has more green squares.

🔒 Compare fractions of a group.

Jen and Maggie each have 6 buttons.

- Shade 3 of Jen's buttons to show the number of buttons that are red. Shade 5 of Maggie's buttons to show the number that are red.

- Write a fraction to show the number of red buttons in each group. Compare the fractions.

Jen's Buttons

Maggie's Buttons

There are the same number of buttons in each group, so you can count the number of red buttons to compare the fractions.

$$3 < \underline{\hspace{1cm}}, \text{ so } \frac{\blacksquare}{6} < \frac{\blacksquare}{6}.$$

So, _____ has a greater fraction of red buttons.

🔑 **Use fraction strips and a number line.**

At the craft store, one piece of ribbon is $\frac{2}{8}$ yard long. Another piece of ribbon is $\frac{7}{8}$ yard long. If Sean wants to buy the longer piece of ribbon, which piece should he buy?

Compare $\frac{2}{8}$ and $\frac{7}{8}$.

- Shade the fraction strips to show the locations of $\frac{2}{8}$ and $\frac{7}{8}$.

- Draw and label points on the number line to represent the distances $\frac{2}{8}$ and $\frac{7}{8}$.

- Compare the lengths.

  $\frac{2}{8}$ is to the left of $\frac{7}{8}$. It is closer to $\frac{0}{8}$, or _____.

  $\frac{7}{8}$ is to the _____ of $\frac{2}{8}$. It is closer to —, or _____.

$\dfrac{}{} < \dfrac{}{}$ and $\dfrac{}{} > \dfrac{}{}$

So, Sean should buy the piece of ribbon that is — yard long.

🔑 **Use reasoning.**

Molly and Omar are decorating same-size bookmarks. Molly covers $\frac{3}{3}$ of her bookmark with glitter. Omar covers $\frac{1}{3}$ of his bookmark with glitter. Whose bookmark is covered with more glitter?

Compare $\frac{3}{3}$ and $\frac{1}{3}$.

- When the denominators are the same, the whole is divided into same-size pieces. You can look at the _____ to compare the number of pieces.

- Both fractions involve third-size pieces. _____ pieces are more than _____ piece. 3 > _____, so $\dfrac{}{} > \dfrac{}{}$.

So, _____ bookmark is covered with more glitter.

MATHEMATICAL PRACTICES

Math Talk **Explain** how you can use reasoning to compare fractions with the same denominator.

Name _____

Share and Show

1. Draw points on the number line to show
$\frac{1}{6}$ and $\frac{5}{6}$. Then compare the fractions.

MATHEMATICAL PRACTICES

Math Talk **Explain** why fractions increase in size as you move right on the number line.

```
←+—+—+—+—+—+—+→
  0   1   2   3   4   5   6
  6   6   6   6   6   6   6
```

Think: $\frac{1}{6}$ is to the left of $\frac{5}{6}$ on the number line.

$\frac{1}{6}$ ◯ $\frac{5}{6}$

Compare. Write <, >, or =.

2. $\frac{4}{8}$ ◯ $\frac{3}{8}$

☑ 3. $\frac{1}{4}$ ◯ $\frac{4}{4}$

4. $\frac{1}{2}$ ◯ $\frac{1}{2}$

☑ 5. $\frac{3}{6}$ ◯ $\frac{2}{6}$

On Your Own

Compare. Write <, >, or =.

6. $\frac{2}{4}$ ◯ $\frac{3}{4}$

7. $\frac{2}{3}$ ◯ $\frac{2}{3}$

8. $\frac{4}{6}$ ◯ $\frac{2}{6}$

9. $\frac{0}{8}$ ◯ $\frac{2}{8}$

H.O.T. Write a fraction less than, greater than, or equal to the given fraction.

10. $\frac{1}{2} < \frac{\square}{\square}$

11. $\frac{\square}{\square} < \frac{12}{6}$

12. $\frac{8}{8} = \frac{\square}{\square}$

13. $\frac{\square}{\square} > \frac{2}{4}$

Problem Solving REAL WORLD

14. Carlos finished $\frac{5}{8}$ of his art project on Monday. Tyler finished $\frac{7}{8}$ of his art project on Monday. Who finished more of his art project on Monday?

_____

15. Ms. Endo made two pies that are the same size. Her family ate $\frac{1}{4}$ of the apple pie and $\frac{3}{4}$ of the cherry pie. Which pie had less left over?

_____

16. **PARCC Test Prep** Todd and Lisa are comparing fraction strips. Which statement is NOT correct?

Ⓐ $\frac{1}{4} < \frac{4}{4}$ Ⓑ $\frac{5}{6} < \frac{4}{6}$ Ⓒ $\frac{2}{3} > \frac{1}{3}$ Ⓓ $\frac{5}{8} > \frac{4}{8}$

 **What's the Error?**

17. Gary and Vanessa are comparing fractions. Vanessa models $\frac{2}{4}$ and Gary models $\frac{3}{4}$. Vanessa writes $\frac{3}{4} < \frac{2}{4}$. Look at Gary's model and Vanessa's model and describe her error.

Vanessa's Model

Gary's Model

- Describe Vanessa's error.

  _____

  _____

- **Explain** how to correct Vanessa's error. Then show the correct model.

  _____

  _____

  _____

  _____

Name _____

Compare Fractions with the Same Numerator

Essential Question How can you compare fractions with the same numerator?

COMMON CORE
Georgia Performance Standard MCC3.NF.3d
Develop understanding of fractions as numbers.

🔑 UNLOCK the Problem · REAL WORLD

Josh is at Enzo's Pizza Palace. He can sit at a table with 5 of his friends or at a different table with 7 of his friends. The same-size pizza is shared equally among the people at each table. At which table should Josh sit to get more pizza?

- Including Josh, how many friends will be sharing pizza at each table?

  _____

- What will you compare?

  _____

  _____

🔓 **Model the problem.**

There will be 6 friends sharing Pizza A or 8 friends sharing Pizza B.

So, Josh will get either $\frac{1}{6}$ or $\frac{1}{8}$ of a pizza.

- Shade $\frac{1}{6}$ of Pizza A.

- Shade $\frac{1}{8}$ of Pizza B.

- Which piece of pizza is larger?

- Compare $\frac{1}{6}$ and $\frac{1}{8}$.

$$\frac{1}{6} \bigcirc \frac{1}{8}$$

So, Josh should sit at the table with _____ friends to get more pizza.

Pizza A   **Pizza B**

---

1. Which pizza has more pieces? _____
   The *more* pieces a whole is divided into,

   the _____ the pieces are.

2. Which pizza has fewer pieces? _____
   The *fewer* pieces a whole is divided into,

   the _____ the pieces are.

MATHEMATICAL PRACTICES

Math Talk Suppose Josh wants two pieces of one of the pizzas above. Is $\frac{2}{6}$ or $\frac{2}{8}$ of the pizza a greater amount? **Explain** how you know.

Use fraction strips.

On Saturday, the campers paddled $\frac{2}{8}$ of their planned route down the river. On Sunday, they paddled $\frac{2}{3}$ of their route down the river. On which day did the campers paddle farther?

Compare $\frac{2}{8}$ and $\frac{2}{3}$.

- Place a ✓ next to the fraction strips that show more parts in the whole.

- Shade $\frac{2}{8}$. Then shade $\frac{2}{3}$. Compare the shaded parts.

- $\frac{2}{8}$ ◯ $\frac{2}{3}$

1							
$\frac{1}{8}$	$\frac{1}{8}$	$\frac{1}{8}$	$\frac{1}{8}$	$\frac{1}{8}$	$\frac{1}{8}$	$\frac{1}{8}$	$\frac{1}{8}$

$\frac{1}{3}$	$\frac{1}{3}$	$\frac{1}{3}$

Think: $\frac{1}{8}$ is less than $\frac{1}{3}$, so $\frac{2}{8}$ is less than $\frac{2}{3}$.

So, the campers paddled farther on _____.

 Use reasoning.

For her class party, Becky baked two cakes that were the same size. After the party, she had $\frac{3}{4}$ of the carrot cake and $\frac{3}{6}$ of the apple cake left over. Was more carrot cake or more apple cake left over?

Compare $\frac{3}{4}$ and $\frac{3}{6}$.

- Since the numerators are the same, look at the denominators to compare the size of the pieces.

$\frac{3}{4}$ ● $\frac{3}{6}$

- The *more* pieces a whole is divided into,

  the _____ the pieces are.

- The *fewer* pieces a whole is divided into,

  the _____ the pieces are.

ERROR Alert

When comparing fractions with the same numerator, be sure the symbol shows that the fraction with fewer pieces in the whole is the greater fraction.

- $\frac{1}{4}$ is _____ than $\frac{1}{6}$ because there are

  _____ pieces.

- $\frac{3}{4}$ ◯ $\frac{3}{6}$

So, there was more _____ cake left over.

Name _____

Share and Show

1. Shade the models to show $\frac{1}{6}$ and $\frac{1}{4}$.

   Then compare the fractions.

   $\frac{1}{6}$ ◯ $\frac{1}{4}$

Compare. Write <, >, or =.

✓ 2. $\frac{1}{8}$ ◯ $\frac{1}{3}$ ✓ 3. $\frac{3}{4}$ ◯ $\frac{3}{8}$ 4. $\frac{2}{6}$ ◯ $\frac{2}{3}$

5. $\frac{4}{8}$ ◯ $\frac{4}{4}$ 6. $\frac{3}{6}$ ◯ $\frac{3}{6}$ 7. $\frac{8}{4}$ ◯ $\frac{8}{8}$

> **Math Talk** **MATHEMATICAL PRACTICES**
> Explain why $\frac{1}{2}$ is greater than $\frac{1}{4}$.

On Your Own

Compare. Write <, >, or =.

8. $\frac{1}{3}$ ◯ $\frac{1}{4}$ 9. $\frac{2}{3}$ ◯ $\frac{2}{6}$ 10. $\frac{4}{8}$ ◯ $\frac{4}{2}$

11. $\frac{6}{8}$ ◯ $\frac{6}{6}$ 12. $\frac{1}{6}$ ◯ $\frac{1}{2}$ 13. $\frac{7}{8}$ ◯ $\frac{7}{8}$

14. **H.O.T.** **Sense or Nonsense?** James ate $\frac{3}{4}$ of his pancake. David ate $\frac{2}{3}$ of his pancake. Both pancakes are the same size. Who ate more of his pancake?

James said he knows he ate more because he looked at the amounts left. Does his answer make sense? Shade the models. **Explain**.

James

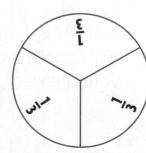

David

_____

_____

🔑 UNLOCK the Problem   REAL WORLD

15. Quinton and Hunter are biking on trails in Katy Trail State Park. They biked $\frac{5}{6}$ mile in the morning and $\frac{5}{8}$ mile in the afternoon. Did they bike a greater distance in the morning or in the afternoon?

a. What do you need to know? _____

b. The numerator is 5 in both fractions, so compare $\frac{1}{6}$ and $\frac{1}{8}$. **Explain**.

_____

c. How can you solve the problem?

d. Complete the sentences.

In the morning, the boys biked

_____ mile.

In the afternoon, they biked

_____ mile.

The boys biked a greater distance

in the _____. $\frac{5}{6}$ ◯ $\frac{5}{8}$

---

16. 🔆 H.O.T. 〉 **Write Math** ▶ Zach has a piece of pie that is $\frac{1}{4}$ of a pie. Max has a piece of pie that is $\frac{1}{2}$ of a pie. Max's piece is smaller than Zach's piece. **Explain** how this could happen. Draw a picture to show your answer.

_____

_____

_____

17. ⭐ **PARCC Test Prep** Before taking a hike, Kate and Dylan each ate part of same-size granola bars. Kate ate $\frac{1}{3}$ of her bar. Dylan ate $\frac{1}{2}$ of his bar. Which of the following correctly compares the amounts of granola bars that were eaten?

Ⓐ $\frac{1}{3} > \frac{1}{2}$

Ⓑ $\frac{1}{2} < \frac{1}{3}$

Ⓒ $\frac{1}{2} > \frac{1}{3}$

Ⓓ $\frac{1}{3} = \frac{1}{2}$

Name _____

Compare Fractions

Essential Question What strategies can you use to compare fractions?

COMMON CORE
Georgia Performance Standard MCC3.NF.3d
Develop understanding of fractions as numbers.

 UNLOCK the Problem REAL WORLD

Luka and Ann are eating the same-size small pizzas. One plate has $\frac{3}{4}$ of Luka's cheese pizza. Another plate has $\frac{5}{6}$ of Ann's sausage pizza. Whose plate has more pizza?

- Circle the numbers you need to compare.
- How many pieces make up each whole pizza?

_____

🔑 Compare $\frac{3}{4}$ and $\frac{5}{6}$.

Missing Pieces Strategy
- You can compare fractions by comparing pieces missing from a whole.

- Shade $\frac{3}{4}$ of Luka's pizza and $\frac{5}{6}$ of Ann's pizza. Each fraction represents a whole that is missing one piece.

- Since $\frac{1}{6}$ ◯ $\frac{1}{4}$, a smaller piece is missing from Ann's pizza.

- If a smaller piece is missing from Ann's pizza, she must have more pizza.

So, _____ plate has more pizza.

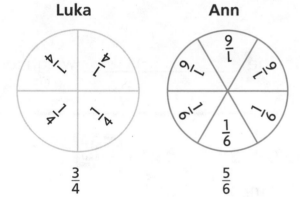

Luka   Ann

$\frac{3}{4}$ $\frac{5}{6}$

MATHEMATICAL PRACTICES

Math Talk Explain how knowing that $\frac{1}{4}$ is less than $\frac{1}{3}$ helps you compare $\frac{3}{4}$ and $\frac{2}{3}$.

Morgan ran $\frac{2}{3}$ mile. Alexa ran $\frac{1}{3}$ mile. Who ran farther?

🔑 Compare $\frac{2}{3}$ and $\frac{1}{3}$.

 $\frac{\square}{3} > \frac{\square}{3}$

Same Denominator Strategy
- When the denominators are the same, you can compare only the number of pieces, or the numerators.

So, _____ ran farther.

Ms. Davis is making a fruit salad with $\frac{3}{4}$ pound of cherries and $\frac{3}{8}$ pound of strawberries. Which weighs less, the cherries or the strawberries?

 Compare $\frac{3}{4}$ and $\frac{3}{8}$.

Same Numerator Strategy
- When the numerators are the same, look at the denominators to compare the size of the pieces.

$\frac{3}{\boxed{}} < \frac{3}{\boxed{}}$

So, the _____ weigh less.

Share and Show MATH BOARD

1. Compare $\frac{7}{8}$ and $\frac{5}{6}$.

   Think: What is missing from each whole?

   Write <, >, or =. $\frac{7}{8} \bigcirc \frac{5}{6}$

Compare. Write <, >, or =. Write the strategy you used.

2. $\frac{1}{2} \bigcirc \frac{2}{3}$

   _____

☑ 3. $\frac{3}{4} \bigcirc \frac{2}{4}$

   _____

☑ 4. $\frac{3}{8} \bigcirc \frac{3}{6}$

   _____

5. $\frac{3}{4} \bigcirc \frac{7}{8}$

   _____

MATHEMATICAL PRACTICES

Math Talk **Explain** how the missing pieces in Exercise 1 help you compare $\frac{7}{8}$ and $\frac{5}{6}$.

On Your Own ....

Compare. Write <, >, or =. Write the strategy you used.

6. $\frac{1}{2}$ ◯ $\frac{2}{2}$

_____

7. $\frac{1}{3}$ ◯ $\frac{1}{4}$

_____

8. $\frac{2}{3}$ ◯ $\frac{5}{6}$

_____

9. $\frac{2}{8}$ ◯ $\frac{0}{8}$

_____

10. $\frac{5}{6}$ ◯ $\frac{5}{6}$

_____

11. $\frac{4}{6}$ ◯ $\frac{4}{2}$

_____

Name a fraction that is less than or greater than the given fraction. Draw to justify your answer.

12. greater than $\frac{2}{3}$ _____

13. less than $\frac{5}{6}$ _____

14. less than $\frac{2}{4}$ _____

15. greater than $\frac{3}{8}$ _____

16. **H.O.T.** **What's the Error?** Jack says that $\frac{5}{8}$ is greater than $\frac{5}{6}$ because the denominator 8 is greater than the denominator 6. Describe Jack's error.

_____

_____

🔑 UNLOCK the Problem — REAL WORLD

17. Tracy is making a blueberry cake. She is using $\frac{4}{4}$ cup of sugar and $\frac{4}{2}$ cups of flour. Which of the following correctly compares the fractions?

Ⓐ $\frac{4}{4} = \frac{4}{2}$ Ⓒ $\frac{4}{2} > \frac{4}{4}$

Ⓑ $\frac{4}{4} > \frac{4}{2}$ Ⓓ $\frac{4}{2} < \frac{4}{4}$

a. What do you need to know?

_____

b. What strategy will you use to compare the fractions?

_____

c. Show the steps you used to solve the problem.

d. Complete the comparison.

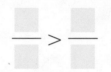

e. Fill in the bubble for the correct answer choice above.

18. Luke and Seth have empty glasses. Mr. Gabel pours $\frac{3}{4}$ cup of orange juice in Seth's glass. Then he pours $\frac{1}{4}$ cup of orange juice in Luke's glass. Which statement is correct?

Ⓐ Luke has less orange juice than Seth.

Ⓑ Luke has more orange juice than Seth.

Ⓒ Seth has less orange juice than Luke.

Ⓓ Luke and Seth have the same amount of orange juice.

Compare and Order Fractions

Essential Question How can you compare and order fractions?

COMMON CORE
Georgia Performance Standard MCC3.NF.3d
Develop understanding of fractions as numbers.

 UNLOCK the Problem REAL WORLD

Harrison, Tad, and Dale ride their bikes to school. Harrison rides $\frac{3}{4}$ mile, Tad rides $\frac{3}{8}$ mile, and Dale rides $\frac{3}{6}$ mile. Compare and order the distances the boys ride from least to greatest.

- Circle the fractions you need to use.
- Underline the sentence that tells you what you need to do.

🔑 Activity 1 Order fractions with the same numerator.

Materials ■ color pencil

You can order fractions by reasoning about the size of unit fractions.

1			
$\frac{1}{4}$	$\frac{1}{4}$	$\frac{1}{4}$	$\frac{1}{4}$

$\frac{1}{8}$	$\frac{1}{8}$	$\frac{1}{8}$	$\frac{1}{8}$	$\frac{1}{8}$	$\frac{1}{8}$	$\frac{1}{8}$	$\frac{1}{8}$

$\frac{1}{6}$	$\frac{1}{6}$	$\frac{1}{6}$	$\frac{1}{6}$	$\frac{1}{6}$	$\frac{1}{6}$

Remember
- The *more* pieces a whole is divided into, the smaller the pieces are.
- The *fewer* pieces a whole is divided into, the larger the pieces are.

STEP 1 Shade one unit fraction for each fraction strip.

_____ is the longest unit fraction.

_____ is the shortest unit fraction.

STEP 2 Shade one more unit fraction for each fraction strip.

Are the shaded fourths still the longest? _____

Are the shaded eighths still the shortest? _____

STEP 3 Continue shading the fraction strips so that three unit fractions are shaded for each strip.

Are the shaded fourths still the longest? _____

Are the shaded eighths still the shortest? _____

$\frac{3}{4}$ mile is the _____ distance. $\frac{3}{8}$ mile is the _____ distance. $\frac{3}{6}$ mile is *between* the other two distances.

So, the distances in order from least to greatest are

_____ mile, _____ mile, _____ mile.

Try This! Order $\frac{2}{6}$, $\frac{2}{3}$, and $\frac{2}{4}$ from greatest to least.

Order the fractions $\frac{2}{6}$, $\frac{2}{3}$, and $\frac{2}{4}$ by thinking about the length of the unit fraction strip. Then label the fractions *shortest*, *between*, or *longest*.

Fraction	Unit Fraction	Length
$\frac{2}{6}$		
$\frac{2}{3}$		
$\frac{2}{4}$		

Math Talk When ordering three fractions, what do you know about the third fraction when you know which fraction is shortest and which fraction is longest? **Explain** your answer.

- When the numerators are the same, think about the

  _____ of the pieces to compare and order fractions.

So, the order from greatest to least is _____, _____, _____.

🔒 Activity 2 Order fractions with the same denominator.

Materials ■ color pencil

Shade fraction strips to order $\frac{5}{8}$, $\frac{8}{8}$, and $\frac{3}{8}$ from least to greatest.

1

| $\frac{1}{8}$ | $\frac{1}{8}$ | $\frac{1}{8}$ | $\frac{1}{8}$ | $\frac{1}{8}$ | $\frac{1}{8}$ | $\frac{1}{8}$ | $\frac{1}{8}$ | Shade $\frac{5}{8}$.

| $\frac{1}{8}$ | $\frac{1}{8}$ | $\frac{1}{8}$ | $\frac{1}{8}$ | $\frac{1}{8}$ | $\frac{1}{8}$ | $\frac{1}{8}$ | $\frac{1}{8}$ | Shade $\frac{8}{8}$.

| $\frac{1}{8}$ | $\frac{1}{8}$ | $\frac{1}{8}$ | $\frac{1}{8}$ | $\frac{1}{8}$ | $\frac{1}{8}$ | $\frac{1}{8}$ | $\frac{1}{8}$ | Shade $\frac{3}{8}$.

- When the denominators are the same, the size of the pieces is the _____.

  So, think about the _____ of pieces to compare and order fractions.

  _____ is the shortest. _____ is the longest.

  _____ is between the other two fractions.

So, the order from least to greatest is _____, _____, _____.

Share and Show MATH BOARD ....

1. Shade the fraction strips to order $\frac{4}{6}$, $\frac{4}{4}$, and $\frac{4}{8}$ from least to greatest.

MATHEMATICAL PRACTICES

Math Talk Explain how you would order the fractions $\frac{2}{3}$, $\frac{1}{3}$, and $\frac{3}{3}$ from greatest to least.

1					
$\frac{1}{6}$	$\frac{1}{6}$	$\frac{1}{6}$	$\frac{1}{6}$	$\frac{1}{6}$	$\frac{1}{6}$

$\frac{1}{4}$	$\frac{1}{4}$	$\frac{1}{4}$	$\frac{1}{4}$

$\frac{1}{8}$	$\frac{1}{8}$	$\frac{1}{8}$	$\frac{1}{8}$	$\frac{1}{8}$	$\frac{1}{8}$	$\frac{1}{8}$	$\frac{1}{8}$

_____ is the shortest. _____ is the longest.

_____ is between the other two lengths. _____, _____, _____

Write the fractions in order from least to greatest.

2. $\frac{1}{2}$, $\frac{0}{2}$, $\frac{2}{2}$ _____, _____, _____

3. $\frac{1}{6}$, $\frac{1}{2}$, $\frac{1}{3}$ _____, _____, _____

On Your Own ....
Write the fractions in order from greatest to least.

4. $\frac{6}{6}$, $\frac{2}{6}$, $\frac{5}{6}$ _____, _____, _____

5. $\frac{1}{8}$, $\frac{1}{4}$, $\frac{1}{2}$ _____, _____, _____

6. $\frac{3}{6}$, $\frac{3}{4}$, $\frac{3}{1}$ _____, _____, _____

7. $\frac{3}{8}$, $\frac{1}{8}$, $\frac{5}{8}$ _____, _____, _____

Write the fractions in order from least to greatest.

8. $\frac{0}{4}$, $\frac{3}{4}$, $\frac{2}{4}$ _____, _____, _____

9. $\frac{2}{4}$, $\frac{2}{6}$, $\frac{2}{8}$ _____, _____, _____

10. H.O.T.

$\frac{6}{3}$, $\frac{6}{2}$, $\frac{6}{8}$ _____, _____, _____

11. H.O.T.

$\frac{4}{2}$, $\frac{2}{2}$, $\frac{8}{2}$ _____, _____, _____

Problem Solving REAL WORLD

12. In fifteen minutes, Greg's sailboat went $\frac{3}{6}$ mile, Gina's sailboat went $\frac{6}{6}$ mile, and Stuart's sailboat went $\frac{4}{6}$ mile. Whose sailboat went the longest distance in fifteen minutes?

_____

Whose sailboat went the shortest distance?

_____

13. **Write Math** ▶ **Pose a Problem** Look back at Exercise 12. Write a similar problem by changing the fraction of a mile each sailboat traveled, so the answers are different from Exercise 12.

_____

_____

_____

_____

SHOW YOUR WORK

14. **H.O.T.** Tom has three pieces of wood. The length of the longest piece is $\frac{3}{4}$ foot. The length of the shortest piece is $\frac{3}{8}$ foot. What might be the length of the third piece of wood?

_____

15. ⭐ **PARCC Test Prep** Jesse ran $\frac{2}{4}$ mile on Monday, $\frac{2}{3}$ mile on Tuesday, and $\frac{2}{8}$ mile on Wednesday. Which list orders the fractions from least to greatest?

Ⓐ $\frac{2}{4}, \frac{2}{3}, \frac{2}{8}$ Ⓒ $\frac{2}{8}, \frac{2}{4}, \frac{2}{3}$

Ⓑ $\frac{2}{3}, \frac{2}{4}, \frac{2}{8}$ Ⓓ $\frac{2}{8}, \frac{2}{3}, \frac{2}{4}$

FOR MORE PRACTICE:
Standards Practice Book

Name _____

Model Equivalent Fractions

Essential Question How can you use models to find equivalent fractions?

COMMON CORE
Georgia Performance Standard MCC3.NF.3a
Develop understanding of fractions as numbers.

Investigate

Materials ■ sheet of paper ■ crayon or color pencil

Two or more fractions that name the same amount are called **equivalent fractions**. You can use a sheet of paper to model fractions equivalent to $\frac{1}{2}$.

A. First, fold a sheet of paper into two equal parts. Open the paper and count the parts.

There are _____ equal parts. Each part is _____ of the paper.

Shade one of the halves. Write $\frac{1}{2}$ on each of the halves.

B. Next, fold the paper in half two times. Open the paper.

Now there are _____ equal parts. Each part is

_____ of the paper.

Write $\frac{1}{4}$ on each of the fourths.

Look at the shaded parts. $\frac{1}{2} = \frac{\boxed{}}{4}$

C. Last, fold the paper in half three times.

Now there are _____ equal parts. Each part is

_____ of the paper.

Write $\frac{1}{8}$ on each of the eighths.

Find the fractions equivalent to $\frac{1}{2}$ on your paper.

So, $\frac{1}{2}$, $\dfrac{\boxed{}}{}$, and $\dfrac{\boxed{}}{}$ are equivalent.

Draw Conclusions

1. **Explain** how many $\frac{1}{8}$ parts are equivalent to one $\frac{1}{4}$ part on your paper.

_____

_____

2. **H.O.T.** **Analyze** What do you notice about how the numerators changed for the shaded part as you folded the paper? _____

What does this tell you about the change in the number of parts? _____

How did the denominators change for the shaded part as you folded? _____

What does this tell you about the change in the size of the parts? _____

Make Connections

You can use a number line to find equivalent fractions.

MATHEMATICAL PRACTICES

Math Talk Explain how the number of sixths in a distance on the number line is related to the number of thirds in the same distance.

Find a fraction equivalent to $\frac{2}{3}$.

Materials ■ fraction strips

STEP 1 Draw a point on the number line to represent the distance $\frac{2}{3}$.

_____

STEP 2 Use fraction strips to divide the number line into sixths. At the end of each strip, draw a mark on the number line and label the marks to show sixths.

_____

STEP 3 Identify the fraction that names the same point as $\frac{2}{3}$. _____

So, $\frac{2}{3} = \frac{}{6}$.

Name _____

Share and Show

Shade the model. Then divide the pieces to find the equivalent fraction.

1.
$$\frac{1}{4} = \frac{}{8}$$

☑ 2.
$$\frac{2}{3} = \frac{}{6}$$

MATHEMATICAL PRACTICES

Math Talk Explain how you decided to divide the pieces in Exercise 2.

Use the number line to find the equivalent fraction.

3.

$$\frac{0}{6} \quad \frac{1}{6} \quad \frac{2}{6} \quad \frac{3}{6} \quad \frac{4}{6} \quad \frac{5}{6} \quad \frac{6}{6}$$

$$\frac{0}{2} \qquad \frac{1}{2} \qquad \frac{2}{2}$$

$$\frac{1}{2} = \frac{}{6}$$

☑ 4.

$$\frac{0}{8} \quad \frac{1}{8} \quad \frac{2}{8} \quad \frac{3}{8} \quad \frac{4}{8} \quad \frac{5}{8} \quad \frac{6}{8} \quad \frac{7}{8} \quad \frac{8}{8}$$

$$\frac{0}{4} \qquad \frac{1}{4} \qquad \frac{2}{4} \qquad \frac{3}{4} \qquad \frac{4}{4}$$

$$\frac{3}{4} = \frac{}{8}$$

5.

$$\frac{0}{8} \quad \frac{1}{8} \quad \frac{2}{8} \quad \frac{3}{8} \quad \frac{4}{8} \quad \frac{5}{8} \quad \frac{6}{8} \quad \frac{7}{8} \quad \frac{8}{8}$$

$$\frac{0}{2} \qquad \frac{1}{2} \qquad \frac{2}{2}$$

$$\frac{1}{2} = \frac{}{8}$$

6.

$$\frac{0}{6} \quad \frac{1}{6} \quad \frac{2}{6} \quad \frac{3}{6} \quad \frac{4}{6} \quad \frac{5}{6} \quad \frac{6}{6}$$

$$\frac{0}{3} \qquad \frac{1}{3} \qquad \frac{2}{3} \qquad \frac{3}{3}$$

$$\frac{3}{3} = \frac{}{6}$$

7. **Write Math** ▶ **Explain** why $\frac{2}{2} = 1$. Write another fraction that is equal to 1. Draw to justify your answer.

_____

_____

Connect to Reading

Summarize

You can *summarize* the information in a problem by underlining it or writing the information needed to answer a question.

Read the problem. Underline the important information.

Mrs. Akers bought three sandwiches that were the same size. She cut the first one into thirds. She cut the second one into fourths and the third one into sixths. Marian ate 2 pieces of the first sandwich. Jason ate 2 pieces of the second sandwich. Marcos ate 3 pieces of the third sandwich. Which children ate the same amount of a sandwich? **Explain.**

The first sandwich was cut into _____.	The second sandwich was cut into _____.	The third sandwich was cut into _____.
Marian ate _____ pieces of the sandwich. Shade the part Marian ate.	Jason ate _____ pieces of the sandwich. Shade the part Jason ate.	Marcos ate _____ pieces of the sandwich. Shade the part Marcos ate.
Marian ate — of the first sandwich.	Jason ate — of the second sandwich.	Marcos ate — of the third sandwich.

Are all the fractions equivalent? _____

Which fractions are equivalent? — = —

So, _____ and _____ ate the same amount of a sandwich.

Name _____

Equivalent Fractions

Essential Question How can you use models to name equivalent fractions?

COMMON CORE
Georgia Performance Standard MCC3.NF.3b
Develop understanding of fractions as numbers.

🔑 UNLOCK the Problem REAL WORLD

Cole brought a submarine sandwich to the picnic. He shared the sandwich equally with 3 friends. The sandwich was cut into eighths. What are two ways to describe the part of the sandwich each friend ate?

Cole grouped the smaller pieces into twos. Draw circles to show equal groups of two pieces to show what each friend ate.

> • How many people shared the sandwich?
>
> _____

There are 4 equal groups. Each group is $\frac{1}{4}$ of the whole sandwich. So, each friend ate $\frac{1}{4}$ of the whole sandwich.

How many eighths did each friend eat? _____

$\frac{1}{4}$ and _____ are equivalent fractions since they both

name the _____ amount of the sandwich.

So, $\frac{1}{4}$ and _____ of the sandwich are two ways to describe the part of the sandwich each friend ate.

Try This! Circle equal groups. Write an equivalent fraction for the shaded part of the whole.

$$\frac{4}{8} = \underline{\quad\quad}$$

Math Talk

MATHEMATICAL PRACTICES

Explain a different way you could have circled the equal groups.

🔒 Example Model the problem.

Heidi ate $\frac{3}{6}$ of her fruit bar. Molly ate $\frac{4}{8}$ of her fruit bar, which is the same size. Which girl ate more of her fruit bar?

Shade $\frac{3}{6}$ of Heidi's fruit bar and $\frac{4}{8}$ of Molly's fruit bar.

- Is $\frac{3}{6}$ greater than, less than, or equal to $\frac{4}{8}$? _____

So, both girls ate the _____ amount.

Heidi

$\frac{1}{6}$	$\frac{1}{6}$	$\frac{1}{6}$
$\frac{1}{6}$	$\frac{1}{6}$	$\frac{1}{6}$

Molly

$\frac{1}{8}$	$\frac{1}{8}$	$\frac{1}{8}$	$\frac{1}{8}$
$\frac{1}{8}$	$\frac{1}{8}$	$\frac{1}{8}$	$\frac{1}{8}$

Try This! Each shape is 1 whole. Write an equivalent fraction for the shaded part of the models.

$$\frac{6}{3} = \frac{\boxed{}}{6}$$

Share and Show MATH BOARD ·

1. Each shape is 1 whole. Use the model to find the equivalent fraction.

$$\frac{2}{4} = \frac{\boxed{}}{2}$$

Math Talk MATHEMATICAL PRACTICES

Explain why both fractions name the same amount.

Each shape is 1 whole. Shade the model to find the equivalent fraction.

✓ 2.

$$\frac{2}{4} = \frac{\boxed{}}{8}$$

3.

$$\frac{12}{6} = \frac{\boxed{}}{3}$$

4. Andy swam $\frac{8}{8}$ mile in a race. Use the number line to find a fraction that is equivalent to $\frac{8}{8}$.

$$\frac{8}{8} = \frac{\boxed{}}{\boxed{}}$$

Name _____

Circle equal groups to find the equivalent fraction.

5.

$$\frac{3}{6} = \frac{\boxed{}}{2}$$

6.

$$\frac{6}{6} = \frac{\boxed{}}{3}$$

On Your Own ....

Each shape is 1 whole. Shade the model to find the equivalent fraction.

7.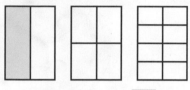

$$\frac{1}{2} = \frac{2}{\boxed{}} = \frac{\boxed{}}{8}$$

8.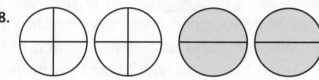

$$\frac{8}{\boxed{}} = \frac{4}{2}$$

Circle equal groups to find the equivalent fraction.

9.

$$\frac{6}{8} = \frac{\boxed{}}{4}$$

10.

$$\frac{2}{6} = \frac{\boxed{}}{3}$$

11. Write the fraction that names the shaded part of each circle.

_____   _____   _____   _____   _____

Which pairs of fractions are equivalent? _____

12. Matt cut his small pizza into 6 equal pieces and ate 4 of them. Josh cut his small pizza, which is the same size, into 3 equal pieces and ate 2 of them. Write fractions for the amount they each ate. Are the fractions equivalent? **Draw** to explain.

_____

Problem Solving REAL WORLD

13. Christy bought 8 muffins. She chose 2 chocolate, 2 banana, and 4 blueberry. She and her family ate the chocolate and banana muffins for breakfast. What fraction of the muffins did they eat? Write an equivalent fraction. Draw a picture.

_____

_____

14. **H.O.T.** **Write Math** ➤ After dessert, $\frac{2}{3}$ of a cherry pie is left. Suppose 4 friends want to share it equally. What fraction names how much of the whole pie each friend will get? Use the model on the right. **Explain** your answer.

_____

_____

15. There are 16 people having lunch. Each person wants $\frac{1}{4}$ of a pizza. How many whole pizzas are needed? Draw a picture to show your answer.

_____

16. Lucy has 5 brownies. Each brownie is cut in half. What fraction names all of the brownie halves? $\frac{\ }{2}$

   What if Lucy cuts each part of the brownie into 2 equal pieces to share with friends? What fraction names all of the brownie pieces now? $\frac{\ }{4}$

   $\frac{\ }{2}$ and $\frac{\ }{4}$ are equivalent fractions.

17. ⭐ **PARCC Test Prep** Mr. Peters made an apple pie. There is $\frac{6}{8}$ of the pie left over. Which fraction is equal to the part of the pie that is left over?

   Ⓐ $\frac{1}{4}$ Ⓑ $\frac{2}{4}$ Ⓒ $\frac{1}{2}$ Ⓓ $\frac{3}{4}$

Name _____

▶ **Vocabulary**

Choose the best term from the box to complete the sentence.

Vocabulary
equivalent fractions
unit fractions

1. _____ are two or more fractions that name the same amount. (p. 427)

▶ **Concepts and Skills**

Compare. Write <, >, or =. MCC3.NF.3d

2. $\frac{1}{6}$ ◯ $\frac{1}{4}$

3. $\frac{2}{8}$ ◯ $\frac{2}{3}$

4. $\frac{4}{2}$ ◯ $\frac{1}{2}$

5. $\frac{7}{8}$ ◯ $\frac{3}{8}$

6. $\frac{5}{6}$ ◯ $\frac{2}{3}$

7. $\frac{3}{4}$ ◯ $\frac{7}{8}$

Write the fractions in order from least to greatest.

MCC3.NF.3d

8. $\frac{1}{5}, \frac{4}{5}, \frac{2}{5}$ _____, _____, _____

9. $\frac{2}{5}, \frac{2}{3}, \frac{2}{4}$ _____, _____, _____

10. $\frac{3}{4}, \frac{2}{4}, \frac{1}{4}$ _____, _____, _____

11. $\frac{4}{6}, \frac{6}{6}, \frac{5}{6}$ _____, _____, _____

Use the model or number line to find the equivalent fraction. MCC3.NF.3a, MCC3.NF.3b

12.

$\frac{2}{3} = \frac{\square}{6}$

13.

$\frac{2}{4} = \frac{\square}{2}$

14.

$\frac{3}{4} = \frac{\square}{8}$

Fill in the bubble for the correct answer choice.

15. Two walls in Tiffany's room are the same size. Tiffany paints $\frac{1}{4}$ of one wall. Jake paints $\frac{1}{8}$ of the other wall. Which of the following correctly compares the fractions? MCC3.NF.3d

Ⓐ $\frac{1}{4} < \frac{1}{8}$ Ⓒ $\frac{1}{4} > \frac{1}{8}$

Ⓑ $\frac{1}{8} = \frac{1}{4}$ Ⓓ $\frac{1}{8} > \frac{1}{4}$

16. Matthew ran $\frac{5}{8}$ mile during track practice. Paul ran $\frac{5}{6}$ mile. Which of the following correctly compares the fractions? MCC3.NF.3d

Ⓐ $\frac{5}{6} = \frac{5}{8}$

Ⓑ $\frac{5}{8} < \frac{5}{6}$

Ⓒ $\frac{5}{8} > \frac{5}{6}$

Ⓓ $\frac{5}{6} < \frac{5}{8}$

17. Eduardo, Max, and Suzie are reading the same book for school. Eduardo has read $\frac{3}{8}$ of the book. Max has read $\frac{2}{8}$ of the book and Suzie has read $\frac{4}{8}$ of the book. Which shows the fractions in order from greatest to least? MCC3.NF.3d

Ⓐ $\frac{4}{8}, \frac{3}{8}, \frac{2}{8}$

Ⓑ $\frac{2}{8}, \frac{3}{8}, \frac{4}{8}$

Ⓒ $\frac{3}{8}, \frac{2}{8}, \frac{4}{8}$

Ⓓ $\frac{4}{8}, \frac{2}{8}, \frac{3}{8}$

Name _____

▶ **Vocabulary**

Choose the best term from the box to complete the sentence.

Vocabulary
equivalent fractions
unit fraction

1. A _____ has 1 as its numerator. (p. 375)

▶ **Concepts and Skills**

Compare. Write <, >, or =. ▌MCC3.NF.3d

2. $\frac{2}{6} \bigcirc \frac{2}{8}$

3. $\frac{1}{4} \bigcirc \frac{1}{8}$

4. $\frac{3}{8} \bigcirc \frac{7}{8}$

5. $\frac{2}{4} \bigcirc \frac{2}{4}$

6. $\frac{3}{3} \bigcirc \frac{2}{3}$

7. $\frac{4}{6} \bigcirc \frac{4}{2}$

Write the fractions in order from least to greatest. ▌MCC3.NF.3d

8. $\frac{1}{6}, \frac{4}{6}, \frac{3}{6}$ _____, _____, _____

9. $\frac{1}{8}, \frac{1}{2}, \frac{1}{3}$ _____, _____, _____

10. $\frac{3}{3}, \frac{1}{3}, \frac{0}{3}$ _____, _____, _____

11. $\frac{4}{8}, \frac{4}{4}, \frac{4}{6}$ _____, _____, _____

Use the model or number line to find the equivalent fraction. ▌MCC3.NF.3a, MCC3.NF.3b

12.

$\frac{3}{4} = \frac{}{8}$

13.

$\frac{2}{8} = \frac{}{4}$

14.

$\frac{1}{3} = \frac{}{6}$

 Assessment Options
Unit Test

Fill in the bubble for the correct answer choice.

15. Tali ran $\frac{3}{8}$ mile at the park. Which distance is less than $\frac{3}{8}$ mile? ▌MCC3.NF.3d

Ⓐ $\frac{1}{8}$ mile   Ⓒ $\frac{4}{8}$ mile

Ⓑ $\frac{7}{8}$ mile   Ⓓ $\frac{3}{8}$ mile

16. Mrs. Harrison has four red flowers for a party. One sixth of the flowers for the party are red. How many flowers does Mrs. Harrison have?

▌MCC3.NF.1

Ⓐ 6   Ⓒ 16

Ⓑ 12   Ⓓ 24

17. David has 12 balloons to share with 6 friends. How many balloons does each friend get? ▌MCC3.NF.1

Ⓐ 2   Ⓒ 12

Ⓑ 6   Ⓓ 24

18. Katherine bakes 40 muffins. One eighth of the muffins are blueberry. How many of the muffins are blueberry? ▌MCC3.NF.1

Ⓐ 20   Ⓒ 10

Ⓑ 15   Ⓓ 5

Fill in the bubble for the correct answer choice.

19. Marissa is decorating a paper plate. She is shading $\frac{1}{4}$ of the plate blue. Which model shows $\frac{1}{4}$ shaded?

MCC3.NF.3a, MCC3.NF.3b

Ⓐ

Ⓒ

Ⓑ

Ⓓ

20. Olivia is painting two same-size tiles for art class. She paints $\frac{7}{8}$ of one tile green. Then Olivia paints $\frac{5}{8}$ of the other tile yellow. Which of the following correctly compares the painted parts of the two tiles? MCC3.NF.3d

Ⓐ $\frac{5}{8} > \frac{7}{8}$

Ⓑ $\frac{7}{8} > \frac{5}{8}$

Ⓒ $\frac{5}{8} = \frac{7}{8}$

Ⓓ $\frac{7}{8} < \frac{5}{8}$

21. Nicholas ran $\frac{5}{6}$ mile on Monday, $\frac{2}{6}$ mile on Tuesday, and $\frac{6}{6}$ mile on Wednesday. Which list orders the fractions from least to greatest?

MCC3.NF.3d

Ⓐ $\frac{2}{6}, \frac{5}{6}, \frac{6}{6}$

Ⓑ $\frac{2}{6}, \frac{6}{6}, \frac{5}{6}$

Ⓒ $\frac{6}{6}, \frac{5}{6}, \frac{2}{6}$

Ⓓ $\frac{5}{6}, \frac{2}{6}, \frac{6}{6}$

▶ **Performance Assessment Task** MCC3.NF.3a, MCC3.NF.3b, MCC3.NF.3d

22. Mrs. Reed baked four same-size cakes for a party.

★ Mrs. Reed cuts one cake into fourths and one into sixths. Which cake has more pieces? Which cake has larger pieces? **Explain**.

_____

_____

_____

★★ Mrs. Reed cuts one cake into thirds, one into fourths, one into sixths, and one into eighths. At the end of the party, there are two pieces from each cake left over. Which cake has the greatest amount left over? **Explain** how you got your answer.

_____

_____

_____

_____

★★★ Mrs. Reed cut the cakes as shown at the right. At the end of the party, equivalent amounts of two pairs of cakes were left over. Shade equivalent amounts on pairs of rectangles to show the cake that might have been left over. Then write two pairs of equivalent fractions. **Summarize** how you got your answer.

_____

_____

_____

_____

Measurement

Show What You Know

Check your understanding of important skills.

Name _____

▶ **Time to the Half Hour** Read the clock. Write the time.

1. _____

2. _____

▶ **Skip Count by Fives**

Skip count by fives. Write the missing numbers.

3. 5, 10, 15, _____, 25, _____, 35   **4.** 55, 60, _____, 70, _____, _____, 85

▶ **Inches** Use a ruler to measure the length to the nearest inch.

5.

6.

about _____ inches   about _____ inch

MATH DETECTIVE

WITH

CARMEN SANDIEGO™

You can look at the time the sun rises and sets to find the amount of daylight each day. The table shows the time the sun rose and set from January 10 to January 14 in Philadelphia, Pennsylvania. Be a Math Detective to find which day had the least daylight and which day had the most daylight.

Sunrise and Sunset Times		
Date	**Sunrise**	**Sunset**
Jan 10	7:22 A.M.	4:55 P.M.
Jan 11	7:22 A.M.	4:56 P.M.
Jan 12	7:22 A.M.	4:57 P.M.
Jan 13	7:21 A.M.	4:58 P.M.
Jan 14	7:21 A.M.	4:59 P.M.

Vocabulary Builder

► **Visualize It** •

Complete the graphic organizer by using the words with a ✓. Write the words in order from the greatest to the least length of time.

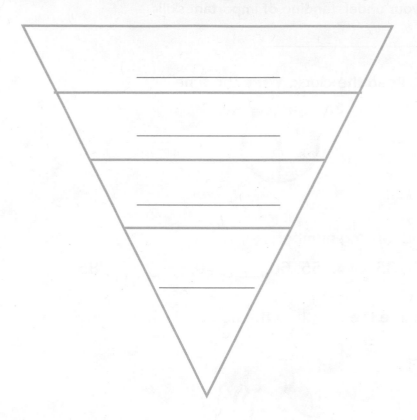

Review Words

fourth

half

✓ half hour

✓ hour (hr)

inch (in.)

✓ quarter hour

Preview Words

A.M.

elapsed time

gram (g)

kilogram (kg)

liquid volume

liter (L)

mass

midnight

✓ minute (min)

noon

P.M.

perimeter

► **Understand Vocabulary** • • • • • • • • • • • • • • • • •

Write the word that answers the riddle.

1. I am written with times after midnight and before noon. _____

2. I am the time when it is 12:00 in the daytime. _____

3. I am the amount of liquid in a container. _____

4. I am the time that passes from the start of an activity to the end of that activity. _____

5. I am the amount of matter in an object. _____

GO **Online** • eStudent Edition • Multimedia eGlossary

Name _____

Time to the Minute

Essential Question How can you tell time to the nearest minute?

COMMON CORE
Georgia Performance Standard MCC3.MD.1
Solve problems involving measurement and estimation of intervals of time, liquid volumes, and masses of objects.

🔑 UNLOCK the Problem REAL WORLD

Groundhog Day is February 2. People say that if a groundhog can see its shadow on that morning, winter will last another 6 weeks. The clock shows the time when the groundhog saw its shadow. What time was it?

- Underline the question.
- Where will you look to find the time?

_____

🔑 Example

Look at the time on this clock face.

- What does the hour hand tell you?

_____

- What does the minute hand tell you?

_____

In 1 **minute**, the minute hand moves from one mark to the next on a clock. It takes 5 minutes for the minute hand to move from one number to the next on a clock.

You can count on by fives to tell time to five minutes. Count zero at the 12.

0, 5, 10, 15, _____, _____, _____, _____

So, the groundhog saw its shadow at _____.

Write: 7:35

Read:

- seven _____

- thirty-five minutes after _____

MATHEMATICAL PRACTICES

Math Talk How does skip counting by fives help you tell the time when the minute hand points to a number?

- Is 7:35 a reasonable answer? **Explain.** _____

_____

Time to the Minute

Count by fives and ones to help you.

🔒 One Way Find minutes after the hour.

Look at the time on this clock face.

- What does the hour hand tell you?

  _____

- What does the minute hand tell you?

  _____

Count on by fives and ones from the 12 on the clock to where the minute hand is pointing. Write the missing counting numbers next to the clock.

When a clock shows 30 or fewer minutes after the hour, you can read the time as a number of minutes *after* the hour.

Write: _____

Read:

- twenty-three minutes after _____

- one _____

🔒 Another Way Find minutes before the hour.

Look at the time on this clock face.

- What does the hour hand tell you?

  _____

- What does the minute hand tell you?

  _____

Now count by fives and ones from the 12 on the clock back to where the minute hand is pointing. Write the missing counting numbers next to the clock.

When a clock shows 31 or more minutes after the hour, you can read the time as a number of minutes *before* the next hour.

Write: 2:43

Read:

- seventeen _____ before three

- two _____

 ERROR Alert

Remember that time *after* the hour uses the previous hour, and time *before* the hour uses the next hour.

Name _____

Share and Show

1. How would you use counting and the minute hand to find the time shown on this clock? Write the time.

_____

Write the time. Write one way you can read the time.

2.

_____ _____

☑ 3.

_____ _____

☑ 4.

_____ _____

> **Math Talk** MATHEMATICAL PRACTICES
> **Explain** how you know when to stop counting by fives and start counting by ones when counting minutes after an hour.

On Your Own

Write the time. Write one way you can read the time.

5.

3:12

_____ _____

6.

_____ _____

7.

_____ _____

Write the time another way.

8. 34 minutes after 5

_____

9. 11 minutes before 6

_____

10. 22 minutes after 11

_____

11. 5 minutes before 12

_____

Problem Solving REAL WORLD

Use the clocks for 12–13.

12. How many minutes later in the day did the groundhog see its shadow in Pennsylvania than in New York?

_____

13. **What if** the groundhog in Pennsylvania saw its shadow 5 minutes later? What time would this be?

_____

Time of Day the Groundhog Saw Its Shadow

NY   PA

14. If you look at your watch and the hour hand is between the 8 and the 9 and the minute hand is on the 11, what time is it?

_____

········ **SHOW YOUR WORK** ········

15. **H.O.T.** What time is it when the hour hand and the minute hand are both pointing to the same number?

_____

16. **Write Math** ➤ Lucy said the time is 4:46 on her digital watch. **Explain** where the hands on the analog clock are pointing when it is 4:46.

_____

_____

_____

_____

17. ★**PARCC Test Prep** What time is shown on this clock?

Ⓐ 4:23   Ⓒ 9:20

Ⓑ 4:47   Ⓓ 9:23

Name _____

A.M. and P.M.

Essential Question How can you tell when to use A.M. and P.M. with time?

COMMON CORE
Georgia Performance Standard MCC3.MD.1
Solve problems involving measurement and estimation of intervals of time, liquid volumes, and masses of objects.

🔑 UNLOCK the Problem REAL WORLD

Lauren's family is going hiking tomorrow at 7:00. How should Lauren write the time to show that they are going in the morning, not in the evening?

You can use a number line to show the sequence or order of events. It can help you understand the number of hours in a day.

- Circle the helpful information that tells about the hiking time.
- What do you need to find?

_____

_____

Think: The distance from one mark to the next mark represents one hour.

12:00 midnight   6:00 A.M.   12:00 noon   **6:00 P.M.**   12:00 midnight

🔓 **Tell time after midnight.**

Midnight is 12:00 at night.

The times after midnight and before noon are written with **A.M.**

7:00 in the morning is written as

7:00 _____

After Midnight and Before Noon

A.M.

So, Lauren should write the hiking time as 7:00 _____

- Find the mark that shows 7:00 A.M. on the number line above. Circle the mark.

Math Talk MATHEMATICAL PRACTICES How are the number line on this page and the clock face alike? How are they different?

🔑 **Tell time after noon.**

Callie's family is going for a canoe ride at 3:00 in the afternoon. How should Callie write the time?

Noon is 12:00 in the daytime.

The times after noon and before midnight are written with **P.M.**

3:00 in the afternoon is written

as 3:00 _____

After Noon and Before Midnight

So, Callie should write the time as 3:00 _____

Share and Show

1. Name two things you do in the A.M. hours.
   Name two things you do in the P.M. hours.

   _____

   _____

Write the time for the activity. Use A.M. or P.M.

2. ride a bicycle

_____

☑ 3. make a sandwich

_____

☑ 4. get ready for bed

_____

5. This morning Sam woke up at the time shown on this clock. Write the time using A.M. or P.M. _____

Math Talk MATHEMATICAL PRACTICES
Explain how you decide whether to use A.M. or P.M. when you write the time.

Name _____

On Your Own ....

Write the time for the activity. Use A.M. or P.M.

6. eat breakfast

_____

7. have science class

_____

8. play softball

_____

9. go to the store

_____

10. leave on a morning airplane flight

_____

11. look up at stars

_____

Write the time. Use A.M. or P.M.

12. quarter after 9:00 in the morning

_____

13. 6 minutes after 7:00 in the morning

_____

14. one half hour past midnight

_____

15. 18 minutes before noon

_____

16. Daylight saving time begins on the second Sunday in March at 2:00 in the morning. Write the time.

Use A.M. or P.M. _____

17. H.O.T. Write Math ▶ From midnight to noon each day, how many times does the minute hand on a clock pass 6? **Explain** how you found your answer.

_____

_____

_____

© Houghton Mifflin Harcourt Publishing Company

🔑 UNLOCK the Problem ▸ REAL WORLD ◂

18. Lea and her father arrived at the scenic overlook 15 minutes before noon and left 12 minutes after noon. Using A.M. or P.M., write the time when Lea and her father arrived at the scenic overlook and the time when they left.

a. What do you need to find? _____

_____

_____

b. What do you need to find first?

_____

c. Show the steps you used to solve the problem.

d. Complete the sentences.

Lea and her father arrived at the

overlook _____ minutes

_____ noon.

They arrived at _____ _____.M.
Lea and her father left the overlook

at _____ minutes _____ noon.

They left at _____ _____.M.

---

19. Lauren was supposed to meet her family at the parking lot at 10:00 in the morning. Lauren arrived 20 minutes early. At what time did Lauren arrive at the parking lot? Use A.M. or P.M.

20. ⭐ **PARCC Test Prep** At which time are most third graders asleep?

Ⓐ 9:23 A.M.

Ⓑ 2:41 P.M.

Ⓒ 7:16 P.M.

Ⓓ 1:38 A.M.

Measure Time Intervals

Essential Question How can you measure elapsed time in minutes?

COMMON CORE
Georgia Performance Standard MCC3.MD.1
Solve problems involving measurement and estimation of intervals of time, liquid volumes, and masses of objects.

🔑 UNLOCK the Problem ⟩ REAL WORLD

Alicia and her family visited the Kennedy Space Center. They watched a movie that began at 4:10 P.M. and ended at 4:53 P.M. How long did the movie last?

To find **elapsed time**, find the amount of time that passes from the start of an activity to the end of the activity.

- What time did the movie begin?

  _____

- What time did the movie end?

  _____

- Underline the question.

🔒 One Way Use a number line.

STEP 1 Find the time on the number line that the movie began.

STEP 2 Count on to the ending time, 4:53. Count on by tens for each 10 minutes. Count on by ones for each minute. Write the times below the number line.

STEP 3 Draw the jumps on the number line to show the minutes from 4:10 to 4:53. Record the minutes. Then add them.

10 min + _____ + _____ + _____ + 1 min + _____ + _____

4:10   4:20   _____ _____ 4:51 _____ _____

$10 + 10 + 10 + 10 + 1 + 1 + 1 =$ _____

The elapsed time from 4:10 P.M. to 4:53 P.M. is _____ minutes.

So, the movie lasted _____ minutes.

Math Talk MATHEMATICAL PRACTICES Describe another way you can use jumps on the number line to find the elapsed time from 4:10 P.M. to 4:53 P.M.

🔑 Other Ways

Start time: 4:10 P.M. End time: 4:53 P.M.

Ⓐ Use an analog clock.

STEP 1 Find the starting time on the clock.

STEP 2 Count the minutes by counting on by fives and ones to 4:53 P.M. Write the missing counting numbers next to the clock.

So, the elapsed time is _____ minutes.

Ⓑ Use subtraction.

STEP 1 Write the ending time. Then write the starting time so that the hours and minutes line up.

STEP 2 The hours are the same, so subtract the minutes.

$$4 : \boxed{} \quad \leftarrow \text{end time}$$
$$- 4 : \boxed{} \quad \leftarrow \text{start time}$$
$$\boxed{} \quad \leftarrow \text{elapsed time}$$

Try This! Find the elapsed time in minutes two ways.

Start time: 10:05 A.M. End time: 10:30 A.M.

Ⓐ Use a number line.

STEP 1 Find 10:05 on the number line. Count on from 10:05 to 10:30. Draw marks and record the times on the number line. Then draw and label the jumps.

Think: Count on using longer amounts of time that make sense.

10:05

STEP 2 Add to find the total minutes from 10:05 to 10:30.

From 10:05 A.M. to _____ is _____ minutes.

So, the elapsed time is _____ minutes.

Ⓑ Use subtraction.

Think: The hours are the same, so subtract the minutes.

$$10 : 30$$
$$- 10 : 05$$
$$\boxed{}$$

MATHEMATICAL PRACTICES

Math Talk Which method do you prefer to use to find elapsed time? **Explain.**

Name _____

Share and Show   ....

1. Use the number line to find the elapsed time
   from 1:15 P.M. to 1:40 P.M. _____

1:15

Find the elapsed time.

✓ 2. Start: 11:35 A.M.   End: 11:54 A.M.

_____

←————————————————————→

_____

✓ 3. Start: 4:20 P.M.   End: 5:00 P.M.

_____

Math Talk 〔MATHEMATICAL PRACTICES〕 **Explain** how to use a number line to find the elapsed time from 11:10 A.M. until noon.

On Your Own ....

Find the elapsed time.

4. Start: 8:35 P.M.   End: 8:55 P.M.

_____

5. Start: 10:10 A.M.   End: 10:41 A.M.

_____

6. Start: 9:25 A.M.   End: 9:43 A.M.

←————————————————————→

_____

7. Start: 2:15 P.M.   End: 2:52 P.M.

←————————————————————→

_____

Problem Solving REAL WORLD

8. John started reading his book about outer space at quarter after nine in the morning. He read until quarter to ten in the morning. How long did John read his book?

_____

SHOW YOUR WORK

9. **What's the Question?** Tim and Alicia arrived at the rocket display at 3:40 P.M. Alicia left the display at 3:56 P.M. Tim left at 3:49 P.M. The answer is Alicia.

_____

_____

10. **H.O.T.** At the space center, Karen bought a model of a shuttle. She started working on the model the next day at 11:13 A.M. She worked until leaving for lunch at 11:51 A.M. After lunch, she worked on the model again from 1:29 P.M. until 1:48 P.M. How long did Karen work on the model?

11. **Write Math** Tim's family toured the Astronaut Hall of Fame from 2:05 P.M. to 2:45 P.M. **Explain** how you know that the tour was more than 30 minutes.

_____

_____

12. ⭐ **PARCC Test Prep** Kira got on the tour bus at 5:15 P.M. She got off the bus at 5:37 P.M. How long was Kira on the bus?

Ⓐ 15 minutes   Ⓒ 37 minutes

Ⓑ 22 minutes   Ⓓ 52 minutes

Name _____

Use Time Intervals

Essential Question How can you find a starting time or an ending time when you know the elapsed time?

COMMON CORE
Georgia Performance Standard MCC3.MD.1
Solve problems involving measurement and estimation of intervals of time, liquid volumes, and masses of objects.

🔑 UNLOCK the Problem

Al begins working on his oceans project at 1:30 P.M. He spends 42 minutes painting a model of Earth and labeling the oceans. At what time does Al finish working on his project?

• What time is given?
_____
_____

• What time do you need to find?
_____
_____

🔓 One Way Use a number line to find the ending time.

STEP 1 Find the time on the number line when Al started working on the project.

STEP 2 Count forward on the number line to add the elapsed time. Draw and label the jumps to show the minutes.

> **Think:** I can break apart 42 minutes into shorter amounts of time.

STEP 3 Write the times below the number line.

1:30 P.M.

MATHEMATICAL PRACTICES
Math Talk Explain how you decided what size jumps to make on the number line.

The jumps end at _____

So, Al finishes working on his project at _____

🔓 Another Way Use a clock to find the ending time.

STEP 1 Find the starting time on the clock.

STEP 2 Count on by fives and ones for the elapsed time of 42 minutes. Write the missing counting numbers next to the clock.

So, the ending time is _____

Find Starting Times

Whitney went swimming in the ocean for
25 minutes. She finished swimming at 11:15 A.M.
At what time did Whitney start swimming?

🔒 One Way Use a number line to find the starting time.

STEP 1 Find the time on the number line when Whitney finished swimming in the ocean.

STEP 2 Count back on the number line to subtract the elapsed time. Draw and label the jumps to show the minutes.

STEP 3 Write the times below the number line.

<--|-->
                                          11:15 A.M.

You jumped back to _____

So, Whitney started swimming at _____

> **Math Talk** MATHEMATICAL PRACTICES
> Explain how the problem on this page is different from the problem on page 401.

🔒 Another Way Use a clock to find the starting time.

STEP 1 Find the ending time on the clock.

STEP 2 Count back by fives for the elapsed time of 25 minutes. Write the missing counting numbers next to the clock.

So, the starting time is _____

Share and Show ....

1. Use the number line to find the starting time if the

elapsed time is 35 minutes. _____

<--|-->
                                          5:10 P.M.

> **Math Talk** MATHEMATICAL PRACTICES
> Explain how to find the starting time when you know the ending time and the elapsed time.

Name _____

Find the ending time.

✓ 2. Starting time: 1:40 P.M.
Elapsed time: 33 minutes

⟵————————————⟶

✓ 3. Starting time: 9:55 A.M.
Elapsed time: 27 minutes

On Your Own ....

Find the starting time.

4. Ending time: 3:05 P.M.
Elapsed time: 40 minutes

⟵————————————⟶

5. Ending time: 8:06 A.M.
Elapsed time: 16 minutes

Find the ending time.

6. Starting time: 10:20 A.M.
Elapsed time: 56 minutes

⟵————————————⟶

7. Starting time: 5:54 P.M.
Elapsed time: 15 minutes

H.O.T. **Algebra** **Complete the table.**

	Starting Time	Ending Time	Elapsed Time
8.	3:13 P.M.		65 minutes
9.		12:17 P.M.	35 minutes

Problem Solving REAL WORLD

10. **Write Math** Suzi began fishing at 10:30 A.M. and fished until 11:10 A.M. James finished fishing at 11:45 A.M. He fished for the same length of time as Suzi. At what time did James start fishing? **Explain**.

_____

_____

_____

11. ⭐ **PARCC Test Prep** Dante's surfing lesson began at 2:35 P.M. His lesson lasted 45 minutes. At what time did Dante's lesson end?

Ⓐ 1:50 P.M.

Ⓑ 2:45 P.M.

Ⓒ 3:20 P.M.

Ⓓ 3:45 P.M.

Connect to Science

Tides

If you have ever been to the beach, you have seen the water rise and fall along the shore every day. This change in water level is called the tide. Ocean tides are mostly caused by the pull of the moon and the sun's gravity. High tide is when the water is at its highest level. Low tide is when the water is at its lowest level. In most places on Earth, high tide and low tide each occur about twice a day.

Use the table for 12–13.

12. The first morning, Courtney walked on the beach for 20 minutes. She finished her walk 30 minutes before high tide. At what time did Courtney start her walk?

_____

13. The third afternoon, Courtney started collecting shells at low tide. She collected shells for 35 minutes. At what time did Courtney finish collecting shells?

_____

Tide Times Atlantic City, NJ		
	Low Tide	High Tide
Day 1	2:12 A.M.	9:00 A.M.
	2:54 P.M.	9:00 P.M.
Day 2	3:06 A.M.	9:36 A.M.
	3:36 P.M.	9:54 P.M.
Day 3	4:00 A.M.	10:12 A.M.
	4:30 P.M.	10:36 P.M.

Name _____

Problem Solving • Time Intervals

Essential Question How can you use the strategy *draw a diagram* to solve problems about time?

 COMMON CORE
Georgia Performance Standard MCC3.MD.1
Solve problems involving measurement and estimation of intervals of time, liquid volumes, and masses of objects.

🔑 UNLOCK the Problem REAL WORLD

Zach and his family are going to New York City. Their airplane leaves at 9:15 A.M. They need to arrive at the airport 60 minutes before their flight. It takes 15 minutes to get to the airport. The family needs 30 minutes to get ready to leave. At what time should Zach's family start getting ready?

Read the Problem

What do I need to find?	**What information do I need to use?**	**How will I use the information?**
I need to find what _____ Zach's family should start _____.	the time the _____ leaves; the time the family needs to arrive at the _____; the time it takes to get to the _____; and the time the family needs to _____	I will use a number line to find the answer.

Solve the Problem

- Find 9:15 A.M. on the number line. Draw the jumps to show the time.

- Count back _____ minutes for the time they need to arrive at the airport.

- Count back _____ minutes for the time to get to the airport.

- Count back _____ minutes for the time to get ready.

So, Zach's family should start getting ready at _____ _____.M.

<————————————————————|→
                                    9:15 A.M.

Math Talk MATHEMATICAL PRACTICES
How can you check your answer by starting with the time the family starts getting ready?

🔑 Try Another Problem

Bradley gets out of school at 2:45 P.M. It takes him 10 minutes to walk home. Then he spends 10 minutes eating a snack. He spends 8 minutes putting on his soccer uniform. It takes 20 minutes for Bradley's father to drive him to soccer practice. At what time does Bradley arrive at soccer practice?

Read the Problem

What do I need to find?	What information do I need to use?	How will I use the information?

Solve the Problem

Draw a diagram to help you explain your answer.

←——————————————————→

1. At what time does Bradley arrive at soccer practice? _____

2. How do you know your answer is reasonable? _____

_____

_____

MATHEMATICAL PRACTICES

Math Talk Do you need to draw jumps on the number line in the same order as the times in the problem? **Explain.**

Name _____

Share and Show

UNLOCK the Problem **Tips**

√ Circle the question.

√ Underline important facts.

√ Choose a strategy you know.

1. Patty went to the shopping mall at 11:30 A.M. She shopped for 25 minutes. She spent 40 minutes eating lunch. Then she met a friend at a movie. At what time did Patty meet her friend?

   First, begin with _____ on the number line.

   Then, count forward _____.

   Next, count forward _____.

   Think: I can break apart the times into shorter amounts of time that make sense.

   SHOW YOUR WORK

   11:30 A.M.

   So, Patty met her friend at _____ _____M.

2. **H.O.T.** **What if** Patty goes to the mall at 11:30 A.M. and meets a friend at a movie at 1:15 P.M.? Patty wants to shop and have 45 minutes for lunch before meeting her friend. How much time can Patty spend shopping?

   _____

3. When Caleb got home from school, he worked on his science project for 20 minutes. Then he studied for a test for 30 minutes. He finished at 4:35 P.M. At what time did Caleb get home from school?

   _____

4. Avery got on the bus at 1:10 P.M. The trip took 90 minutes. Then she walked for 32 minutes to get home. At what time did Avery arrive at home?

   _____

On Your Own

Choose a STRATEGY

Act It Out
Draw a Diagram
Find a Pattern
Make a Table

SHOW YOUR WORK

5. Olivia modeled her number with 3 hundreds blocks and 9 tens blocks. Todd modeled his number with 2 hundreds, 6 tens, and 5 ones blocks. Who has the greater number? How much greater?

_____

6. **H.O.T.** Kyle and Josh have a total of 64 CDs. Kyle has 12 more CDs than Josh. How many CDs does each boy have?

_____

7. Jamal spent 60 minutes using the computer to play games and do research for his report. He spent a half hour of the time playing games and the rest of the time researching his report. How many minutes did Jamal spend researching his report?

_____

8. **Write Math ▶** Miguel played video games each day for a week. On Monday, he scored 83 points. His score went up 5 points each day. On what day did Miguel score 103 points? **Explain** how you found your answer.

_____

_____

9. ★**PARCC Test Prep** When Laura arrived at the library, she spent 40 minutes reading a book. Then she spent 15 minutes reading a magazine. She left the library at 4:15 P.M. At what time did Laura arrive at the library?

Ⓐ 3:20 P.M.

Ⓑ 3:35 P.M.

Ⓒ 4:00 P.M.

Ⓓ 5:10 P.M.

Module 21 Assessment

▶ Vocabulary

Choose the best term from the box.

Vocabulary
A.M.
minute
P.M.

1. In one _____, the minute hand moves from one mark to the next on a clock. (p. 443)

2. The times after noon and before midnight are written with _____. (p. 448)

▶ Concepts and Skills

Write the time for the activity. Use A.M. or P.M. MCC3.MD.1

3. play ball	4. eat breakfast	5. do homework	6. sleep
_____	_____	_____	_____

Find the elapsed time. MCC3.MD.1

7. Start: 10:05 A.M.   End: 10:50 A.M.

10:05

_____

8. Start: 5:30 P.M.
   End: 5:49 P.M.

_____

Find the starting time or the ending time. MCC3.MD.1

9. Starting time: _____
   Elapsed time: 50 minutes
   Ending time: 9:05 A.M.

9:05 A.M.

10. Starting time: 2:46 P.M.
    Elapsed time: 15 minutes

    Ending time: _____

Fill in the bubble for the correct answer choice.

11. Lori started walking to school at 7:45 A.M. She arrived at school 23 minutes later. At what time did Lori arrive at school? MCC3.MD.1

    Ⓐ 8:03 A.M.   Ⓒ 8:08 A.M.

    Ⓑ 8:05 A.M.   Ⓓ 8:23 A.M.

12. The third-grade art class ends at 3 minutes before 2:00. Which clock shows the time the art class ends? MCC3.MD.1

    Ⓐ   Ⓒ

    Ⓑ   Ⓓ

13. Matt went to his friend's house. He arrived at 5:10 P.M. He left at 5:37 P.M. How long was Matt at his friend's house? MCC3.MD.1

    Ⓐ 10 minutes   Ⓒ 37 minutes

    Ⓑ 27 minutes   Ⓓ 47 minutes

14. Ruthie's train leaves at 7:30 A.M. She needs to arrive 10 minutes early to buy her ticket. It takes her 20 minutes to get to the train station. At what time should Ruthie leave her house? MCC3.MD.1

    Ⓐ 7:00 A.M.   Ⓒ 8:00 A.M.

    Ⓑ 7:40 A.M.   Ⓓ 8:30 A.M.

15. At which time are most third graders in school?

    MCC3.MD.1

    Ⓐ 10:12 A.M.   Ⓒ 7:34 P.M.

    Ⓑ 4:41 P.M.   Ⓓ 2:03 A.M.

Name _____

Measure Length

Essential Question How can you generate measurement data and show the data on a line plot?

COMMON CORE
Georgia Performance Standard MCC3.MD.4
Represent and interpret data.

CONNECT You have learned how to measure length to the nearest inch. Sometimes the length of an object is not a whole unit. For example, a paper clip is more than 1 inch but less than 2 inches.

You can measure length to the nearest half inch or fourth inch. The half-inch markings on a ruler divide each inch into two equal parts. The fourth-inch markings divide each inch into four equal parts.

Math Idea

A ruler is like a number line.

$\frac{0}{4}$ $\frac{1}{4}$ $\frac{2}{4}$ $\frac{3}{4}$ $\frac{4}{4}$

$\frac{0}{2}$ $\frac{1}{2}$ $\frac{2}{2}$

inches

UNLOCK the Problem REAL WORLD

Example 1 Use a ruler to measure the glue stick to the nearest half inch.

- Line up the left end of the glue stick with the zero mark on the ruler.

- The right end of the glue stick is between the half-inch marks for

  _____ and _____.

- The mark that is closest to the right end of the glue stick is for _____ inches.

So, the length of the glue stick to the

nearest half inch is _____ inches.

Example 2 Use a ruler to measure the paper clip to the nearest fourth inch.

- Line up the left end of the paper clip with the zero mark on the ruler.

- The right end of the paper clip is between the fourth-inch marks for

  _____ and _____.

- The mark that is closest to the right end of the paper clip is for _____ inches.

So, the length of the paper clip to the

nearest fourth inch is _____ inches.

🔑 Activity   Make a line plot to show measurement data.

Materials ■ inch ruler ■ 10 crayons

Measure the length of 10 crayons to the nearest half inch.
Complete the line plot. Draw an **X** for each length.

Length of Crayons Measured to the Nearest Half Inch

- **Describe** any patterns you see in your line plot.

_____

_____

Try This! Measure the length of your fingers to the nearest fourth inch. Complete the line plot. Draw an **X** for each length.

MATHEMATICAL PRACTICES

Math Talk How do you think your line plot compares to line plots your classmates made? **Explain.**

Length of Fingers Measured to the Nearest Fourth Inch

Share and Show . . . .

1. Measure the length to the nearest half inch. Is the key closest to $1\frac{1}{2}$ inches, 2 inches, or $2\frac{1}{2}$ inches?

_____ inches

Name _____

Measure the length to the nearest half inch.

2. ____ inches

Measure the length to the nearest fourth inch.

3. ____ inches

MATHEMATICAL PRACTICES
Math Talk **Explain** why you would want to measure to the nearest half inch or fourth inch.

On Your Own

Measure the length to the nearest half inch.

4.

____ inches

5.

____ inches

Measure the length to the nearest fourth inch.

6. ____ inches

7. ____ inches

Practice: Copy and Solve Use the lines for 8–9.

8. Measure the length of the lines to the nearest half inch and make a line plot.

9. Measure the length of the lines to the nearest fourth inch and make a line plot.

Problem Solving

REAL WORLD

SHOW YOUR WORK

10. Tara's hand is $4\frac{3}{4}$ inches long. This length is between which two inch-marks on a ruler?

_____

11. **H.O.T.** **What's the Error?** Joni says that this piece of ribbon is $3\frac{1}{2}$ inches long. Describe her error. How long is the ribbon?

_____

_____

_____

_____

12. Find two objects in your desk that are different sizes. Measure the length of each object to the nearest fourth inch. Then use < or > to compare the lengths.

Object _____ Length _____

Object _____ Length _____

_____ ◯ _____

13. ⭐ **PARCC Test Prep** What is the length of the pencil to the nearest half inch?

Ⓐ $3\frac{1}{2}$ inches   Ⓒ $5\frac{1}{2}$ inches

Ⓑ 4 inches   Ⓓ 6 inches

Name _____

Estimate and Measure Liquid Volume

Essential Question How can you estimate and measure liquid volume in metric units?

COMMON CORE
Georgia Performance Standard MCC3.MD.2
Solve problems involving measurement and estimation of intervals of time, liquid volumes, and masses of objects.

🔑 UNLOCK the Problem REAL WORLD

Liquid volume is the amount of liquid in a container. The **liter (L)** is the basic metric unit for measuring liquid volume.

🔓 Activity 1

Materials ■ 1-L beaker ■ 4 containers ■ water ■ tape

STEP 1 Fill a 1-liter beaker with water to the 1-liter mark.

STEP 2 Pour 1 liter of water into a container. Mark the level of the water with a piece of tape. Draw the container below and name the container.

STEP 3 Repeat Steps 1 and 2 with three different-sized containers.

Container 1	Container 2
_____	_____
Container 3	Container 4
_____	_____

Math Talk MATHEMATICAL PRACTICES
What can you say about the amount of liquid volume in each container?

1. How much water did you pour into each container? _____

2. Which containers are mostly full? **Describe** them.

_____

3. Which containers are mostly empty? **Describe** them.

_____

© Houghton Mifflin Harcourt Publishing Company

Module 22 469

Compare Liquid Volumes

A full glass holds less than 1 liter.

A water bottle holds about 1 liter.

A fish bowl holds more than 1 liter.

🔒 Activity 2 Materials ■ 1-L beaker ■ 5 different containers ■ water

STEP 1 Write the containers in order from the one you think will hold the least water to the one you think will hold the most water.

_____, _____, _____,

_____, _____

STEP 2 Estimate how much each container will hold. Write *more than 1 liter*, *about 1 liter*, or *less than 1 liter* in the table.

STEP 3 Pour 1 liter of water into one of the containers. Repeat until the container is full. Record the number of liters you poured. Repeat for each container.

Container	Estimate	Number of Liters

STEP 4 Write the containers in order from the least to the greatest liquid volume.

_____, _____, _____,

_____, _____

MATHEMATICAL PRACTICES

Math Talk Was the order in Step 1 different than the order in Step 4? **Explain** why they may be different.

Name _____

Share and Show

1. The beaker is filled with water. Is the amount *more than 1 liter, about 1 liter,* or *less than 1 liter*?

_____

Estimate how much liquid volume there will be when the container is filled. Write *more than 1 liter, about 1 liter,* or *less than 1 liter.*

2. cup of tea	✓ 3. kitchen sink	✓ 4. teapot
_____	_____	_____

On Your Own

MATHEMATICAL PRACTICES

Math Talk Explain how you could estimate the liquid volume in a container.

Estimate how much liquid volume there will be when the container is filled. Write *more than 1 liter, about 1 liter,* or *less than 1 liter.*

5. pitcher	6. juice box	7. punch bowl
_____	_____	_____

Use the pictures for 8–10. Ginger pours punch into four bottles that are the same size.

8. Did Ginger pour the same amount into each bottle? _____

9. Which bottle has the least amount of punch? _____

10. Which bottle has the most punch? _____

Problem Solving REAL WORLD

H.O.T. **Use the containers for 11–14. Container A is full when 1 liter of water is poured into it.**

A   D

B

11. **Write Math** ▶ **What if** you poured 1 liter of water into Container B? Describe the way the water fills the container. **Explain** how you know.

_____

_____

_____

12. Estimate how many liters will fill Container C and how many liters will fill Container E. Which container will hold more water when filled?

_____

_____

C   E

13. Name two containers that will be filled with about the same number of liters of water. **Explain**.

_____

_____

14. **Write Math** ▶ **What's the Error?** Samuel says that you can pour more liters of water into Container E than into Container D. Is he correct? **Explain**.

_____

_____

_____

15. ⭐ **PARCC Test Prep** The bottles of tea are all the same size. Which bottle has the most tea in it?

Ⓐ Bottle J   Ⓒ Bottle L

Ⓑ Bottle K   Ⓓ Bottle M

J   K   L   M

Name _____

Estimate and Measure Mass

Essential Question How can you estimate and measure mass in metric units?

COMMON CORE
Georgia Performance Standard MCC3.MD.2
Solve problems involving measurement and estimation of intervals of time, liquid volumes, and masses of objects.

🔑 UNLOCK the Problem REAL WORLD

🔒 Peter has a dollar bill in his pocket. Should Peter measure the mass of the dollar bill in grams or kilograms?

The **gram (g)** is the basic metric unit for measuring **mass**, or the amount of matter in an object. Mass can also be measured by using the metric unit **kilogram (kg)**.

A small paper clip has a mass of about 1 gram.	A box of 1,000 paper clips has a mass of about 1 kilogram.

Think: The mass of a dollar bill is closer to the mass of a small paper clip than it is to a box of 1,000 paper clips.

So, Peter should measure the mass of the dollar bill in _____.

🔑 Activity 1

Materials ■ pan balance ■ gram and kilogram masses

You can use a pan balance to measure mass.

Do 10 grams have the same mass as 1 kilogram?

• Place 10 gram masses on one side of the balance.

• Place a 1-kilogram mass on the other side of the balance.

Think: If it is balanced, then the objects have the same mass. If it is not balanced, the objects do not have the same mass.

• Complete the picture of the balance above by drawing masses to show your balance.

   The pan balance is _____.

So, 10 grams and 1 kilogram _____ the same mass.

MATHEMATICAL PRACTICES

Math Talk Which has a greater mass, 10 grams or 1 kilogram? **Explain**.

🔒 Activity 2

Materials ■ pan balance ■ gram and kilogram masses ■ classroom objects

STEP 1 Use the objects in the table. Decide if the object should be measured in grams or kilograms.

STEP 2 Estimate the mass of each object. Record your estimates in the table.

STEP 3 Find the mass of each object to the nearest gram or kilogram. Place the object on one side of the balance. Place gram or kilogram masses on the other side until both sides are balanced.

STEP 4 Add the measures of the gram or kilogram masses. This is the mass of the object. Record the mass in the table.

▲ 189 marbles have a mass of 1 kilogram.

Mass		
Object	**Estimate**	**Mass**
crayon		
stapler		
eraser		
marker		
small notepad		
scissors		

Math Talk MATHEMATICAL PRACTICES
How did your estimates compare with the actual measurements?

• Write the objects in order from greatest mass to least mass.

_____, _____, _____,

_____, _____, _____

Share and Show

1. Five bananas have a mass of about _____.

   Think: The pan balance is balanced, so the objects on both sides have the same mass.

© Houghton Mifflin Harcourt Publishing Company

Name _____

**Choose the unit you would use to measure the mass.
Write *gram* or *kilogram*.**

2. strawberry

_____

☑ 3. dog

_____

**Compare the masses of the objects. Write
is less than, *is the same as*, or *is more than*.**

4.

The mass of the bowling pin

_____ the mass of
the chess piece.

☑ 5.

The mass of the erasers

_____ the mass of
the clips.

On Your Own . . . .

**Choose the unit you would use to measure the mass.
Write *gram* or *kilogram*.**

6. chair

7. sunglasses

8. watermelon

**Compare the masses of the objects. Write
is less than, *is the same as*, or *is more than*.**

9.

The mass of the pen _____
the mass of the paper clips.

10.

The mass of the straws _____
the mass of the blocks.

11. Put the sports balls shown at the right in order from greatest mass to least mass.

_____

_____

Golf ball

Table tennis ball

Bowling ball

12. Choose two objects that have about the same mass. Draw a balance with one of these objects on each side.

13. Choose two objects that have different masses. Draw a balance with one of these objects on each side.

Baseball

Tennis ball

14. **H.O.T. Pose a Problem** Write a problem about the objects you chose in Exercise 13. Then solve your problem.

SHOW YOUR WORK

_____

_____

15. **Write Math** ▶ **Sense or Nonsense?** Amber is buying produce at the grocery store. She says that a Fuji apple and a green bell pepper would have the same mass because they are the same size. Does her statement make sense? **Explain**.

_____

_____

_____

_____

16. ⭐**PARCC Test Prep** Dan wants to find the mass of a large pumpkin. Which unit should he use?

Ⓐ inch   Ⓒ kilogram

Ⓑ gram   Ⓓ liter

Name _____

Solve Problems About Liquid Volume and Mass

Essential Question How can you use models to solve liquid volume and mass problems?

COMMON CORE
Georgia Performance Standard MCC3.MD.2
Solve problems involving measurement and estimation of intervals of time, liquid volumes, and masses of objects.

🔑 UNLOCK the Problem   REAL WORLD

A restaurant serves iced tea from a large container that can hold 24 liters. Sadie will fill the container with the pitchers of tea shown below. Will Sadie have tea left over after filling the container?

🔓 Example   Solve a problem about liquid volume.

_____ L   _____ L   _____ L   _____ L

Since there are _____ equal groups of _____ liters, you can multiply.

_____ ◯ _____ = _____

Circle the correct words to complete the sentences.

_____ liters is *greater than / less than* 24 liters.

So, Sadie *will / will not* have tea left over.

Try This! Use a bar model to solve.

Raul's fish tank contains 32 liters of water. He empties it with a bucket that holds 4 liters of water. How many times will Raul have to fill the bucket?

_____ ◯ _____ = _____

So, Raul will have to fill the bucket _____ times.

times

4 L   4 L

32 L

🔒 Activity Solve a problem about mass.

Materials ■ pan balance ■ glue stick ■ gram masses

Jeff has a glue stick and a 20-gram mass on one side of a balance and gram masses on the other side. The pan balance is balanced. What is the mass of the glue stick?

STEP 1 Place a glue stick and a 20-gram mass on one side of the balance.

STEP 2 Place gram masses on the other side until the pans are balanced.

STEP 3 To find the mass of the glue stick, remove 20 grams from each side.

> **Think:** I can remove 20 grams from both sides and the pan balance will still be balanced.

STEP 4 Then add the measures of the gram masses on the balance.

The gram masses have a measure of _____ grams.

So, the glue stick has a mass of _____ .

MATHEMATICAL PRACTICES

Math Talk What equation can you write to find the mass of the glue stick? **Explain.**

Try This! Use a bar model to solve.

A bag of peas has a mass of 432 grams.
A bag of carrots has a mass of 263 grams.
What is the total mass of both bags?

_____ ◯ _____ = _____

So, both bags have a total mass of _____ grams.

_____ g   _____ g
_____ g

Share and Show ....

1. Ed's Delivery Service delivered three packages to Ms. Wilson. The packages have masses of 9 kilograms, 12 kilograms, and 5 kilograms. What is the total mass of the three packages? Use the bar model to help you solve.

___ kg   _____ kg   ___ kg
_____ kg

_____

478

Name _____

Write an equation and solve the problem.

2. Ariel's recipe calls for 64 grams of apples and 86 grams of oranges. How many more grams of oranges than apples does the recipe call for?

____ ◯ ____ = ____ ____

3. Dan's Clams restaurant sold 45 liters of lemonade. If it sold the same amount each hour for 9 hours, how many liters of lemonade did Dan's Clams sell each hour?

____ ◯ ____ = ____ ____

On Your Own . . . .

Math Talk | **MATHEMATICAL PRACTICES** **Explain** how you could model Exercise 2.

Write an equation and solve the problem.

4. Sara's box holds 4 kilograms of napkins and 29 kilograms of napkin rings. What is the total mass of the napkins and napkin rings?

____ ◯ ____ = ____ ____

5. Josh has 6 buckets for cleaning a restaurant. He fills each bucket with 4 liters of water. How many liters of water are in the buckets?

____ ◯ ____ = ____ ____

6. **H.O.T.** **Write Math** Ellen will pour water into Pitcher *B* until it has 1 more liter of water than Pitcher *A*. How many liters of water will she pour into Pitcher *B*? **Explain** how you found your answer.

Pitcher *A*   Pitcher *B*

_____

_____

7. **Practice: Copy and Solve** Use the pictures to write two problems. Then solve your problems.

Grape Juice   Apple Juice   Cereal   Coffee

8. Ken's Café serves hot cocoa. Each serving has 9 grams of chocolate. How many grams of chocolate are in 8 servings of hot cocoa?

Ⓐ 1 gram Ⓒ 72 grams

Ⓑ 17 grams Ⓓ 89 grams

a. What do you need to find? _____

_____

b. What operation will you use to find the answer? _____

c. Draw a diagram to solve the problem.

d. Complete the sentences.

There are _____ servings with

_____ grams of chocolate in each.

Since each serving is an _____

group, you can _____.

_____ ◯ _____ = _____

So, there are _____ grams of chocolate in 8 servings of hot cocoa.

e. Fill in the bubble for the correct answer choice above.

9. Alison has a container filled with 12 liters of water. Daniel has a container filled with 16 liters of water. What is the total liquid volume of the containers?

Ⓐ 4 liters Ⓒ 28 liters

Ⓑ 24 liters Ⓓ 32 liters

10. A jar holds 21 grams of salad dressing. Sam pours 3 grams of salad dressing on each salad plate. If Sam uses all the dressing, how many salad plates are there?

Ⓐ 24 Ⓒ 8

Ⓑ 18 Ⓓ 7

Name _____

Module 22 Assessment

▶ **Vocabulary**

Choose the best term from the box to complete the sentence.

Vocabulary
kilograms
liquid volume
liters

1. _____ is the amount of liquid in a container. (p. 469)

2. Mass can be measured in units such as

_____ (p. 473)

▶ **Concepts and Skills**

Measure the length to the nearest fourth inch. MCC3.MD.4

3.

_____ inches

Estimate how much liquid volume there will be when the container is filled. Write *more than 1 liter*, *about 1 liter*, or *less than 1 liter*. MCC3.MD.2

4. bathtub	5. shampoo bottle	6. bottle of hand soap
_____	_____	_____

Choose the unit you would use to measure the mass. Write *gram* or *kilogram*. MCC3.MD.2

7. headphones	8. lamp	9. boots
_____	_____	_____

Fill in the bubble for the correct answer choice.

10. Dora placed a pencil on one side of a balance. What is the mass of the pencil? ▶MCC3.MD.2

Ⓐ 1 gram

Ⓑ 6 grams

Ⓒ 1 kilogram

Ⓓ 6 kilograms

11. Which equation can you use to find the total liquid volume of the containers? ▶MCC3.MD.2

Ⓐ 4 + 3 = 7   Ⓒ 3 × 4 = 12

Ⓑ 10 + 4 = 14   Ⓓ 3 × 10 = 30

12. Megan is using a red crayon to draw a picture.

Which is closest to the length of the crayon? ▶MCC3.MD.4

Ⓐ $2\frac{1}{2}$ inches   Ⓒ $3\frac{1}{2}$ inches

Ⓑ 3 inches   Ⓓ 4 inches

13. The bottles of water are all the same size. Which bottle has the least amount of water? ▶MCC3.MD.2

Ⓐ Bottle W

Ⓑ Bottle X

Ⓒ Bottle Y

Ⓓ Bottle Z

W   X   Y   Z

Model Perimeter

Essential Question How can you find perimeter?

COMMON CORE
Georgia Performance Standard MCC3.MD.8
Geometric measurement: recognize perimeter as an attribute of plane figures and distinguish between linear and area measures.

Investigate

Perimeter is the distance around a shape.

Materials ■ geoboard ■ rubber bands

You can find the perimeter of a rectangle on a geoboard or on dot paper by counting the number of units on each side.

A. Make a rectangle on the geoboard that is 3 units on two sides and 2 units on the other two sides.

B. Draw your rectangle on this dot paper.

←— 1 Unit

C. Write the length next to each side of your rectangle.

D. Add the number of units on each side.

_____ + _____ + _____ + _____ = _____

E. So, the perimeter of the rectangle

is _____ units.

• How would the perimeter of the rectangle change if the length of two of the sides was 4 units instead of 3 units?

_____

_____

Draw Conclusions

1. **Describe** how you would find the perimeter of a rectangle that is 5 units wide and 6 units long.

   _____

2. A rectangle has two pairs of sides of equal length. **Explain** how you can find the unknown length of two sides when the length of one side is 4 units, and the perimeter is 14 units.

   _____

   _____

   _____

3. **Evaluate** Jill says that finding the perimeter of a shape with all sides of equal length is easier than finding the perimeter of other shapes. Do you agree? **Explain.**

   _____

   _____

Make Connections

You can also use grid paper to find the perimeter of shapes by counting the number of units on each side.

Start at the arrow and trace the perimeter. Begin counting with 1. Continue counting each unit around the shape until you have counted each unit.

MATHEMATICAL PRACTICES

Math Talk If a rectangle has a perimeter of 12 units, how many units wide and how many units long could it be? **Explain.**

A

← 1 Unit

Perimeter = _____ units

B

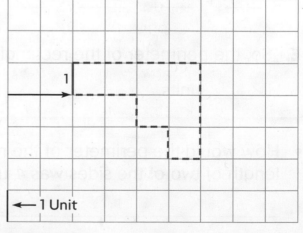

← 1 Unit

Perimeter = _____ units

Name _____

Share and Show

Find the perimeter of the shape. Each unit is 1 centimeter.

1.

_____ centimeters

☑ 2.

_____ centimeters

3.

_____ centimeters

4.

_____ centimeters

Find the perimeter.

5. A shape with four sides that measure 4 centimeters, 6 centimeters, 5 centimeters, and 1 centimeter

_____ centimeters

☑ 6. A shape with two sides that measure 10 inches, one side that measures 8 inches, and one side that measures 4 inches

_____ inches

7. **H.O.T.** **Write Math** Explain how to find the length of each side of a triangle with sides of equal length, and a perimeter of 27 inches.

_____

_____

Problem Solving ....

 What's the Error?

8. Kevin is solving perimeter problems. He counts the units and says that the perimeter of this shape is 22 units.

Look at Kevin's solution.   **Find Kevin's error.**

Ⓐ
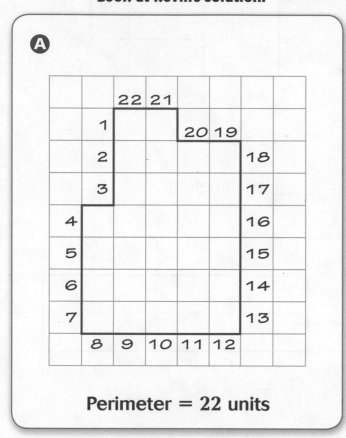

Perimeter = 22 units

Ⓑ
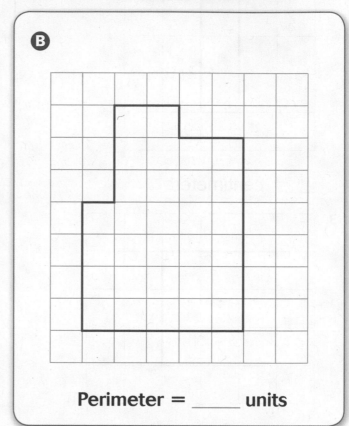

Perimeter = _____ units

- Use the grid on the right to find the correct perimeter of the shape above.

_____

- Describe the error Kevin made.

_____

_____

_____

- Circle the places in the drawing of Kevin's solution where he made an error.

FOR MORE PRACTICE:
Standards Practice Book

Name _____

On Your Own

Use a ruler to find the perimeter.

6.

_____ in.

_____ in.   _____ in.

_____ in.

_____ inches

7.

_____ cm

_____ cm

_____ cm   _____ cm

_____ cm

_____ cm

_____ centimeters

8. Use the grid paper to draw a shape that has a perimeter of 24 centimeters. Label the length of each side.

← 1 cm

Problem Solving · REAL WORLD

Model • Reason • Make Sense

MATHEMATICAL
PRACTICES

Use the photos for 9–10.

9. Which of the animal photos has a perimeter of 26 inches?

_____

5 in.

8 in

5 in.

7 in.

8 in.   4 in.

4 in.

7 in.

10. How much greater is the perimeter of the bird photo than the perimeter of the cat photo?

_____

SHOW YOUR WORK

11. **H.O.T.** Erin is putting a fence around her square garden. Each side of her garden is 3 meters long. The fence costs $5 for each meter. How much will the fence cost?

_____

12. **H.O.T.** **Write Math** Gary's garden is shaped like a rectangle with two pairs of sides of equal length, and it has a perimeter of 28 feet. **Explain** how to find the lengths of the other sides if one side measures 10 feet.

_____

_____

_____

_____

13. ⭐ **PARCC Test Prep** Austin's class is making a poster for Earth Day. What is the perimeter of the poster?

Ⓐ 20 feet   Ⓒ 24 feet

Ⓑ 21 feet   Ⓓ 30 feet

9 ft

6 ft

6 ft

9 ft

© Houghton Mifflin Harcourt Publishing Company

Find Unknown Side Lengths

Essential Question How can you find the unknown length of a side in a
plane shape when you know its perimeter?

COMMON CORE
Georgia Performance Standard MCC3.MD.8
Geometric measurement: recognize perimeter as an
attribute of plane figures and distinguish between
linear and area measures.

 UNLOCK the Problem REAL WORLD

Chen has 27 feet of fencing to put around
his garden. He has already used the lengths
of fencing shown. How much fencing does
he have left for the last side?

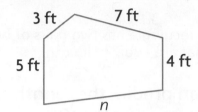

🔑 **Find the unknown side length.**

Write an equation for the perimeter.

$$5 + 3 + \underline{\quad} + \underline{\quad} + n = 27$$

Think: If I knew the length of n, I would add
all the side lengths to find the perimeter.

$$5 + 3 + 7 + 4 + n = 27$$

Add the lengths of the sides you know.

$$\underline{\quad} + n = 27$$

Think: Addition and subtraction are
inverse operations.

Write a related equation.

$$n = 27 - 19$$

So, Chen has _____ feet of fencing left.

$$\underline{\quad} = 27 - 19$$

Math Idea
A symbol or letter can stand
for an unknown side length.

Try This!

The perimeter of the shape is 24 meters.
Find the unknown side length, w.

So, the unknown side length, w, is _____ meters long.

🔑 Example Find unknown side lengths of a rectangle.

5 ft

Lauren has a rectangular blanket. The perimeter is 28 feet. The width of the blanket is 5 feet. What is the length of the blanket?

l   *l*

Hint: A rectangle has two pairs of opposite sides that are equal in length.

You can predict the length and add to find the perimeter. If the perimeter is 28 feet, then that is the correct length.

5 ft

Predict	Check	Does it check?
l = 7 feet	5 + ____ + 5 + ____ = ____	**Think:** Perimeter is not 28 feet, so the length does not check.
l = 8 feet	5 + ____ + 5 + ____ = ____	**Think:** Perimeter is not 28 feet, so the length does not check.
l = 9 feet	5 + ____ + 5 + ____ = ____	**Think:** Perimeter is 28 feet, so the length is correct. ✓

So, the length of the blanket is _____ feet.

Try This! Find unknown side lengths of a square.

The square has a perimeter of 20 inches. What is the length of each side of the square?

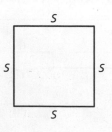

s

s   *s*

s

Think: A square has four sides that are equal in length.

You can multiply to find the perimeter.

- Write a multiplication equation for the perimeter. $4 \times s = 20$

- Use a multiplication fact you know to solve. $4 \times$ _____ $= 20$

So, the length of each side of the square is _____ inches.

Name _____

Share and Show

Find the unknown side lengths.

1. Perimeter = 25 centimeters

$9 + \underline{\quad} + \underline{\quad} + n = 25$

$\underline{\quad} + n = 25$

$\underline{\quad} = \underline{\quad} - \underline{\quad}$

$n = \underline{\quad}$ centimeters

2. Perimeter = 34 meters

$j = \underline{\quad}$ meters

3. Perimeter = 12 feet

$r = \underline{\quad}$ feet

On Your Own

Math Talk MATHEMATICAL PRACTICES
Explain how you can use division to find the length of a side of a square.

Find the unknown side lengths.

4. Perimeter = 32 centimeters

$k = \underline{\quad}$ centimeters

5. Perimeter = 8 meters

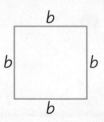

$b = \underline{\quad}$ meters

6. Perimeter = 16 inches

$n = \underline{\quad}$ inches

7. H.O.T. Perimeter = 42 feet

$g = \underline{\quad}$ feet

UNLOCK the Problem REAL WORLD

8. Latesha wants to make a border with ribbon around a shape she made and sketched at the right. She will use 44 centimeters of ribbon for the border. What is the unknown side length?

Ⓐ 3 centimeters   Ⓒ 9 centimeters

Ⓑ 6 centimeters   Ⓓ 13 centimeters

3 cm
8 cm
13 cm
6 cm
5 cm
h

a. What do you need to find? _____

b. How will you use what you know about perimeter to help you

solve the problem? _____

_____

c. Write an equation to solve the problem.

d. Complete the sentences.

The perimeter is _____ centimeters.

The sum of the sides I know is _____ centimeters.

A related subtraction equation is

_____ = _____ − _____.

So, the length of side *h* is

_____ centimeters.

e. Fill in the bubble for the correct answer choice above.

9. A rectangle has a perimeter of 34 inches. The left side is 6 inches long. What is the length of the top side?

Ⓐ 6 inches

Ⓑ 11 inches

Ⓒ 28 inches

Ⓓ 40 inches

10. Eleni wants to put up a fence around her square garden. The garden has a perimeter of 28 meters. How long will each side of the fence be?

a
a   *a*
a

Ⓐ 6 meters   Ⓒ 8 meters

Ⓑ 7 meters   Ⓓ 14 meters

Same Perimeter, Different Areas

Essential Question How can you use area to compare rectangles with the same perimeter?

COMMON CORE
Georgia Performance Standard MCC3.MD.8
Geometric measurement: recognize perimeter as an attribute of plane figures and distinguish between linear and area measures.

🔑 UNLOCK the Problem

Toby has 12 feet of boards to put around a rectangular sandbox. How long should he make each side so that the area of the sandbox is as large as possible?

• What is the greatest perimeter Toby can make for his sandbox?

_____

🔒 Activity

Materials ■ square tiles

Use square tiles to make all the rectangles you can that have a perimeter of 12 units. Draw and label the sandboxes. Then find the area of each.

Sandbox 1	Sandbox 2	Sandbox 3
__1__ ft	___ ft	___ ft
__5__ ft	___ ft	___ ft

Find the perimeter and area of each rectangle.

	Perimeter	Area
Sandbox 1	__5__ + __1__ + __5__ + __1__ = __12__ feet	__1__ × __5__ = ____ square feet
Sandbox 2	____ + ____ + ____ + ____ = ____ feet	____ × ____ = ____ square feet
Sandbox 3	____ + ____ + ____ + ____ = ____ feet	____ × ____ = ____ square feet

The area of Sandbox _____ is the greatest.

So, Toby should build a sandbox that is

_____ feet wide and _____ feet long.

Math Talk   MATHEMATICAL PRACTICES
How are the sandboxes alike? How are the sandboxes different?

🔑 Examples Draw rectangles with the same perimeter and different areas.

Ⓐ Draw a rectangle that has a perimeter of 20 units and an area of 24 square units.

The sides of the rectangle measure

_____ units and _____ units.

Ⓑ Draw a rectangle that has a perimeter of 20 units and an area of 25 square units.

The sides of the rectangle measure

_____ units and _____ units.

MATHEMATICAL PRACTICES

Math Talk Explain how the perimeters of Example *A* and Example *B* are related. Explain how the areas are related.

Share and Show [MATH BOARD] . . . .

1. The perimeter of the rectangle at the right is

_____ units. The area is _____ square units.

2. Draw a rectangle that has the same perimeter as the rectangle in Exercise 1 but with a different area.

3. The area of the rectangle in Exercise 2 is

_____ square units.

☑ 4. Which rectangle has the greater area?

_____

5. If you were given a rectangle with a certain perimeter, how would you draw it so that it has the greatest area?

_____

MATHEMATICAL PRACTICES

Math Talk Explain how you knew what the rectangle for Exercise 5 would look like.

Name _____

Find the perimeter and the area. Tell which rectangle has a greater area.

6.

    A

    B

A: Perimeter = _____; Area = _____

B: Perimeter = _____; Area = _____

Rectangle ____ has a greater area.

On Your Own ....

Find the perimeter and the area. Tell which rectangle has a greater area.

7.

    A

    B

A: Perimeter = _____;

   Area = _____

B: Perimeter = _____;

   Area = _____

Rectangle ____ has a greater area.

8.

    B

    A

A: Perimeter = _____;

   Area = _____

B: Perimeter = _____;

   Area = _____

Rectangle ____ has a greater area.

9. Draw a rectangle with the same perimeter as Rectangle C, but with a smaller area. What is the area?

Area = _____

    C

Problem Solving REAL WORLD

10. **What's the Question?** Todd's flower garden is 4 feet wide and 8 feet long. The answer is 32 square feet.

_____

11. **PARCC Test Prep** Which shape has a perimeter of 20 units and an area of 16 square units?

Ⓐ   Ⓒ

Ⓑ   Ⓓ

Connect to Reading

Cause and Effect

Sometimes one action has an effect on another action. The *cause* is the reason something happens. The *effect* is the result.

Sam wanted to print a digital photo that is 3 inches wide and 5 inches long. **What if** Sam accidentally printed a photo that is 4 inches wide and 6 inches long?

Sam can make a table to understand cause and effect.

Cause	Effect
The wrong size photo was printed.	Each side of the photo is a greater length.

Use the information and the strategy to solve the problems.

12. What effect did the mistake have on the perimeter of the photo?

_____

_____

13. What effect did the mistake have on the area of the photo?

_____

_____

Name _____

Same Area, Different Perimeters

Essential Question How can you use perimeter to compare rectangles with the same area?

COMMON CORE
Georgia Performance Standard MCC3.MD.8
Geometric measurement: recognize perimeter as an attribute of plane figures and distinguish between linear and area measures.

 UNLOCK the Problem REAL WORLD

Marcy is making a rectangular pen to hold her rabbits. The area of the pen should be 16 square meters with side lengths that are whole numbers. What is the least amount of fencing she needs?

• What does the least amount of fencing represent?

_____

 Activity Materials ■ square tiles

Use 16 square tiles to make rectangles. Make as many different rectangles as you can with 16 tiles. Record the rectangles on the grid, write the multiplication equation for the area shown by the rectangle, and find the perimeter of each rectangle.

Math Talk MATHEMATICAL PRACTICES
Explain how you found the rectangles.

Area: _____ × _____ = 16 square meters   Perimeter: _____ meters

Area: _____ × _____ = 16 square meters   Perimeter: _____ meters

Area: _____ × _____ = 16 square meters   Perimeter: _____ meters

To use the least amount of fencing, Marcy should make a rectangular

pen with side lengths of _____ meters and _____ meters.

So, _____ meters is the least amount of fencing Marcy needs.

Try This!

Draw three rectangles that have an area of 18 square units on the grid. Find the perimeter of each rectangle. Shade the rectangle that has the greatest perimeter.

Share and Show

1. The area of the rectangle at the right is

   _____ square units. The perimeter is _____ units.

2. Draw a rectangle that has the same area as the rectangle in Exercise 1 but with a different perimeter.

3. The perimeter of the rectangle in Exercise 2 is

   _____ units.

4. Which rectangle has the greater perimeter?

   _____

5. If you were given a rectangle with a certain area, how would you draw it so that it had the greatest perimeter?

   _____

Math Talk Did you and your classmate draw the same rectangle for Exercise 2? Explain.

MATHEMATICAL PRACTICES

© Houghton Mifflin Harcourt Publishing Company

Name _____

Find the perimeter and the area. Tell which rectangle has a greater perimeter.

6.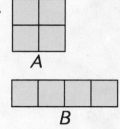

A: Area = _____; Perimeter = _____

B: Area = _____; Perimeter = _____

Rectangle _____ has a greater perimeter.

On Your Own ....

Find the perimeter and the area. Tell which rectangle has a greater perimeter.

7.
A

B

8.
A

B

A: Area = _____;

Perimeter = _____

B: Area = _____;

Perimeter = _____

Rectangle _____ has a greater perimeter.

A: Area = _____;

Perimeter = _____

B: Area = _____;

Perimeter = _____

Rectangle _____ has a greater perimeter.

9. **H.O.T.** **Sense or Nonsense?** Dora says that of all the possible rectangles with the same area, the rectangle with the largest perimeter will have two side lengths that are 1 unit. Does her statement make sense? **Explain.**

UNLOCK the Problem REAL WORLD

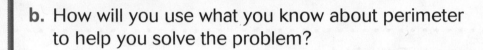

10. Ed has 12 tiles. Each tile is 1 square inch. He will arrange them into a rectangle and glue 1-inch stones around the edge. How can Ed arrange the tiles so that he uses the least number of stones?

a. What do you need to find? _____

_____

b. How will you use what you know about perimeter to help you solve the problem?

_____

c. Draw possible rectangles to solve the problem, label them *A*, *B*, and *C*.

d. Complete the sentences.

Rectangle *A* has side lengths

_____ and _____ with

a perimeter of _____.

Rectangle *B* has side lengths

_____ and _____ with a

perimeter of _____.

Rectangle *C* has side lengths

_____ and _____

with a perimeter of _____.

So, Ed should arrange
the tiles like Rectangle _____.

---

11. ⭐ **PARCC Test Prep** Which shape has an area of 15 square units and a perimeter of 16 units?

Ⓐ

Ⓒ

Ⓑ

Ⓓ

FOR MORE PRACTICE:
Standards Practice Book

Name _____

 Module 23 Assessment

▶ **Vocabulary**

Choose the best term from the box.

Vocabulary
area
perimeter
square unit

1. The distance around a shape is the _____. **(p. 483)**

2. The measure of the number of unit squares needed to cover a shape with no gaps or overlaps is the _____.

▶ **Concepts and Skills**

Find the perimeter of the shape. Each unit is 1 centimeter. MCC3.MD.8

3.

_____ centimeters

4.

_____ centimeters

Find the unknown side lengths. MCC3.MD.8

5. Perimeter = 33 centimeters

10 cm
4 cm
6 cm
g
10 cm

g = _____ centimeters

6. Perimeter = 32 feet

12 ft
k   k
12 ft

k = _____ feet

Find the perimeter and the area. Tell which rectangle has a greater area. MCC3.MD.8

7.
A

B

A: Perimeter = _____ Area = _____;

B: Perimeter = _____ Area = _____;

Rectangle _____ has a greater area.

Fill in the bubble for the correct answer choice.

8. Adrienne is decorating a square picture frame. She glued 36 inches of ribbon around the edge of the frame. What is the length of each side of the picture frame? MCC3.MD.8

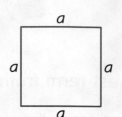

Ⓐ 6 inches

Ⓑ 9 inches

Ⓒ 30 inches

Ⓓ 32 inches

9. Jeff is making a poster for a car wash for the Campout Club. What is the perimeter of the poster? MCC3.MD.8

Ⓐ 8 feet

Ⓑ 6 feet

Ⓒ 4 feet

Ⓓ 3 feet

10. A rectangle has two side lengths of 8 inches and two side lengths of 10 inches. What is the perimeter of the rectangle? MCC3.MD.8

Ⓐ 18 inches

Ⓑ 28 inches

Ⓒ 32 inches

Ⓓ 36 inches

11. Which rectangle has a perimeter of 16 units and an area of 12 square units?
MCC3.MD.8

Ⓐ Rectangle *A*

Ⓑ Rectangle *B*

Ⓒ Rectangle *C*

Ⓓ Rectangle *D*

Unit 7 Assessment

▶ Vocabulary

Choose the best term from the box to complete the sentence.

Vocabulary
elapsed time
mass
perimeter

1. _____ is the amount of time that passes from the start of an activity to the end of the activity. (p. 451)

2. The distance around a shape is the _____. (p. 483)

▶ Concepts and Skills

Write the time for the activity. Use A.M. or P.M. MCC3.MD.1

3. eat lunch

4. play outside

5. watch a sunset

6. have math class

_____

Choose the unit you would use to measure the mass. Write _gram_ or _kilogram_. MCC3.MD.2

7.

8.

9.

_____

Find the perimeter of the shape. Each unit is 1 centimeter. MCC3.MD.8

10.

11.

_____ centimeters   _____ centimeters

GO Online Assessment Options Unit Test

Fill in the bubble for the correct answer choice.

12. Todd arrived at the soccer game at sixteen minutes before four. Which is one way to write the time? MCC3.MD.1

    Ⓐ 3:00   Ⓒ 4:16

    Ⓑ 3:44   Ⓓ 4:44

13. Pilar began exercising at 2:15 P.M. She finished at 2:55 P.M. How long did Pilar exercise? MCC3.MD.1

    Ⓐ 55 minutes   Ⓒ 45 minutes

    Ⓑ 50 minutes   Ⓓ 40 minutes

14. Alexa is drawing with a blue marker.

    Which is closest to the length of the marker? MCC3.MD.4

    Ⓐ $4\frac{1}{2}$ inches   Ⓒ 4 inches

    Ⓑ $4\frac{1}{4}$ inches   Ⓓ $3\frac{1}{4}$ inches

15. What is the perimeter of the shape ? Each unit is 1 centimeter. MCC3.MD.8

    Ⓐ 9 centimeters   Ⓒ 20 centimeters

    Ⓑ 18 centimeters   Ⓓ 23 centimeters

PARCC TEST PREP

Fill in the bubble for the correct answer choice.

16. Susan cuts a piece of fabric with side lengths of 3 feet and 8 feet. What is the perimeter of the piece of fabric? MCC3.MD.8

    (A) 22 feet

    (B) 24 feet

    (C) 32 feet

    (D) 64 feet

17. Jacob built a toolbox with a perimeter of 70 inches. What is the length of side m? MCC3.MD.8

    (A) 10 inches

    (B) 20 inches

    (C) 25 inches

    (D) 50 inches

18. Allen started his homework at 8:10 P.M. and worked for 45 minutes. Then he phoned a friend and talked for 20 minutes. He went to bed when he finished the call. At what time did Allen go to bed? MCC3.MD.1

    (A) 8:30 P.M.   (C) 9:15 P.M.

    (B) 8:55 P.M.   (D) 9:45 P.M.

19. A garden has two side lengths of 6 feet and two side lengths of 10 feet. What is the perimeter of the garden? MCC3.MD.8

    (A) 18 inches

    (B) 28 inches

    (C) 32 inches

    (D) 36 inches

20. Mr. Carter coaches a neighborhood basketball team. The table shows the activities the team does during practice.

Practice Activities	
Activity	**Elapsed Time**
Passing skills	22 minutes
Dribbling skills	30 minutes
Running laps	28 minutes
Practice game	45 minutes

★ Practice starts at 9:15 A.M. with passing skills. At what time is the team finished with passing skills? **Explain** how you got your answer.

_____

_____

_____

★★ If practice starts at 9:15 A.M., at what time does practice end? **Explain** how you got your answer.

_____

_____

_____

★★★ This Saturday, practice ended at 12:10 P.M. The team took a 10-minute break between the dribbling skills and running laps. At what time did practice begin? **Explain** how you know your answer is reasonable.

_____

_____

_____

_____

_____

**Unit Project
Building Houses**

Project

Materials ■ centimeter ruler

You are managing the construction of a new house. You are in charge of making sure that the work is done correctly, ordering supplies, and paying the workers.

▶ **Plan**

You are helping to plan and build a patio for the house. The patio will be a rectangle with a perimeter of 20 yards. Which of these has the correct shape and perimeter?

Design 1

6 yards

6 yards   6 yards

6 yards

Design 2

6 yards   6 yards

6 yards

Design 3

6 yards

4 yards   4 yards

6 yards

Design 4

8 yards

4 yards   4 yards

6 yards

Correct shape and perimeter: _____

▶ Put It Together

The final design of the patio is a rectangle that is 8 yards long and 4 yards wide.

A. Draw the patio on the grid below.

B. Label the length and width. What is the area of the patio?

_____

The customer wants the patio to be divided into 4 equal sections. One section will be yellow, one section will be green, one section will be brown, and one section will be white.

C. Draw lines to divide your patio into 4 equal sections.

D. Now shade the part of the patio that will be green. What fraction of the patio will be green?

_____

Name _____

Reflect

The patio will be made of concrete pavers.
You need 56 pavers for each section.

A. How many groups of 8 pavers do you need for
each section?

_____

B. You can buy 8 pavers for $20. How much will the
pavers for one section cost?

_____

How much will the pavers for the whole patio cost?

_____

You have 3 workers building the patio. The table shows
how much each worker earns for one day. It takes
2 days to finish the patio. Complete the table.

Earnings		
Worker	One Day	Two Days
1	$125	
2	$145	
3	$160	

C. How much more does Worker 3 earn than
Worker 2 for 2 days of work?

_____

D. How much will you pay the 3 workers in
all for building the patio?

_____

▶ Go Beyond

The bar graph shows the numbers of workers that have been working on the house for the past 5 weeks.

Workers in Past 5 Weeks

A. Use the graph to complete these sentences.

In the past 5 weeks, a total of _____ workers worked on the house.

The number of workers in Week 1 is

_____ the number of workers in Week 4.

The number of workers in Week 2 is greater than

the total number of workers in Weeks _____ and _____.

B. The number of workers in Week 6 is 2 less than twice the number of workers in Week 4. How many workers is this? Show Week 6 in the graph.

_____

512

Name _____

1. There are 37 second graders and 27 third graders in the soccer club. How many students are in the soccer club?

_____

2. The number of people who watched a popular cartoon on television last week was 564. This week, 215 people watched the cartoon. How many more people watched the cartoon last week than this week?

_____

3. Students in two third-grade classes each measured a bean plant to the nearest inch. The data are in the tally table.

Bean Plant Heights	
Height in Inches	Tally
7	JHT IIII
8	JHT III
9	JHT JHT II
10	JHT IIII

How many **fewer** bean plants were 8 or less inches tall than 9 or more inches tall?

_____

4. Freddie drew an array to show how the members of the chorus would stand.

Write a multiplication sentence that shows the total number of members of the chorus.

_____

5. Mia wrote the multiplication facts for 5. What digits will always be in the ones place of the products?

_____

6. Jack's scout troop made cereal bars and put each bar in a plastic bag. They used 4 boxes of plastic bags to wrap all of the bars. Each box has 50 plastic bags. How many cereal bars did Jack's scout troop make?

_____

7. Roni is counting wheels on cars. The table shows how many wheels are on the different numbers of cars. Which two numbers come next?

Cars	2	3	4	5	6
Wheels	8	12	16	▪	▪

_____

8. Miller has 20 blocks. He makes 5 equal groups. How many blocks does Miller put in each group?

_____

9. Tinley buys 56 hamburger buns for the team party. The hamburger buns come in packages of 8. Write a related multiplication fact for this problem.

_____

10. Hector read for the same amount of time each day for 2 days. He read for 6 hours total. How many hours did Hector read each day?

_____

11. Andrea used 35 craft sticks to make 7 picture frames. She used the same number of craft sticks for each picture frame. How many craft sticks did Andrea use for each picture frame?

_____

12. Enrique shaded a model to show the amount of pie that was left after dessert.

What fraction of the pie was left after dessert?

_____

13. Sylvia has 16 flower stickers. One fourth of the stickers she already had before buying more.

How many flower stickers did Sylvia already have?

_____

14. Of all the houses that are on Main Street, $\frac{1}{4}$ are blue and $\frac{1}{6}$ are yellow. What symbol correctly compares the fractions? Write <, >, or =.

$$\frac{1}{4} \bigcirc \frac{1}{6}$$

15. Sarah looked at her watch before she began mowing the grass. The hour hand was between the 9 and the 10. The minute hand was on the 7. At what time did Sarah begin mowing the grass?

_____

16. Casey brought 16 liters of iced tea to a party. She put the iced tea into 8 containers. The same amount of iced tea is in each container. How many liters of iced tea are in each container?

_____

Name _____

17. Roberto drew a rectangle that has an area
of 16 square centimeters. Each unit square
represents 1 square centimeter. Draw a
rectangle that could be Roberto's rectangle.

18. Warwick drew these rectangles.

Explain how the perimeters and areas of the
rectangles are related.

B

A

_____

_____

_____

19. Lisa made a pennant out of cardboard.
The pennant has 3 angles. Write the shape
Lisa made.

_____

20. Dena used a Venn diagram to sort shapes.
Write a label she could use for circle A.

A   Polygons with
            Right Angles

_____

_____

21. The craft store had 151 bags of beads. It sold 128 bags. How many bags of beads are left?

Ⓐ 37

Ⓑ 33

Ⓒ 27

Ⓓ 23

22. Mavis and her friends collected bottle caps. The table shows how many bottle caps each person collected.

Which is the **best** estimate of the total number of bottle caps Mavis and Pedro collected?

Ⓐ 100

Ⓑ 200

Ⓒ 300

Ⓓ 400

Bottle Caps Collected

Name	Number of Bottle Caps
Karen	372
Mavis	255
Pedro	121
John	315

23. Dakota is playing a math game with Madison. Dakota wrote:

$$7 + 7 + 7 + 7$$

Which is another way to show what Dakota wrote?

Ⓐ 7×7 Ⓒ 4×7

Ⓑ 28×7 Ⓓ $4 + 7$

24. The picture graph shows the number of books that Jim owns.

How many books does Jim own altogether?

Ⓐ 60

Ⓑ 62

Ⓒ 63

Ⓓ 64

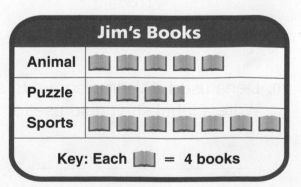

Jim's Books

Animal	
Puzzle	
Sports	

Key: Each 📖 = 4 books

25. Monica looked in 5 fish tanks. In each fish tank she saw 0 fish. Which sentence represents the total number of fish Monica saw?

Ⓐ $5 + 0 = 5$

Ⓑ $5 \times 0 = 0$

Ⓒ $5 \times 1 = 5$

Ⓓ $5 - 5 = 0$

26. Gail has 5 sticker books. She has 3 stickers in each book. How many stickers does Gail have?

Ⓐ 15

Ⓑ 12

Ⓒ 10

Ⓓ 8

27. There are 8 teams setting up booths for the school fair. There are 7 people on each team. How many people are setting up booths?

Ⓐ 28

Ⓑ 48

Ⓒ 56

Ⓓ 64

28. Karen has 15 tennis balls. She puts an equal number in each of 3 groups.

How many tennis balls are in each group?

Ⓐ 3

Ⓑ 5

Ⓒ 8

Ⓓ 15

29. José made a design with 30 tiles equally arranged in 6 rows. How many tiles are in each row?

Ⓐ 3

Ⓑ 4

Ⓒ 5

Ⓓ 6

30. The Parker Produce Company displays 40 apples grouped by the types of apples. There are an equal number of apples in each of the 5 groups. How many apples are in each group?

Ⓐ 8

Ⓑ 9

Ⓒ 35

Ⓓ 40

31. Holly is making 4 veggie trays for a party. She wants to divide 36 carrot sticks equally among the trays. How many carrot sticks will she put on each tray?

Ⓐ 7

Ⓑ 8

Ⓒ 9

Ⓓ 32

32. Stevie divided a rectangle into equal parts. What is the name for the parts?

Ⓐ eighths

Ⓑ sixths

Ⓒ fourths

Ⓓ thirds

Name _____

33. Mitch bought 12 flowers. He gave $\frac{1}{4}$ of the flowers to his Aunt Edee. How many flowers did he give to Aunt Edee?

Ⓐ 3   Ⓒ 8

Ⓑ 4   Ⓓ 9

34. Elaine brought $\frac{7}{8}$ pound of potato salad to a picnic. Jake brought $\frac{2}{8}$ pound of macaroni salad. Which statement correctly compares the fractions?

Ⓐ $\frac{2}{8} = \frac{7}{8}$

Ⓑ $\frac{2}{8} > \frac{7}{8}$

Ⓒ $\frac{7}{8} < \frac{2}{8}$

Ⓓ $\frac{7}{8} > \frac{2}{8}$

35. Mr. Carver spent 45 minutes making dinner. Then he spent 18 minutes eating dinner. He finished eating at 6:15 P.M. At what time did Mr. Carver start making dinner?

Ⓐ 5:12 P.M.   Ⓒ 5:30 P.M.

Ⓑ 5:22 P.M.   Ⓓ 6:12 P.M.

36. Roberto uses an inch ruler to measure the flower. What is the height of the flower to the nearest fourth inch?

Ⓐ 1 inch

Ⓑ $1\frac{1}{4}$ inches

Ⓒ $1\frac{2}{4}$ inches

Ⓓ $1\frac{3}{4}$ inches

37. Willie is building two gardens. The rose garden is 4 feet long and 2 feet wide. The vegetable garden is the same width as the rose garden. The area of the vegetable garden is twice the area of the rose garden. What is the length of the vegetable garden?

(A) 1 foot

(C) 4 feet

(B) 2 feet

(D) 8 feet

38. Amanda uses a ruler to draw a square. The perimeter of the square is 24 centimeters. What is the length of each side of the square?

(A) 4 centimeters

(B) 6 centimeters

(C) 8 centimeters

(D) 12 centimeters

39. Which shape is **not** a polygon?

(A)

(B)

(C)

(D)

40. Henry drew a quadrilateral with 4 right angles and 2 pairs of sides of equal length. Which shape did he draw?

(A) hexagon

(C) rectangle

(B) pentagon

(D) trapezoid